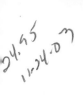

Next of Kin

Next of Kin

A Brother's Journey
to Wartime Vietnam

THOMAS L. REILLY

Brassey's, Inc.
Washington, D.C.

Library of Congress Cataloging-in-Publication Data

Reilly, Thomas L., 1950–
  Next of kin : a brother's journey to wartime Vietnam / Thomas L. Reilly.— 1st ed.
      p. cm.
Includes index.
  ISBN 1-57488-595-2 (hardcover : alk. paper)
  1. Vietnam—Description travel. 2. Vietnamese Conflict, 1961–1975—Personal narratives, American. 3. Reilly, Thomas L., 1950–
l. Title

  DS559.5.R47 2003
  959.704'3'092
                          2003004490

Printed in the United States of America on acid-free paper that meets the American National Standards Institute Z39-48 Standard.

Brassey's, Inc.
22841 Quicksilver Drive
Dulles, Virginia 20166

First Edition

10 9 8 7 6 5 4 3 2

The events described in this book are based on the author's recollections of how they occurred at the time. Other than family, names have been changed for most of the people mentioned out of respect for their privacy.

*Dedicated to Shana, who encouraged me
to begin writing this book,
And to my wife, Arliss, who encouraged
me to finish writing it.*

*And, of course,
to the loving memory of my older brother and hero, Ron,
whose spirit lives on throughout these pages.*

Contents

Prologue

This is the true story of one of the 58,226 names engraved in the cool black granite of the Vietnam Veterans Memorial in Washington, D.C. It is a story about a journey of love and hero worship by the kid brother of one of the real people represented by a name on The Wall.

In July of 1970, I was nineteen years old when, as official "Next of Kin," I was notified of my older brother's death in Vietnam. Sgt. First Class Ronald H. Reilly, thirteen years my senior, was my hero. Even though he was a "lifer" in the U.S. Army and was away most of the time, he had always been there for me—in one way or another.

He was there for me when our parents died unexpectedly just a week apart when I was seven years old. He was there for me, from afar, when I lived on my own as a young teenager, after running away from my court-appointed guardian's farm. He was there to teach me the ways of the world by allowing me to tour a Mexican border town with him, while I was on my way to manhood. He was certainly there to guide me towards the collegiate path, so that, in his words, "you can have a better life than I did." Yes, throughout the early phases of my life, Ron was always there for me, at least in thought and sound advice, if not in person.

Then suddenly he was gone, taken from me by a confusing war that took place halfway around the world from innocent, rural Wisconsin where we had grown up. By a war that most people in this country didn't seem to understand.

This is the story of my tribute to him. It is the memoir of a teenage civilian who, in 1970, traveled to Vietnam in the midst of the war in search of the details of how his hero died, and to see the very piece of ground on which he fell. This daring quest was taken without the knowledge, permission, or assistance of either the U.S. or the South Vietnamese governments, or anyone else for that matter. Because of that, major difficulties sprang up along the way, such as being denied entry into South Vietnam, winding up in Thailand and Cambodia, before eventually being smuggled into South Vietnam by the Southeast Asian black market via the "back door"—across the notorious Communist-controlled Ho Chi Minh Trail.

Once in Vietnam, using only notes from Ron's personal effects that had been sent to me by the Army, I was able to make my way from sleazy Tu Do Street in Saigon to his base camp north of the city. It was there that I finally was able to complete the tribute to my brother, which he so greatly deserved for setting me on the right path before his untimely death at age thirty-two.

Every soldier, sailor, airman, and Marine has a designated Next of Kin. This is the story of a special relationship with an older brother and the unique and sometimes dangerous journey one such Next of Kin took to honor that brother who died in Vietnam.

Chapter 1

First Rite of Passage

"Tommy, now bring your tricycle in on the porch, and let's get your clothes changed, you're going to the hospital with me! *Right now, Tommy, let's go!*" My mother's face was nearly as red as my faded trike, which had been bleached by previous summers like this one in the hot Brandon, Wisconsin, sun. Her voice today conveyed an urgency uncommon to her usual calm and loving demeanor. Brave though she seemed, she was confused and frightened by her husband's—my father's—condition in the small Waupun Municipal Hospital nine miles away.

Leonard Reilly had reluctantly entered that institution two days earlier. It was the first time in his forty-nine years as a carpenter, machinist, and provider that he had ever had a reason to see a doctor, let alone be admitted to the sanitized and strange environment of a hospital. But all of a sudden his headaches had gotten worse. No longer could he dull the pain with a pint of Jack Daniels that hung hidden on a three-foot string inside the basement cistern wall. I remember seeing him once as he sat on his favorite wooden crate along the stone wall of the cistern in the half-dark, musty cellar of our old house. He cradled his forehead in his hands, propped up by his knees, and winced in agony. A small and well-used piece of wood was clenched between his teeth. I didn't understand at the time, but he bit on

1

this rough piece of pine to quiet any sounds of discomfort that might be heard by my mother, who was doing dishes in the kitchen directly above him.

When the wincing subsided, the wood jiggled, as he unclenched his jaw, and that rugged but drained man slowly rose, leaning on the stone wall. With one hand massaging his forehead, he felt along the uppermost edge of the wall for the protruding nail anchored in the mortar between the stones. It didn't take long to find, since this nail held an old and comforting friend. After a swig or two, he carefully returned his "medicine" to the cool darkness of the cistern to wait for his next emergency. It was only a few long seconds until he received some relief from the overused anvil in his forehead. Then, after taking a few bites of raw potato or onion from the stores that were drying on the boards of the cellar floor, to disguise his booze breath from my more puritanical mother, my dad was ready to settle down in a chair upstairs and read the *Milwaukee Journal*.

I was mystified by my one and only observance of that ritual. I knew it happened nearly every night when he came home from a hard day's work. He always disappeared into the dim cellar for a half hour or so. When he reappeared, it was like he had just visited some witch doctor dwelling in our cellar who had performed a miracle on him. Since it all seemed so private, I decided never to watch him in there again. I was afraid that if I, an outsider, were caught witnessing that ritual, I would be captured by the creatures that were living in the dark inner regions of that old basement. At age seven, I wasn't ready yet for any rite of passage, or so I thought.

But now the basement ritual wasn't enough, and neither was the second half-pint of medicine I knew was concealed in the bottom of the toolbox he carried to work.

Two days ago the combination of headaches and hot sun had caused him to collapse while reshingling a barn roof just outside our small town. He couldn't hide that incident or the accompanying delirium from his coworkers. He was brought home and the town's only doctor was summoned to the house. An hour later, my mother was driving my dad to the area's only hospital.

He was semiconscious and rambling, out of his senses, about Sputnik, the Braves winning another World Series, and how "Tommy is sick and should go to the hospital." It was strange to see him like this. I thought perhaps the witch doctor in the basement was making him say these things, and I made up my mind never to open that cellar door again as long as I lived.

The doctors had been good to me when I was in that hospital for dental problems the year before, so I assumed they would be even better to a man as important as my dad.

They weren't.

I knew when my mother said I was going to the hospital with her to see my dad that something wasn't right. At first I suspected some sort of deception on my mother's part, since kids weren't allowed hospital visiting rights. But she didn't normally resort to trickery—only when I was incorrigible or throwing a temper tantrum, which I did with regularity, much to my mother's utter embarrassment. My favorite maneuver was to wrap all four limbs around a parking meter on a busy main street and yell at the top of my lungs that I wasn't moving until I got what I wanted. However, this day I was just quietly playing on my tricycle without any hint of incorrigibility, and not a parking meter in sight. Something had to be seriously wrong with my dad.

After two days, as his condition steadily worsened, the doctors had informed my mother that her husband was, in fact, dying and would probably not wake up from the coma he had lapsed into earlier that day.

I kept hearing the word *stroke* being spoken by the adults. I didn't know what it meant, but I knew it had to be bad. I gathered that, because of the sad looks on the faces of my older brothers, Ron, Gary, and Jim, and because of the quiet tears I saw streaming down my sister Jean's pale cheeks. Because they were all adults between the ages of eighteen and twenty-four, their reactions conveyed to me the gravity of my dad's situation. Then there was the lost and frightened expression on my mother's face. If my dad's condition was all that bad, I really wanted to see how *he* felt about it and what *he* had to say.

I was allowed to go into his hospital room with my mother for a brief visit later that evening. It was uncommonly dark in the room, eerily lit by only a small hidden headboard bulb and a streetlight outside the window near his bed. Because of the room's darkness, I thought maybe he wasn't being ministered to by the white-coated doctors, but instead again by the basement witch doctor. Whoever was taking care of him must have been finished, because he was just lying in bed asleep. He didn't look sick to me. He wasn't holding his forehead or wincing, or biting down on his piece of wood. He was just lying there, asleep on his back, with white linen all around him. But something about his arms and legs seemed unnatural. Then I saw what it was. In the dim light, I could see a yellow leather strap wrapped around his right wrist. The other end of the strap was buckled to

3

the railing, which was raised just over the edge of the bed. I ran around the bed to the other side and found that his left wrist was tethered in the same manner. I went to the foot of the bed and lifted the covers by his feet. My God, his ankles were also strapped to the bed frame! Why, I wondered. Was my father a prisoner of the doctors, or worse yet, the witch doctor? My mother quickly rearranged the covers over his wrists and ankles, and trying not to cry, explained that the straps were there so "Daddy won't hurt himself in his sleep." How ridiculous! How could my dad, a skilled carpenter, hurt himself while he slept so peacefully? I was certain some sort of trickery was involved here.

�֎ ✖ ✖

I had never slept sitting in a chair before, but it seemed to be the thing to do that night. My mother, Ron, and Jean made attempts at sleeping in a half-lit waiting room just down the hall from my dad's room. That old waiting room looked like an office that had been deserted, with only the venetian blinds and a few uncomfortable chairs left behind. I figured I had it the easiest, since I was the smallest and could get more comfortable in the chairs than Ron or Jean. I knew I was more comfortable than my mother, because she was a rather large lady and seemed to be squeezed into her chair in an upright position. It occurred to me, however, that she didn't really want to sleep, anyway. She spent the next several hours just sitting in that chair, weeping. I woke up several times, and each time she was awake with wet eyes and an ever-growing pile of wadded tissues on the floor next to her chair. I had a hard time understanding why we were all huddled in this ugly little room, where rest was nearly impossible, while my father was sleeping so peacefully in a bed just down the hall.

Just before dawn, a stranger came into the gloomy waiting room and shook me awake in my chair, and I realized I was alone in the room. The man acted as if he were on some sort of mission to take me somewhere. He took my hand and led me, half-awake, down the hall to my father's room. Dad's room was still nearly dark, and the gray dawn was just making its presence known outside. A priest was mumbling unintelligible phrases over my dad, while my mother, Ron, and Jean were huddled at the foot of the bed. Both women were crying uncontrollably, and Ron was just staring out the window.

The man, leading me by the hand, took me up to my mother, who tried to compose herself. She guided me to the head of the bed and said, "Tommy, I want you to take a last look at your father, because you'll never see him again." I sensed everyone in the room was staring at me through the dimness. I also sensed that now my mother wasn't trying to trick me.

I looked at my father, who appeared to still be asleep, only now his hands weren't strapped to the bed, but rested peacefully, unrestrained across his chest. He seemed so incredibly still that I wondered why the solemn chanting of the priest hovering over him didn't wake him up.

He never did wake up, and he never again needed the secret bottle from the basement cistern. The next day I felt that my mother had told me a small lie when she said I'd never see my dad again. For I saw him again, still asleep, but this time he was dressed in his one and only suit, which he wore to church on Sundays. It was faded brown, with overly padded shoulders and baggy pants. But the pants didn't really matter, since his legs disappeared in the large bronze-colored bed they told me was called a casket.

This first major social event in my life, my father's funeral, came and went with hazy confusion. That confusion was more on the part of everyone else in the family than mine. The grown-ups were the ones that had to arrange things, like not forgetting to contact my mother's great-aunt Jen, who someone thought lived outside of Indianapolis. Then there was the important matter of selecting the pallbearers, and what type of potato salad to have at the house when all the relatives came over after the funeral.

I felt that my dad and I really had the least to do with all of this, and I liked it that way. All I was responsible for was being clean and in the proper clothes at the right time, and not to fidget too much. And all my dad had to do was lie there in his half-open casket, while the relatives made chitchat in the large room of the funeral home. Before each one left, it seemed necessary to walk up to the casket, become very solemn, and mumble something about "How good he looked." Personally, I thought he looked better alive, and in his carpenter's work clothes.

I learned several new words and their meanings during the days involved with my dad's funeral. Words like *casket, sympathy, cemetery,* and *burial*. Of course, I didn't know it at the time, but I had a suspicion that the words were important and I should keep them readily retrievable for use in the future.

My mother took the ordeal of my father's funeral well. I knew this to be a concrete fact, since I heard it from some aunt or uncle nearly every five minutes while we were at the funeral home. But, just as I disagreed with all the relatives milling around saying that my father "looked good" in the casket, I had reason to doubt that my mother was "taking it well." Even at seven years old, I could read the sad expression on her face during those long days. She was quiet, but sociable, when others tried to converse with her. She responded politely to little conversational tidbits from friends and relatives, like, "Leonard was too young to die" or "You'll be all right."

Merrill, my mother, was seven years younger than my dad, and right then, at age forty-two, although she didn't realize it, she only had a few more days left to feel so terribly alone.

�֍ ✤ ✤

I can't vividly recall those next five days. For some reason they just didn't seem important to me. I do remember, however, that on one night during that period my older brother Ron came to me when I couldn't sleep. He rubbed my back to help me relax on that humid July night, and as he did, he just stared out the window through the torn screen and tried to comfort me. Even at my young age, I knew that I didn't demand as much comforting over my dad's death as my mother and Jean did. He tried so hard to justify our father's death to me and to let me know everything would be all right. He rationalized our loss by saying things like, "It could be a lot worse, boy; they could *both* have been killed in a car accident together," and, "At least we still have Mom." I can still remember thinking that night that it really could have been worse. I agreed with Ron that our mother could have been taken from us, too, and that would definitely be worse. Jean could also be taken from us, I realized, but for me personally, to have Ron taken from me would be the most devastating scenario my fast-maturing seven-year-old mind could comprehend. He was not only my big brother and protector, he was my idol.

At twenty years old, Ron symbolized what I wanted to be like when I got older. I didn't consciously know exactly what becoming a man meant at my age—an age when I shouldn't even have been thinking about growing up yet, but I did know that Ron had whatever it was. He had looks, both rugged and gentle. He was friendly, but uniquely reserved, and had a charm that put nearly everyone who came close to him at ease. His refined Steve McQueen looks, combined with his controlled charisma, also made him extremely popular with the opposite sex.

I was constantly being introduced to his new girlfriends. At least twice, when I embarrassed him in front of new dates by mentioning another girl's name, I received a couple of the worst private tongue-lashings of my young life. After that, when he found it necessary to introduce me to a new member of his harem, he would always point out that I was his "*mute* little brother, Tommy," so that I would take my cue and just smile a lot, from ear to ear, dimpled cheeks fully accentuating my pleasure to meet her.

But Ron put his busy social life aside for those few days following our dad's funeral. I think he felt that he was the one who had to stay in control, had to pull the family together and keep it together. Since he always treated me like I was a lot older than I was, he told me he was concerned for me, but not worried about me. He said that he knew I would be all right, but that he would always be there if I needed any help along the way. He was, however, very worried about our mother's distraught condition, resulting from all the grief she was suffering. He knew that life had to go on after a personal tragedy and, after a few days, felt responsibile to help get our mother's life back on some sort of productive course.

At that time, Jean had been married about a year and lived with her husband on a dairy farm about twenty-five miles away. Ron and Jean decided that maybe a weekend stay at the farm would help our mother by just getting her away from the house she and our father had shared for so long.

Although she was apprehensive about the idea, Mother agreed to go. So the next day, Friday, the seventh day after our dad died, Ron and I packed up his light blue 1955 Ford Fairlane, and the three of us drove off over the country roads of central Wisconsin, en route to Jean's farm.

Mother was feeling better that day, once we left Brandon and got into the open country. The bright mid-July sun illuminated the flatland crops that were maturing in the neatly fenced ten- and twenty-acre fields. Jamaican laborers, "imported" by the big canning factories in the area, were toiling in the fields, harvesting peas. Since my mom was very intelligent and always had the correct answers, she told me where and what Jamaica was, and explained why these workers were in the fields. She mentioned it had something to do with "cheap wages" and "mundane work."

Just before we arrived at Jean's farm, Ron pointed to a small plane that was diving into a field right next to the road. I was both excited and afraid, because I thought the plane was about to crash. But just before what I thought would be a sure explosion, the pilot pulled the plane out of its dive, leveled off, and went skimming across the field just above the fence tops. A white cloud was trailing behind the plane, coming from a pipe along the back of the wings. When the plane reached the end of the green field, the white cloud stopped and the plane pulled almost straight up after passing under the utility wires along the road. It was my first time seeing a crop duster in action. I was thrilled to be in such close proximity to a man doing something so daring and dangerous. I had knowledge of World War II, with all its action and heroes, and I knew that some men led exciting lives, but that was always so far away, like around the world or out West. Surely nothing so daring and exciting ever happened in sleepy little central Wisconsin. But there, right in front of me, was a man in a plane actually risking his life for his job. I made a quick, but deep mental note that if at all possible, I would include a lot of excitement and heart-stopping action in my life.

We made it to the farm later that morning, and our mom was in great spirits, almost as if she hadn't experienced all that grief during the previous week. There was a normal dose of small talk about how bright Jean's freshly painted yellow kitchen walls looked, and about what her husband, Gerhardt, was currently doing with his three hundred acres of choice Wisconsin farmland.

Later that morning, Gerhardt came in from the fields for a cool glass of lemonade and to see how the "town people" were getting along. He was several years older than Jean and had a rather gruff, yet gentle, air about him. He was a husky man, in strong physical condition—a man with weathered features who had never taken a vitamin or an aspirin, because he was just naturally healthy. When he smiled, which was often around visitors, his white teeth shone in distinct contrast to his dark, tanned skin.

Gerhardt, not being a man to waste a lot of time sitting in the house sipping refreshments on a workday, suggested that Ron and I ride along with him in his pickup to do an errand. He had to return some borrowed tools to a neighbor "just down the road," and wanted to do so before lunch. Since there was only room for one passenger in the cab, if I went, I'd have to ride in the open back of the pickup truck. My adrenaline leapt at the thought of riding in the open. I could pretend I was a "desert rat" soldier, riding in the back of an Army jeep, with the wind blowing through my hair as my mounted machine gun blazed away at the enemy.

Because I knew this sounded almost as dangerous as crop dusting to my mother, I was afraid I wouldn't be allowed to ride in the back of the truck. My fear was instantly confirmed, because not only could I not ride in the back, I couldn't go at all. The female side of my family thought I would be exposed to too many things a seven-year-old should not be exposed to, since there was apt to be a lot of crude conversation among Gerhardt, Ron, and the neighbor men. How was I supposed to grow up, I wondered, if I never got to hear any of the good stuff?

I was to find out later there are other ways of growing up.

Nevertheless, even with Ron pulling for me, it was decided I was too young and would remain at the house with the women. Even though I didn't like the decision, I assumed I could keep myself occupied. After all, the farm had a lot of room for real or imagined adventures for a young town kid.

As soon as the men left and Gerhardt's pickup truck could be heard sputtering down the road, I asked Jean if I could go out in the nearby pasture to get a closer look at the cows and new calves. Jean said she thought that was a good idea, but asked if I would postpone it for a while. She had a basket of wash to hang out, and said she would prefer it if I stayed in the house with Mom until she got done. This seemed a little unnecessary to me, since our Mom was an adult and seemed to be doing fine. But I knew because of the serious look Jean gave me, she meant what she said.

So, I stayed in the house and opened a box of dominoes on the kitchen table, while Jean went about her laundry duties outside.

My mother remained in the kitchen as well. She was seated in a large old-fashioned chair, located at one end of Jean's huge kitchen. The chair was made of solid oak, with a worn, padded leather seat and back, and large, bare, wooden arms. It reminded me of a chair that Ebenezer Scrooge would have in his uncomfortably decorated office. What that chair was doing in the kitchen, in front of the windows with Jean's lacy yellow-and-white curtains, was anybody's guess. Actually, I had seen Gerhardt sit there before to take off his heavy work boots. The austere ruggedness of that chair seemed compatible with Gerhardt and his work boots, but my mother's feminity looked unnatural in so massive a piece of furniture. But, nonetheless, she sat there looking at a recent issue of *Life* magazine, while I carefully and deliberately arranged the dominoes in straight lines on the table.

All of a sudden I looked across the room at my mother. She had a strange, perplexed expression on her face, as if something were happening to her, but she didn't know what or why. Her right hand reached for the side of her forehead, near the temple. At the same time, she gasped the words, "My God! I have a *terrible* headache." The last word, *headache*, came out slurred. The *Life* magazine slipped from her left hand and fell to the floor in disarray. My mother's head slumped forward, and her right hand fell from her temple to an awkward position dangling over the arm of the old chair. All this seemed to happen in less than a heartbeat. I rushed over to her, now slumped forward and to the right in the chair. A large, ugly bruise was visible over her right temple, and she appeared unconscious, or worse. I didn't know what to do for her, so I ran out the kitchen door, onto the porch, and screamed for Jean, who was only a few yards away at the clothesline. She and I ran back into the kitchen, where our mother was still motionless in the chair. I wished that somehow she would have moved during the time I went outside to get Jean. When I saw her again in the chair, I sensed she would never again move under her own power.

She was gone, too, just seven days after my father's death.

It all seemed like a recurring bad dream, as I stood in the cemetery again in the hot July sun. Ron had bought me a new sports jacket and bow tie just a week before to wear to our dad's funeral. Since it had been purchased for such a special occasion, I thought I would grow out of it before ever having to wear it again. But here I was, standing among the same relatives I had just seen a week ago, in the same peaceful back corner of that little country cemetery.

The last time I left the cemetery, my dad's shiny bronze-colored casket had still been sitting on a weird mechanical frame over a large open grave. Now, there was just a slight mound of rich Wisconsin topsoil remaining where his casket used to be. I understood that his casket was now deep underground, just as my mother's would be shortly. Her casket looked identical to his, and was now sitting on the same type of metal frame over an open grave not more than a foot from my dad's. I thought it strange that someone had to go to all the work of digging a second hole in the ground for her casket. Why didn't they just reopen the first grave, so they could both be together again, just like they had been in life for so many years, rather than having a foot of ground separating them?

Ron and I were the last to leave the cemetery that day. We left just as some burly cemetery workers were lowering our mother's sealed casket into the ground. He looked at me as we were walking to his car and said, "Boy, sometimes life is hell, and you just can't tell what's gonna happen." I told him that I thought it was death that was hell. He just looked at me, then looked far away, sighed, and slowly nodded his head, adding, "We all have to die someday."

Even then, I hoped that his "someday" would come long after mine, so I would be spared the loss of someone who was now, without a doubt, the most important person in my life.

Chapter 2

Strengthening Brotherly Ties

Throughout the ordeal of my parents' deaths and funerals, my psychological and emotional states grew far beyond those of my chronological age. I somehow instinctively knew that I had to look at the world around me differently than I had only a month before. Actually, like any other seven-year-old, I had never really looked at the outside world before, or at the small speck that *I* represented in that world. That was left up to the others, mostly my mother and, to a lesser degree, the sibling I felt closest to, Ron. But even at that young age, I knew that I no longer had the luxury of living in the comforting cocoon that had sheltered me so well for the first seven years of my life.

Oh, of course, I knew that "somebody" would take care of me; that's what adults and other family members were supposed to do, weren't they? But I also knew that God and society had assigned the job of raising a child to *parents,* not necessarily to older siblings or other relatives. But now that both of my parents were gone, the assignment of raising me would have to be completed by someone of lesser authority. Who that authority might be was unknown to me at the time, but, I was determined somehow to become part of the process. After all, it was *my* life we were talking about here.

The first essential step in my part of the process was to assess what options I had. Little did I know, that at the same time, my older family members, as well as a local juvenile court system, were making the same assessment.

My mother had always been the dominant factor in my life and present on a daily basis to take care of all of my needs and most of my wants. My father had been more mercurial; his presence was always felt, but he was more in the background of things. This was corroborated years later when I found a few snapshots of my father and me. I was always the "star" of the photo, with him doing something else several yards behind me, almost as part of a backdrop.

So, the initial assessment of responsible grown-ups who could raise me could no longer consider my mother and father. Next came my siblings, who were eleven to seventeen years older than me. I quickly eliminated my next oldest brother, Gary. He had just turned eighteen and wasn't handling our parents' deaths well himself. I accepted this, because, after all, he had known them more than ten years longer than I had. He was already talking about enlisting in the Army to get away from small-town Wisconsin and to see the world.

But there was another, more subtle, reason I eliminated him from taking any responsibility for my future upbringing. Gary had been the "baby" of the family for ten years, and according to my older siblings, had enjoyed the fruits of that position until I came along. According to psychologists, birth order is a very important factor shaping relationships. That was no exception in my family. Gary and I were never close while our parents were alive; he was always finding ways to "pick on me" when he knew it wouldn't be noticed by anyone else. Once our parents died, this teenage-type needling turned to open hostility, induced by the added attention that "poor little Tommy" was receiving. Gary basically turned his back on me, and I often thought his desire to join the Army was his way of extracting himself from what he saw as a painful emotional situation. Years later I would understand the dynamics of it all, and be at peace with his response during this time of his life. But at the time, I had to eliminate him as someone who could help support me.

Then there was my eldest brother, Jim, seventeen years my senior. At twenty-four, Jim had secured a relatively good job at a factory in a town twenty miles away, was married with a child, and was planning on having more children. In short, when our parents died, Jim was on his way in the outside world, and no one doubted he would settle into his piece of the American Dream. I had always admired him for this.

However, after that fateful July 1958 when our parents died, my other siblings made me aware that there was tension between them and Jim. I was never exactly sure what the basis of the tension was, but, according to what Ron and Gary told me, they had the feeling that Jim, being the oldest, tried to take too much control after our parents died. Moreover, they felt he took this control simply based on the fact that he was the oldest. But in Jim's defense, he was in the awkward position of trying to hold the family together, which included dealing with the newfound independence of two slightly younger brothers, a recently married sister, and me, the youngest, only seven. Tough job for anyone.

Even though we all lived together for the next year in the same rented house in Brandon after our parents died, my other siblings influenced me not to get involved in any relationship with Jim.

In the simpler time of the late 1950s, and in the simpler setting of rural Wisconsin, this arrangement for my welfare was legally acceptable. After all, the immediate family unit, for all outward appearances, was staying together. What could a court do better for a child of seven? It also seemed like a good plan to me. I could put my assessment process on hold for the time being and live with all of my older brothers.

However, by the next spring, tensions increased and things began to unravel. Gary did, in fact, leave for the Army. And worse yet, Ron, the brother I was closest to and the main person that now cared for me, announced that he, too, was going to join the Army.

The thought of Ron being physically out of my life devastated me. He assured me this was something he had to do, but I could tell he was torn between his restless urge to get out into the world and the responsibility of being there to help with my upbringing.

With Ron and Gary both leaving, I immediately became concerned about who was left to take care of me, now at age eight. Jim and Jean were the only ones left, and they each had two children by that time and were forming their own family units. I believed that Jim and Jean's growing families helped prod Ron into leaving for parts unknown via the military. He was definitely not the family man type. His swashbuckling was what made me admire him so much, and it also helped me understand why he *had* to leave at that time.

Before enlisting, Ron reassured me that one of his main concerns was my welfare and upbringing. He promised me he would stay in close touch through letters and telephone calls. But, more importantly, he had a plan for me that he had been discussing with our sister Jean and the local court system. It was very comforting for me to know that Ron considered me so important in his life, because he sure was in mine.

He was convinced I would have a much better life living on the farm near Beaver Dam with Jean and her growing family than I would in Brandon. He felt that living in the country and learning a work ethic early would serve me well as an adult. Because it was Ron telling me this, I was easily convinced. I had always gotten along with Jean, even though she had spent most of her late teens and young adult years living away from home with an aunt and uncle.

Of course, I also realized that because of Ron's relationship with Jim, Ron would feel more comfortable if I were not living with Jim. With little urging, Ron convinced Jean that she, too, wanted me to move to the farm with her and her husband, Gerhardt, who also gave the plan his blessing. This seemed like a win-win situation for all concerned. So, when I finished second grade in May 1959, I moved the twenty-five miles from Brandon to Jean's farm just outside of Beaver Dam.

Shortly thereafter, I went with Ron and Jean to a nearby county court-house to have documents drawn up making Jean my legal guardian. At one point during the proceedings, the judge asked Ron and Jean to leave the mahogany-paneled courtroom. Then the judge and I were alone, separated only by an enormous wooden desk. I felt like I was in a *Perry Mason* episode, only in color instead of black and white.

The judge, apparently realizing I was too short to approach the bench like an adult, came down from his high seat and sat next to me on a churchlike pew. I was very surprised by his action, since I had never seen a judge on *Perry Mason* come out from behind his bench. So here I was, alone in a real courtroom with just this gray-haired stranger who wore glasses, a long black robe.

"Seems to me your brother and sister think you're pretty important, 'specially that brother of yours, Ron," the judge declared in a low, comforting tone.

I could only nod in response, because I had no idea why the judge was talking to me without Ron or Jean present.

"I know what *they* think is best for you," he continued, "but I don't know what *you* think is best for you, or where you would like to live until you turn eighteen."

Then I realized why this stranger was talking to me privately. Even at the young age of eight, I felt the judge wanted me to take more control of my life, and I suddenly felt very special.

"I know Ron really thinks it's best for me to live on the farm with Jean and not with my oldest brother, Jim," I said very quietly, looking down at my feet.

"I know you have a lot of love and respect for Ron, but is that what you want, too?" asked the judge in an even more compassionate tone.

"Yes, I think I would like to live on the farm with Jean, but do I have to stay there until I'm eighteen?" *Eighteen* seemed a few lifetimes away.

"No, Tommy, you don't have to stay, but we at the court would like you to if everything works out well," replied the judge.

This was about the longest conversation I had ever had with a stranger, but I could tell it was important.

"Are you sure, Tommy?"

I was amazed at how big of a role I seemed to be playing in all this. It was scary, yet exhilarating at the same time.

I finally just looked directly at the judge's worn face and nodded. I really wasn't sure, because I had no idea of what to expect on the farm, but I knew Ron thought it was a good thing, so I figured it had to be my best option.

So, as a result, a month or so after the courtroom visit, my sister Jean, then twenty-three, was appointed as my "legal guardian." I had no idea what that really meant, I only knew that she had become *legally* responsible for me.

❈ ❈ ❈

The farm was a three-hundred-acre dairy operation located in south central Wisconsin, three miles outside the town of Beaver Dam. Beaver Dam, located on the shore of Beaver Dam Lake (and most likely named for the lake's furry, flat-tailed inhabitants), was a town of about thirteen thousand people. Most of its residents were either employed by the local Kraft Foods plant, a shoe factory, or a local foundry. The rest of the businesses in Beaver Dam played a large role in supporting the surrounding rural agricultural population.

At that time, in the late 1950s, farming was still a popular and integral part of American society, particularly in southern Wisconsin. More specifically, in Beaver Dam and surrounding Dodge County, dairy farming was the preferred choice and the most profitable kind of farming. Small family farms were neatly spaced about a quarter-mile apart along the pastoral back roads. The mostly red, or sometimes white, barns and equipment sheds, with one to three silos, metal dome tops shining in the summer sun, were signs of the region's continuing postwar prosperity.

The one-family farms were usually in their third or fourth generation, indicating a stable and healthy way of life for the families who were willing to perform the enormous amount of work required by farming.

Dairy farming at that time, even though somewhat automated by electric milking machines and pipelines to carry milk from the barn to the milk house, where it was stored overnight, was considered by many to be the hardest kind of farming. Each dairy farmer had a herd of between twenty to forty holstein or Brown Swiss milk cows. That was about all a single farmer, with the help of his male sons or hired hands, could effectively handle. These cows had to be milked twice a day, once in the early morning and then again in the evening, *without exception*. An average milking would take about two hours, depending on the size of the herd and available labor.

Four hours of work a day doesn't sound like much to a city worker. But milking made up only a fraction of the farmers' daily workload. *Everything* in a dairy farmer's life revolved around the milk herd. The cows, of course, had to be fed twice daily, as well as taken to pastures during the summer. The barn and all milk-handling equipment had to be cleaned each day to meet the strict grading requirements of the local dairy processing plants. The grade helped determine the price the farmer received for his milk. Also, the small herd of heifers, or pre-milk cows, as well as young calves, had to be cared for daily.

Each of the dairy farms was situated on two hundred to five hundred acres. About 10 percent of the tillable land was used for cash crops, like peas or sweet corn, and the rest was planted with oats, alfalfa, and field corn—all used as feed for the dairy herd, heifers, and calves.

The science and art of planting, nurturing, and harvesting these crops was handed down from generation to generation. And even though modern farm equipment helped the process considerably, the dairy farmer's work was never finished. From May to November, fourteen- to sixteen-hour workdays were the rule rather than the exception for the dairy farmer. Rainy days or equipment breakdowns were the only obstacles to slow down a day's work during spring, summer, and autumn. But such delays would only cause frustration about getting behind. The fieldwork and twice daily milking routines were a carefully orchestrated balancing act performed instinctually by the farmers.

Jean's husband, Gerhardt, was one such dairy farmer. A strong, burly man of about thirty when Jean married him, he was third-generation Polish American, but his farming lifestyle had been instilled in him by his European ancestors long before his grandfather came to America. His father started the farm outside Beaver Dam in 1915 and called it Railroad View Dairy Farm, because the house and barn were situated about a hundred yards from a local train track. After his father's death, Gerhardt and his two brothers worked the farm. By the time he married Jean, he had bought out his brothers' shares. His strong work ethic, considered by some to be unlimited, allowed him to work his very successful operation alone, with limited help from his brothers and an occasional live-in hired hand.

Gerhardt simply loved to work the farm, although like many of his counterparts, he openly cursed the cows, the land, and farming in general, on a daily basis. Such negativism was only superficial statements all farmers were expected to make. After all, if one indicated he loved *anything,* including his livelihood, he was considered less of a man.

Gerhardt had dropped out of grade school at a young age so that he could work on the family farm that would eventually be his. He stayed in school long enough to learn reading, writing, and arithmetic, all essentials for successful farming. Subjects like history, geography, or civics would have been of no interest to him, because he knew at a young age what he would be doing for a living, and exactly where he would be doing it. The only history that mattered to him were the weather patterns over the past few years so he could better judge his crop fieldwork. The only geography that mattered to him was his three hundred acres of the planet, and maybe a curiosity about his neighbors' acreage surrounding his own land. And, the only civics lessons that concerned him were centered around the taxes he knew he had to pay.

It was this type of work ethic that Ron saw in Gerhardt and thought—accompanied by a wholesome farm life—would be beneficial to me. But then, Ron, being a "townie" all of his life, had no idea what life was really like on a dairy farm, particularly the one run by Jean's husband. Almost immediately upon moving to the farm, I started to find out what my life was going to be like.

"Tom . . . Tom . . . Tom, wake up!" This was my first night at the farm; it was still dark, and I kept hearing this refrain repeated over and over. "Tom, wake up." I didn't even know where it was coming from. I got out of bed and went to my partially opened bedroom door, but nobody was there. "Tom . . . Tom, come on, time for work."

I stumbled over to a window, and there, two floors below, in the darkness outside stood Gerhardt, fully dressed in his work clothes, looking up at me.

He smiled when he saw I was finally awake, albeit not yet coherent. "Come on, I'll show you how to get the cows from the pasture," he said with far too much enthusiasm for what I considered to be still the middle of the night. I had just gotten out of school a few days earlier and was looking forward to a fun and carefree summer vacation. "Come on, let's go!" Gerhardt said, sounding more impatient.

I looked at the old alarm clock on my dresser, which I hadn't bothered to set because it was summer vacation; it was only 4:45 A.M! As I pulled on my jeans, shirt, and shoes, I realized there was probably not going to be any summer vacation, only summer work for me in my new setting.

Over the next several days, my time was spent with Gerhardt teaching me the fine art of rounding up the cows in their pasture while it was still dark (and thus, stepping in numerous "cow pies") as well as teaching me how to do the other daily chores. I learned to shovel manure out of the barn floor gutters, sweep out all thirty-six stanchions, where the cows stood while being milked, spread absorbent lime on the barn floor, and put a shovelful of a corn-and-oats mixture in each of the thirty-six feed troughs. These were the daily routine chores Gerhardt assigned to me; some needed to be done twice a day. Then there were the special projects, like cleaning all the cobwebs off the interior rafters of the barn and several other toolsheds and grain buildings, and sweeping all of them at least weekly.

Within about two weeks, I graduated to helping with the fieldwork, which had to be done during the main part of the workday between the routine chores. A good portion of fieldwork consisted of several hours spent in the hot sun "picking stones." Even though the soil was rich, it was still rocky in places. Each year's tilling would turn up stones the size of baseballs and larger, which had to be cleared from the fields by hand to prevent damage to the equipment that might occur while cultivating or harvesting the crops. This was particularly backbreaking and dirty, demeaning work, especially for a "townie" like me.

Other jobs I learned that first summer on the farm were equally grueling. In my "spare time," meaning the time between doing daily chores and other special work projects, I was expected to do two equally repulsive tasks: cutting weeds and thistles around the perimeter fence lines of all the fields, and pulling up wild mustard, which grew at will in the alfalfa fields.

Cutting weeds was to be accomplished with a handheld sickle, commonly called a "corn knife" by the farmers. This was simply a sharp, curved, heavy metal blade with a wooden handle. It was a fairly lightweight and effective hand tool for a grown man, but to an eight-year-old town kid, it was heavy and cumbersome.

The fields I was assigned to cut away the unwanted vegetation were twenty to forty acres in size. This meant I was supposed to cut away three or four feet of weeds and prickly thistles, some the size of small saguaro cactus, along *miles* of fence line with a handheld blade. Even to an eight-year-old, who was still trying to keep an open mind about the value of living on a farm, this was utterly ridiculous! First, Wisconsin has a short growing season, followed by a bitterly harsh winter. All these weeds would die anyway in a few months. Secondly, with all the pesticides and herbicides sprayed on the crops, the perimeter fence line weeds didn't stand a chance of wandering into the crops.

When I asked Gerhardt why he didn't also spray the fence lines with weed killers and other chemicals of the day, I got a very simple two-part answer: "It costs money to spray those weeds," and "If I did, you wouldn't have anything to do!" *Yeah, fat chance!*

The other dreaded job I was taught that first summer on the farm was the fine art of pulling mustard. The wild mustard plant, or so it was named by Gerhardt, was a bright yellow blossoming weed, which stood about eighteen inches high and grew in random colonies, particularly in open pastures and in alfalfa fields. According to Gerhardt, the presence and procreation of this weed meant the certain ruination of all agriculture and the overall destruction of life on the planet. The only solution was to destroy any presence of it immediately upon sight. The only way to destroy it was to pull each plant out by its roots. According to Gerhardt, the faster and easier attack of cutting it would not do; it would only keep growing if the roots were left in the ground. And, as a result of our discussion about the fence row weeds, I knew better than to suggest to Gerhardt that he use herbicide to spray those dastardly yellow plants.

No, the only way to eliminate this nuisance of a weed and save all creation was to have *me* pull it out of all the fields where it grew, by hand. And grow it did; sometimes nearly half of a twenty-acre field sported more yellow mustard plants than alfalfa or other precious crops. This meant tens of thousands of these weeds in each field. Not only was this task daunting, it had to be completed in addition to my other daily chores and special projects.

Then there was the problem of actually pulling this weed out by the roots. Demonstrating this newest task to me, Gerhardt, with his six-foot, 250-pound frame, easily reached over, grabbed the pesky perpetrator midway down the main stalk and pulled it out by the roots. When my eight-year-old body reached over to do the same thing, I was amazed that not only did the weed *not* come out, I felt as though it was trying to pull *me* down into the ground. By increasing my determination and strength, I was able to pull and wiggle a mustard plant out of the soil, getting *most* of the root bundle. I assured Gerhardt I had the hang of it, so he trudged out of the field and told me not to forget to get the cows from their pasture at 5:30 P.M.; that was at 1:20 P.M. So, one mustard weed down, 987,343 to go in that field; but I had *over four hours* in the hot sun in which to do so!

❋   ❋   ❋

So went my first summer at my new home on the farm. A summer spent as a child slave from before sunrise to well after sunset, seven days a week. I reminisced about previous times when my summers had been filled with fun, laughter, and the carefree days of childhood. And even though most children reach an age of impatience where they wish they were growing up faster, I was uncomfortable with being so quickly catapulted into an adult life of constant hard work. I sensed the sheer quantity of work was even more than what most grown-ups had to endure in their professional lives. Surely, I thought, most adults took *some* time off for nonwork activities.

In order to realize at least some sense of childhood play, I began incorporating little boy fantasies into my daily work regimen. When cutting weeds along the fence lines, I imagined I was a soldier hacking his way through dense jungle of the South Pacific islands with a machete, as I had seen in World War II movies. Only three more days of this sweaty, tiring slicing, and I would link up my platoon with Merrill's Marauders main force, then on to victory!

One of my main responsibilities during that summer was driving the cows to their nighttime pastures after the evening milking. The pasture was located about a half-mile away from the house down a gravel road. The cows really seemed to know where they were going, but I had to follow along on my bicycle just to make sure they stayed to the side of the road when the infrequent vehicle used the road at the same time.

I must admit, this assignment was enjoyable compared to most of my other chores. I made it even more enjoyable by imagining I was a real cowboy on the Chisholm Trail, working for Mr. Gil Favor of *Rawhide*, the television show. My bicycle was transformed into a chestnut cutting horse.

"Get 'em up, move 'em out!" was my dusty trail mantra as I drove the herd into the western sunset each night towards their pasture.

The only true escape from chores I got during the next several years was the time I spent in school. Unlike my peers, I actually looked forward to and counted the days towards each summer's end when I could return to the classroom, which represented a respite from spending the entire day working on the farm. During the school year, I only had to do routine chores for two hours before and three hours after school each day. Schoolwork was something I enjoyed and was naturally good at, and it contrasted vividly to farmwork, which I hated for the most part and was not good at anyway—a judgment that was constantly reinforced by Gerhardt.

Advancing through grade school taught me about the world beyond the farm, which I thirsted to be part of someday.

My brothers Ron and Gary were both in the Army stationed in Germany during my first years on the farm. Ron would write to me weekly, sending postcards and gifts, which I would take to Highland Prairie Elementary School and proudly show to my classmates and teachers.

Upon entering the fifth grade in 1961, and being asked to write about something interesting that happened over the previous summer, I wrote a story that was accompanied by a dozen Kodak color slides about the Berlin Wall crisis that had just occurred. The slides were from Ron, who, along with Gary, was stationed there at the time. As I showed the slides to the class while reading my essay, I proudly wore a dark blue satin jacket that Ron had sent to me from Germany. It had my name stitched on the front breast panel, his military unit patch on the sleeve, reading "Seven Steps to Hell," and a full needlepoint map of Germany on the back, showing Berlin. Talk about a presentation to a grade school class! Even my teacher thought this was great, but asked me not to wear my prized jacket to school again unless I removed the military patch that bore the word *Hell*.

Even though I wrote back to Ron consistently, I was reluctant to tell him anything about my dislike of living on the farm because of my heavy work-load. I didn't want to disappoint him, and I knew he thought he had done something good by promoting my move to the farm. And after all, I figured he was off helping save the world in interesting foreign places and shouldn't be bothered by the whining of a kid brother.

The summer I was twelve, Ron wrote to say he was coming to the farm for a ten-day leave before reporting for duty in Okinawa. He said he wanted to spend some time with me and see how I was really doing. I knew Jean had become very concerned about how hard Gerhardt was working me. I actually heard the occasional muffled arguments between her and Gerhardt, with my farmwork being the main topic. I sensed she had also written something of this to Ron.

After weeks of excruciating impatience on my part, Ron finally arrived. He had flown to Milwaukee and taken a Greyhound bus to Beaver Dam, where Jean and I picked him up. There he was in his Army uniform, looking every bit the hero he was to me. Nobody, but nobody, I determined, would ever ask *him* to remove the patch reading "Seven Steps to Hell" from his shoulder.

After reminiscing late into the night that first evening, Ron said he wanted to spend the next week just hanging around with me and helping me with some of my chores. At first I thought this was super, but soon began feeling pangs of embarrassment. I was actually embarrassed to show my worldly hero what my life on the farm was like, particularly in the summer months. But since this was time to be spent with Ron, I naturally agreed. Gerhardt, too, thought this was a good idea, since he would be gaining a temporary "hired" hand.

By this time, I had graduated from doing chores around the barn, cutting weeds, and pulling mustard, to operating equipment in the field to support Gerhardt's crop growing and harvesting. But I hadn't graduated *out* of the previous work, I was just expected to do both chores *and* fieldwork each day.

The next morning I was up and out of bed at my usual 5:00 A.M. Ron was still sleeping in the extra bedroom, so I woke him up as well. He was surprised at the time. He groggily explained to me that even though he was in the Army, his workday usually started at a more civilized 8:00 a.m. Regardless, he dutifully got dressed, grabbed a quick cup of instant coffee, and we were off to get the cows from the pasture.

After we helped Gerhardt with the morning milking, we ate a hurried breakfast, then it was back to clean the barn and put out the evening feed for each cow. The rest of the morning was spent picking stones out of a portion of a twenty-acre field. I drove a yellow 1940s Willis jeep pickup truck out into the middle of the field, and Ron and I would gather up the stones, throw them into the jeep bed, and move on to another part of the field. When the pickup bed was full, we drove to the end of the field and unloaded the stones, by hand, onto a rock pile in a ditch. This was exhausting, backbreaking, dirty work, which Ron uttered several commentaries about as the morning progressed.

During the noon meal, Gerhardt announced the afternoon would be spent baling hay. Ron had absolutely no idea what this entailed, but I assured him it was a notch or two better than the stone picking we had done that morning.

The art of baling hay consisted of me sitting on the seat of a huge Farm-all International Model M tractor, that pulled an ancient New Holland automatic baler with a flatbed wagon connected, and steering around the raked rows of cut alfalfa. Gerhardt stood on the deck of the wagon with a metal hook in his right hand. He had the hard job. After the baling machine compacted, shaped, and tied each bale with two strands of wire, Gerhardt would pull the heavy bales out of the machine's back chute and stack them on the wagon. This was incredibly hard physical work for Gerhardt, as the bales were heavy and difficult to maneuver. Gerhardt neatly stacked the bales in interlocking rows on the wagon, six to eight high, until that wagon was filled and exchanged for an empty one.

Ron was sort of odd man out that day for the baling process. He rode along on the tractor between my driver's seat and the rear wheel fender. He tried to carry on a conversation by shouting directly into my ear, but the machines were still too loud. Besides, he was distracting me from Gerhardt's ever-present hand signals. Shortly after starting, Gerhardt suggested that Ron join him as an extra loader on the wagon and do "some real work."

After the first load was completed, Ron suggested it was time for a cold beer, a shade tree, and a nap. After all, it was two in the afternoon, and he had been working since 5:00 A.M. He was visibly irritated when Gerhardt smugly informed him we had three more loads to get in before milking that evening. And following supper and the milking, the four baled wagons would have to be unloaded and stacked into the hay barn in case of rain the next morning. Quitting time that night would be about eleven; that meant we would have worked a strenuous eighteen-hour day, only stopping three times for meals. On his very first day on the farm, Ron was beginning to get a good idea of what real farm life was all about.

By evening of the fourth day of nearly round-the-clock work, Ron walked along with me as I herded the cows to their nighttime pasture. As I slowly walked my bike next to him along the country road at sunset, I could tell Ron had something troubling on his mind. Although a twelve-year-old is somewhat unnerved at seeing his hero become quiet and distant, out of respect, he doesn't attempt to ascertain the reason.

After walking a few dozen yards, Ron finally spoke. "You know, I've spent the last four days with you here, and I'm a little concerned."

"What about?" I asked, hoping I hadn't done or said anything to upset him.

"Is this what your life is *really* like here on the farm? I mean, is all your time spent working?"

A wave of both relief and fear came over me listening to his questions. By his tone, I could tell that Ron not only realized the extent of my responsibilities on the farm but was actually perturbed by what he was witnessing. I was relieved at the validation of what I had always felt, and that the validation was coming from someone I loved and respected. I knew something would surely happen if Ron got involved and protested to Gerhardt about my working conditions. But I also knew Gerhardt, based on his view of things, did not have the capacity to understand.

"Yeah, pretty much this is what my days are like, especially in the summertime," I quietly answered him.

"Don't you have any time for yourself or to play ball with your friends, go into town, you know, stuff boys your age should be doing?" Ron pressed.

"Not really. Gerhardt is a hard worker and expects the same from me, I guess. I do get to go to the county fair for a few afternoons in late August each summer, though," I said, trying to soften the impact a little, but, why, I didn't know.

"That's *bullshit,* boy, bullshit! And so is about half the work you do around here. Nobody gives a damn about weeds growing along the fences. He makes you do that shit just to keep you busy, you gotta know that, don't you?"

"Yeah, I know, but I'm living here, and it wouldn't do any good for me to refuse to work. Gerhardt would just get mad and start yelling at me. Plus, I'd still have to do the work, anyway."

"Tom, this is not at all what I thought your life would be like here on the farm. I thought the fresh air and outdoor life would be good for your growing up. I didn't think you'd be turned into a goddamned slave, for Christ's sake!"

I knew from the impassioned way he was expressing his views that Ron was going to try to change things.

"You know, Jean wrote me in Germany a couple of times telling me she thought Gerhardt was working you too hard. She said she even fought with him sometimes over it, but it didn't do any good," Ron continued. "I thought she may have been overreacting, but now I've seen it for myself, and goddamn it, *I'll* do something about it. I'll tell Gerhardt to knock off some of the bullshit. He's robbing you of your childhood, and I don't like it at all!"

But I knew Ron was only going to be there a few days longer. He could talk, or even yell at Gerhardt all he wanted, but I knew after he left for

Okinawa, halfway around the world from the farm, that my life wouldn't change. It couldn't. I had another six years until I turned eighteen.

"You know, Tom, ever since our folks died, I've had high hopes for you. I'm glad to see your grades are so good in school. Don't know how you do so well, with all your chores here, but I'm glad," Ron's tone had calmed somewhat as he started talking about my schoolwork.

"I like school. I get to learn about what's out there in the world, and I like that. Someday, maybe I can even go to places you've traveled to," I told him.

"Yeah, well . . . but you're gonna do better than me. You need to go to college, then you can get a good job and maybe see the world that way. I'd like to see you go to the University of Wisconsin. Madison's a great city to live in. I'd even like to move there someday when I get out of the Army."

Wow! I could always feel Ron's caring for me, if only through his letters. But, as he talked about college, I realized he had some sort of master plan for me. Nobody had ever discussed my going to college before that day.

"Tell you what. If Jean doesn't need the car for anything tomorrow, I'll borrow it, and we'll drive to Madison and check out the campus. I thought about going there to college once before I enlisted. Hell, it's only about forty miles away!"

I was exhilarated by the thought of going to a city with Ron, but knew his idea would cause problems. "I think Gerhardt is planning on us helping him bale hay again tomorrow, if the weather holds," I said nervously.

"To hell with him! I'll take care of that, it won't be a problem, I assure you!"

Somehow I knew Ron meant what he said.

Later that night, after I had gone to bed, I was awakened by loud voices downstairs. Because of the solidly constructed old house, I couldn't understand exactly what was being said, but Ron's voice was the loudest and seemed quite angry. Occasionally I heard Jean's and Gerhardt's voices as well, but it was apparent that Ron was the one controlling the argument. I knew he was doing what he said he would, making it "no problem" to get me away from work for a day. I was sure he was letting Gerhardt know exactly what he thought of my constant workload. It was possible this confrontation could even help my future on the farm, but I still had doubts at that point.

Ron slept through the next morning's milking, and Gerhardt never said a word to me as I went about my chores in the barn trying to avoid any physical proximity with him. Ron joined all of us for breakfast after the milking and seemed quite upbeat. Both Jean and Gerhardt remained quiet, and the atmosphere at the table was tense.

Ron was the first to speak, and he directed his words to me across the table. "Tom, you and I are gonna take the rest of the day off and drive to Madison. I want to show you the city and the university campus where you'll be attending someday. We'll be leaving right after breakfast," he said in a calm and confident manner.

Gerhardt said nothing. Ron was merely officially informing me that he had won the argument and would get his way, at least today.

My one word answer to him was, "Okay," not wanting to upset Gerhardt, because the weather had stayed dry, meaning the hay needed to be baled that afternoon.

Just as I answered, a bright red truck drove up into the circular driveway. It was Bob, Gerhardt's younger brother. Bob, a rather stout man who occasionally helped with some of the larger farm projects, entered the kitchen, poured himself a cup of coffee, and asked Gerhardt, "What chores do you want me to do this morning before we start baling hay?"

So that was the solution for the day. Ron and I drove to Madison with me feeling the excitement of my day's reprieve from servitude. I was confident it would be one of the best days of my young life up to that point.

We began with a walk around Capital Square, the hub of all activity in the state's capital city. The massive light gray capital building, with its large dome resembling that of the U. S. Capitol in Washington, D.C., is an impressive sight for one of any age to behold.

After relaxing a while on the immense tree-shaded lawn of the capital building, Ron decided we needed a sandwich, and he a cold beer. This was easily accomplished when he found a local tavern a few yards off the square on one of the diagonal streets that began on each of the square's corners.

After cheeseburgers and a cold Pabst Blue Ribbon beer for Ron and a soda (or "pop" as upper Midwesterners called it) for me, it was time for a walk down State Street. This was the most direct street linking Capital Square, in the heart of the city, to the UW campus about six blocks away. State Street was lined on both sides with business establishments mostly supporting the university's thirty-five thousand students. This meant an assortment of book stores, coffee shops, restaurants, beer-only bars, inexpensive clothing stores, and at least one art deco–style movie theater. Strolling down such a street was a first for me, and the experience was enhanced by the fact that Ron was my tour guide.

At the other end of State Street begins the long, nearly half-mile walk up Bascom Hill, the focal point of the university campus. This is an expansive open lawn with old tree-lined parallel sidewalks leading up to Bascom Hall, the main administrative building for the university. Several old stone or brick classroom buildings, each for different subjects, are situated along the perimeters of Bascom Hill.

My heart pounded as we made the climb up that hill, partly from the exertion, but mostly from Ron explaining that someday *I* would be attending classes in these very same halls of higher learning.

Upon completing our extraordinary tour of the sprawling campus, even checking out the dormitory areas, we walked back to State Street on a wooded campus footpath along the shore of Lake Mendota, which borders the university's western boundary. Ron and I stopped for some late afternoon nourishment and refreshments at a restaurant and bar called "Nick's" on State Street, just before Capital Square. The food there was great and tasted even better because I had spent the whole day with my brother.

This was the *real world* I longed to be involved with someday. Even this brief glimpse, far ahead of my time in both years and education, only served to increase my impatience. If only I didn't have to spend another six long, hard, tedious years of what I considered a very limiting (and overworked) life on the farm.

I knew on the ride home at the end of that day that somehow I would find a way to change my circumstances, even if I had to take charge myself, as I had always admired Ron for doing.

Chapter 3

A Ride Towards Independence

In a few days Ron said good-bye to me, as Jean and I took him to the Greyhound bus station in Beaver Dam. He was en route to his new duty station in Okinawa, where he would spend the next two years. He promised to stay in touch with me, and I knew he would.

I was particularly sad to see him go this time. He had expressed genuine concern about the conditions of my life on the dairy farm, realizing it wasn't the best thing for me after all. It was apparent he felt he had let me down by suggesting that I move there. But he had no way of knowing what it would be like at the time. He told me privately at the bus station that he had talked to Gerhardt on my behalf, telling him I needed more time to enjoy my childhood. But even Ron was doubtful this would help, because it was apparent Gerhardt was trying to mold me into a farm boy—the only life he knew.

Before boarding his bus, Ron told me never to lose sight of his hopes of me attending the University of Wisconsin in Madison, and that it was important to keep my grades high in order to be admitted to college when the time came. Then, with a firm handshake and a smile, he was gone.

I endured for the rest of that summer and throughout the next school year. As promised, Ron stayed in touch with a series of red-and-blue-bordered airmail envelopes that arrived about every two weeks. And, as I assured him, I continued to get good grades and thoroughly enjoyed my time in school.

But as May arrived at the end of seventh grade, I dreaded another long summer of constant hard work on the farm. A resentment of both farm life and my brother-in-law, Gerhardt, was building, fueled by the natural early adolescent yearnings for independence. I also felt like I was becoming a burden to Jean and Gerhardt, who were raising their own children. I felt ready to assert some control over my life—a feeling that grew stronger every day.

I wrote to Ron about these growing feelings of restlessness, hoping for some sort of validation that I could take matters into my own hands and try to change my living conditions.

Much to my surprise, I got it, or, at least what I rationalized to be his approval. In one of his letters he said that he fully understood the way I was feeling. He said he was sorry for putting me into a life I hated, even though he thought it was the best thing for me at the time. But, most importantly, he said he would support any ideas I might have, but cautioned me about making *sensible* changes and not doing anything that I might regret in future years.

That was all I needed! In June 1964, when I was thirteen, I began to plot my "escape" from the farm. I would run away.

I had heard about teenage runaways and the trouble many got into. But that happened in big cities like New York or Los Angeles. There were no runaway teens that I knew of in my small area of Wisconsin. Besides, I didn't even like the term *runaway*. I rationalized that I would be *running to* a better life—one that I would have control over. And I would do it sensibly, as Ron expected. I knew many runaway teens just wanted to get away from their parents so they could have the freedom to party, drink beer, or do drugs. I didn't seek the freedom to do any of those things. To me, kids who ran to this type of lifestyle were just immature jerks who would eventually get caught and returned home, or worse. I wanted to escape to a positive and responsible life, one that I was willing to work hard for.

But where? At that time my oldest brother, Jim, was living in Ripon, a town thirty-five miles north of Beaver Dam. I had stayed at Jim's house for a week the previous summer. Ripon was a nice town of about seven thousand people. It had a small private college, a cookie factory, and a Speed Queen washer and dryer assembly plant. I just knew that I could make a life for myself in Ripon, if I could get there and get a job that summer. But the question was, how does a thirteen-year-old get there? And, if he does, how does he go about getting a job and a place to live?

I was determined to do *something* that summer. After about ten days of agonizing over various scenarios, I came up with a plan: I would ride my bicycle the thirty-five miles from the farm to Ripon some night, leaving after Jean's family was asleep and arriving early the next morning. I knew the route well, especially a backcountry road where I could avoid the main state highways for much of the way.

My plan was to ride to Ripon and be at Jim's home before he left for his factory job at six in the morning. I also had to arrive in Ripon before Gerhardt started looking for me to fetch the cows for the morning milking. I figured actually *doing* this before discussing it with either Jim or Jean would show them how serious I was about changing my life. The plan simply had to work.

My hope was to be able to stay with Jim's family just long enough for me to get a summer job so I could afford a small studio apartment or boardinghouse room of my own. Then, when school started in the fall, I could work before and after classes, and on weekends to support myself. I knew, too, that Jean had been receiving about sixty dollars a month in Social Security survivor benefits for me since our father's death. This money was intended to help support me; I hoped I could convince her to send it directly to me. Between the Social Security money and my part-time jobs, I figured I would do okay on my own.

I wrote a long letter to Ron explaining my plan, but didn't mail it immediately. I knew it took about five days for a letter to reach him via airmail, and I didn't want to send it until I was sure things would work out. If I had to abort and reschedule for later in the summer, I would need the element of surprise, even with Ron.

I started narrowing down dates for my escape. I closely followed weather reports to see what conditions would be like for the next several days. Finally, like General Eisenhower at Normandy, I decided on my own D—for departure—Day. I would leave the night of July 15–16. The weather was to be dry, and there would be a half-moon—good enough to light my way, but not too bright for me to be seen clearly from a distance.

Finally I mailed the letter to Ron, then wrote a similar one to Jean, explaining I could not and would not live on the farm any longer. I outlined my plan for what I thought would be a sensible alternative and asked for her support. I planned to leave this letter on my bed when I left.

Logic told me that I had to travel light, so the day before I planned to leave, I packed a small knapsack with a quart jar of water, a few packaged cookies, and some beef jerky I swiped from a supply Gerhardt liked to keep handy in the kitchen. I also had a small flashlight I could clip onto my belt.

On the day of my planned departure, I checked the air in my bicycle tires and oiled the chain. I covertly duct-taped a small hand-operated air pump to the frame, just in case I got a flat tire. The only thing I couldn't prepare for was staying up all night. I had never stayed awake all night before, but I figured I could do it since my plan was important. I also counted on the fresh night air to help keep me alert for this adventure!

That night I went to bed about nine as usual, except I kept my clothes on. I was excited and filled with anticipation—and a bit of fear—as I waited the two hours it took for me to be sure everyone else was asleep.

Fortunately, the beginning of my plan went smoothly, as the family went to bed on schedule—around 10:30 P.M. I spent about ten minutes listening for sounds or movement at my partially opened door, then got up the courage to pull my knapsack from under my bed and leave my second-floor bedroom. Each bare wooden step seemed to make a deafening groan as I slowly started down the stairs. It felt like it took hours to traverse the dozen or so steps from my room to the kitchen, but I made it without waking anyone.

The doors from the kitchen to the outside yard were the next noisy obstacles I had to overcome. Doors in old houses creek when they are opened and closed, and they seem to be louder at night when one is trying to sneak through them. These doors were no exception. And, although they were, in my opinion, loud enough to compete with a John Philip Sousa marching band, no one woke up.

Soon I was out of the house, and with the gait and caution of a burglar, I made my way across the circular driveway to the equipment shed where, earlier that evening, I had stashed my bike. After securing my knapsack to the rear carrying rack and squeezing the tires one more time, I was riding down the farm driveway.

The night was still and warm, but not too muggy, as late July nights can be in Wisconsin. The only sounds were the constant chirping of crickets and the occasional distant hum of a cicada. There were no vehicles in sight as I rode out onto Prospect Road, the narrow blacktop that went past the farm. I couldn't believe I was actually doing this! And I knew all hell would break loose in the morning.

But for the time being, I had to concentrate on the journey ahead. After a couple of miles, Prospect Road intersected with County Trunk A, a slightly wider, more well-traveled road. I knew this road was under construction that July, with several miles covered with loose gravel, pending resurfacing. As I passed the smudge pots of burning oil that marked the beginning of the gravel, the going got awfully tough. I was able to keep my tires in a track that had been packed smoother by vehicles that had driven the road before me. This slowed my pace somewhat, but I knew the gravel portion only lasted for a couple of miles—no major setback.

About three miles from the farm, I turned off the graveled County Trunk A onto Buckhorn Road. Even though I had encountered no vehicles before reaching this junction, I knew there was even less likelihood of meeting traffic on this road. It was a seldom-used twelve-mile stretch of road that went from outside Beaver Dam to Waupun, the next town. I chose it for that very reason. The highway, which also connected the two towns, was too heavily traveled.

As I pedaled along the flat and straight Buckhorn Road, I began to believe I was really going to escape. I was making good time and felt fine. So far, the adrenaline was not letting any fatigue set in.

One thing I hadn't planned for were farm dogs. I encountered the first one several miles down Buckhorn Road. The sudden barking and howling of a large dog in the middle of a still night has the same effect as sirens and floodlights being switched on during an escape attempt from a prison. It curdles the blood of the escapee and alerts the guards—or, in my case, the sleeping farm family. Moreover, most farm dogs run loose and are quick to chase strange things passing their farmyards.

I thought I could outpedal the first dog, but I couldn't. The yard light came on just as I made it past where it could illuminate me, but the dog—some sort of German shepherd mix—ran at full speed to catch me. And he was mean! Barking, growling, and snapping at my ankles as I frantically pedaled.

I knew I had to do something or the farmer would come out thinking there was a threat to his family or crops. I suddenly stopped my bike, which made the mongrel back off a bit in surprise. In a quiet voice, I tried to calm him down, but it only partially worked; he came closer, still growling and baring his teeth. I remembered the beef jerky I'd brought along. While the dog was threatening and growling, I slowly reached into the knapsack and pulled out an eight-inch strip of the dried, spicy beef. It worked! As soon as he got a whiff of it, I flung it several yards behind me, and he went over to it and lay down on the pavement and started gnawing on the leatherlike treat. I took that opportunity to ride quickly away.

Just before reaching the end of Buckhorn Road, where it intersected with County Trunk AW, I spotted headlights coming from behind. A car was closing in on me fast. My first thought was that it was Jean or Gerhardt, or both, tracking me down after realizing I was gone. I didn't know how they could have discovered me missing, but there is a certain amount of paranoia that accompanies every escapee, and I was no different. My fear of being caught was far worse than my fear of some farm dog mauling me along the route. I knew about Gerhardt's quick temper, and I certainly didn't want to be on the receiving end of it out on a deserted road in the middle of the night.

As the car got closer, I knew I had to do something to get out of sight before it was close enough to cast its headlights on me and the red reflector on the back fender of my bike. But there was no place to hide. No trees, no rock fences, no buildings. There was a shallow ditch along the road with weeds growing about two feet high. I pulled off the road and laid my bike flat in the ditch, hurriedly pulling weeds out by the roots to cover the shiny red-and-white fenders. I was especially careful to cover the red reflectors. As the vehicle noise grew louder, I too got down in the ditch and quickly covered myself with weeds. I covered my face with my arm just as the headlights cast their glow over the area where I was—I hoped—concealed.

The car sped by without slowing down. As it passed, I raised up to look, and to my great relief, it was not one that I recognized.

It was then that I realized that in my haste, I had pulled up some large thistles with my bare hands. My hands stung and burned, but I considered them inconsequential wounds for such a mission. I got back on my bike and started to ride again.

By that time fatigue, both from being up all night and from extended physical exertion, was setting in. I had to get off and walk my bike up some of the gentle hills along the route. Also setting in was the realization that I was actually accomplishing my plan. And every mile I traveled reinforced my anticipation of having the freedom to live my own life. At that point, I knew I would finish my nighttime journey on schedule, and I would also accomplish my goal of attaining independence, despite what surely would happen in a few hours, when all this was discovered.

Three hours later, I was coasting by the Ripon city limits sign, just as dawn was beginning to illuminate the eastern sky. Lights were being turned on in the houses along the back streets I took to Jim's house. The local townspeople were beginning a new day.

When I arrived at Jim's house, his car was in the driveway and his kitchen light was on in the rear of the house. This meant he was up and about but hadn't left for work yet. My plan was still working.

I was so fatigued and drained of energy, that it was all I could do to get off my bike and collapse in a lawn chair a few feet from his car. There I would wait for him to come out, so as not to awaken the rest of his family. I was hoping it would only be a few minutes before he left for work, because I had to concentrate my remaining strength on keeping my eyes open.

Soon Jim came out the back door carrying his lunch box to receive what must have been one of the shocks of his life, to see his kid brother half-asleep in one of his lawn chairs at 5:00 A.M. Obviously, my escape plan had remained a secret; Jean or Gerhardt apparently had not yet noticed I was gone, or surely they would have already called Jim.

He was surprised to see me, but also was sympathetic and concerned when he found me in his yard. My presence also put him in a dilemma, because he was supposed to pick up some coworkers and drive them to their factory jobs twenty miles away, and he didn't have time to deal with me right then. He took me into the house, woke his wife, then telephoned Jean. On our way inside, I told him I had run away from the farm and wanted to stay with him just long enough to find a job and a place to live.

I wasn't privy to his phone conversation with Jean, but after he hung up, he assured me everything would be worked out when he got home that evening. For now, I should get some rest. His wife fixed up an extra bedroom for me, and I slept the entire day, satisfied that I had accomplished my "escape" from the farm. I was determined to stay away and begin the next phase in my quest for independence.

And, as promised, that night—and for the next week—my fate was discussed back and forth among Jim, Jean, and me. I was adamant about not going back to the farm under any circumstances, temporary or otherwise.

Ron received my letter by the end of the first week of my stay at Jim's house. He immediately called me on a military line from Okinawa. He said he was a bit surprised at my boldness, but, more importantly, he wasn't disappointed in me for leaving the farm. He told me he thought it took a lot of guts and he was proud of me for that. He said he would continue to support me and would also send money if I needed it. He said he would try to get some leave in a few months to come and see me, but for now he felt I should "just stay put" at Jim's until he could do more.

Ron's input had a major impact on all concerned in this situation. He convinced Jean that I was ready to take care of myself and made her agree, at the very least, that the farm was not the place for me to live.

I was elated! My plan had worked, and I was victorious!

Within two weeks of arriving in Ripon, I got an afternoon and Sunday morning paper route, where I earned fifty dollars a month with tips. Within another month, two ladies running a Sears Roebuck catalog store along my paper route offered me a second part-time position doing odd jobs, such as sweeping, uncrating displays, and packing up returned merchandise. I did this job for two hours each day after my paper route, and all day on Saturdays, which provided me with nearly another hundred dollars a month. I could maintain both of these jobs without interfering with school or homework, which was of vital importance, because of Ron's constant insistence that I keep my grades up.

Jean remained my legal guardian, but Jim assumed daily custody of me. This situation quickly grew strained on both sides. Jim and his family had reluctantly agreed to take me in, and I fully understood his reluctance. He had had his kid brother shoved down his throat by circumstances, and it was a big imposition on him. He never showed his frustration, but I knew it had to be there.

Around Thanksgiving that first year in Ripon, I received some great news from Ron. He was coming home on a thirty-day leave to see how I was doing and to offer more of his help. For the next two weeks, it was extremely difficult for me to concentrate on school, but I knew I had to in order to prove to him my plan could work.

When the day finally came for Ron's arrival, I met him on my bike at the old Sunoco gas station that doubled as Ripon's Greyhound bus terminal. I was nearly exploding with the joy of seeing him again and with the excitement of sharing with him so many things about my new life.

Ron could immediately see the difference in me compared to how I was on the farm. He concluded that, although it might have been difficult, living on Gerhardt's farm had taught me a good work ethic, which I should be thankful for. Actually, I was thankful for that; but now I was channeling that work ethic into a life I enjoyed and could control.

After proudly showing off my jobs and most recent grades to Ron, I broached what I knew would be a delicate subject. I wanted to live on my own, away from Jim's family. Not really to my surprise, Ron listened intently to what I had to say, but didn't say much about it. The next day, after finishing school and work, I stopped in to see him at the hotel where he was staying. When I got there, he was reading the classifieds in the Ripon newspaper. When I asked why he was reading the ads, he calmly stated that he was looking for an apartment that would be right for me, and then he smiled.

He had come through for me again, convincing Jim and Jean that I really could live on my own as a young teenager! His only conditions were what I would have guessed: Keep my grades up and stay out of trouble. I readily agreed to those conditions, because it was what I intended to do anyway.

While I was at school the next day, Ron went apartment hunting in Ripon. We had agreed to a "cover story." He would not tell prospective landlords the apartment would be for a lone teenager. Rather, he would explain he had just gotten out of the Army and had landed a job as a salesman who would be on the road a lot, but still needed a small place to call home. He would also say he had a younger brother who would help look after his affairs while he was gone.

By the time I returned from school and work that night, Ron said he had the perfect place for me. It was a small, furnished studio apartment above a drugstore on Watson Street, Ripon's main business thoroughfare. It rented for forty-five dollars a month, and the money order could be mailed each month to the landlord who lived in another part of town. It had an entrance on the main street, as well as another backstairs entrance from an alley that afforded more privacy. I arranged to meet Ron there the following day on my school lunch break. He would have the key so I could inspect the apartment before he signed the rental agreement.

It was perfect! Small, but perfect. The apartment was more like a long hallway that was about three feet wider at one end to accommodate the length of a small sleeper sofa and an old stuffed chair. A kitchenette, resembling a galley on a small fishing boat, was along one wall in the narrow part of the hall. A tiny bathroom with a tub and shower was at the other end. For a newly emancipated teen living on his own, it was more than sufficient. Who cared if you had to move the stuffed chair each time you wanted to open the tiny closet door in the living/bedroom?

The next day, Ron signed the paperwork and told me he had paid three months' rent to give me some breathing room. The following Sunday, after my morning paper route, he helped me move my things in, including a small used black-and-white TV he had bought me. For the remainder of Ron's leave, we spent the nights with him sleeping on the sofa and me on the frayed carpeted floor. There wasn't enough room to fold out the single sleeper *and* have another person sleep on the floor. But, I thought the cramped arrangements were just fine, and Ron didn't seem to mind either.

Too soon, I was again standing with Ron at Ripon's Greyhound bus stop. He was back in uniform, returning to finish his tour in Okinawa. He told me he would try to get another leave after he completed that assignment. He said he was interested in then doing a tour in a place called Vietnam. This was a place I was just beginning to hear about, as I watched Walter Cronkite on the display TV sets while mopping the floor at the Sears catalog store each night. But, no matter where Ron was stationed, I *always* felt his presence and support, as though he were standing right there beside me. If only every teenage guy could have an older brother like him!

After Ron left, I settled into my life as a teenager living on my own in Ripon. The apartment Ron had found for me was indeed perfect. It was very small, but large enough for me. I decided it was best to keep my living arrangements a secret from my friends and acquaintances, who were always looking for ways to "escape" from their parents. I didn't want my apartment to become a hangout for other teens. I took the responsibility of living on my own with more maturity than other kids my age could understand. I didn't want to blow it.

And, of course, I felt I owed it to Ron to prove I was responsible, in exchange for assisting me in this whole emancipation process. I wanted to show him I could live alone, work my part-time jobs, and keep my grades up in school. After all, college was only a couple of years away.

Actually, I found it exciting to keep up the charade of sharing the apartment with my older brother. Ron did, in fact, change his Army records to reflect "our" apartment address as his official home address. I simply told those who were curious, or had a specific need to know, that my brother worked for the government and traveled a lot. I certainly wasn't being untruthful on either count, just stretching reality a bit.

Then there were times when some of my peers suggested coming over to the apartment for some special occasion. I would quickly counter such proposals by saying Ron just got in late, or was expected at any time, especially if I thought they had an inkling I was alone for a few days. I either became so good at being the Artful Dodger, or so unbelievable, that before long, suggestions of "we can meet at Tom's apartment" were no longer made. Either way, I protected my situation.

I also had to use the same cover story around adults I dealt with in Ripon. I had heard a rumor that if the local school board found out I was living on my own, without parents or guardians paying into the school's tax base, I would have to pay private tuition—as much as six hundred dollars a year—to attend the public high school. Ron advised me to maintain a low profile, but assured me that if the rumor was in fact true and my independence was discovered, he would pay the tuition if needed.

I heeded Ron's advice as usual, and kept my big secret, even from my employers. I just kept collecting part-time jobs as time went by. I maintained my paper route and part-time position at the Sears catalog store until I was sixteen. Then I traded in the paper route for jobs delivering pizzas at two competing restaurants in Ripon. They provided the delivery vehicles, complete with portable sterno ovens in the backseat. More importantly, each restaurant also gave me a free meal with every four-hour shift I worked. This was a great benefit for me. I worked six nights a week, three for each restaurant, which meant that each week I got to eat six hot dinners of anything they served.

I also got an additional part-time job at a veterinary hospital in Ripon. I would go in very early each morning before school and on weekends for about two hours to clean the kennels, feed the animals, and perform general janitorial work. I loved animals and at one time thought about becoming a veterinarian. I also learned to admire Dr. Statler, the vet who owned and operated the hospital. I respected his combination of professional knowledge, business sense, and customer service. During the next few summers, I worked full-time for him. Sometimes I went with him in the mornings on his farm appointments, and in the afternoons, I assisted him with small animal surgeries at his hospital. As Ron was, Dr. Statler was quite the role model for me at the time.

Ron finished his assignment in Okinawa and came home for another leave shortly after I got my driver's license. Of course, this was the time for me to parade him around Ripon, so everyone could see he did, in fact, exist.

Ron's biggest concern was that I was working too many hours a week at my accumulated jobs, and that it could affect my schooling. After he acclimated himself to the local time zone, I took Ron on a typical day with me. We were up at 5:00 A.M. and at the vet hospital by 5:30, finishing work there by 7:30. He went back to the apartment while I attended school until 3:30. I met him again at the Sears store, where I worked until 5:00, then back to the vet hospital until 6:30. Finally, I was off delivering pizzas until about eleven o'clock. He wanted to know when I did my homework, so I explained that most weeknights were slow for pizza delivering, so I was allowed to read or study while on the clock. Also, I pointed out that I could now pay my own living expenses, meaning Jean could bank my monthly Social Security checks in a college fund.

He, of course, thought this was too much work and compared it to my previous life on the farm. I assured him I enjoyed being busy and earning money and hot meals, and that I was fine. Besides, I reminded him all my report cards showed A's and B's, except for math, where I only earned a C, making me reconsider becoming a veterinarian.

Ron said he would remain concerned, but was satisfied that I was happy and said he admired my work ethic. He also saw that I needed my own transportation to shuttle between all of my jobs. The following week he bought me a 90 cc Suzuki motorcycle. His only stipulation was that I wear a helmet when riding it outside of town. Now, thanks to him, I had complete freedom!

Another thing that concerned Ron while on that particular leave was his choice of his next duty station. He had volunteered to go to Vietnam. By then it was early 1967, and Vietnam had been creeping into American households with more and more regularity via the evening news.

I had mixed feelings about him going to a war zone. On one hand, it was exciting for me to think of him in Vietnam, a place where a career soldier like Ron could really put his skills and training to good use. But, on the other hand, I had the very selfish fear of possibly losing the most important person in my life.

Ron explained all the "benefits" of his volunteering for Vietnam in an attempt to rationalize it to me, and maybe to himself. He pointed out the extra combat pay each month, no federal income taxes in a war zone, and faster promotions in rank. And, by the way, there was also the free postage on all letters to the States from Vietnam. It certainly made me feel better that since he would be risking his life, he would at least get *free* postage!

He assured me he would be all right, and somehow I just had to believe him. But when he left Wisconsin for Vietnam, I could only imagine how painful it would be for me if he never came back.

It took about two weeks for his first letter to arrive, and sure enough, the airmail envelope had the word *FREE* handwritten by him in the corner where the stamp should be. Vietnam was already paying off for him.

He told me in that first letter that he had arrived safely in Vietnam and was assigned to a unit with the 25th Infantry Division, in a place called Cu Chi. He assured me the 25th had a solid and distinguished history in both World War II and Korea prior to its deployment to Vietnam. He also said it was located in a relatively "safe" part of the country, only about twenty-five miles northwest of Saigon, in Tay Ninh Province.

His one-page letters would arrive at my apartment about every ten days or so. Sometimes he would send a Polaroid picture of him in and around the Cu Chi base camp. One time he even sent me a picture of him with M-16 in hand, squatting over a dead North Vietnamese soldier.

About a week after receiving each letter, I would rush home to check my mailbox for the next red, white, and blue airmail envelope. One time, after his year in Vietnam was nearly completed, there was a large official look-ing manila envelope from the "Department of the Army" leaning next to the row of apartment mailboxes in my building's hallway. My heart sank as I slumped down, all alone, on the stairs near the mailbox to open it, as I feared the worst. Inside was a green plastic-covered plaque and a small black box that had the words *BRONZE STAR MEDAL* engraved on the outside. The plaque was the official award of the Bronze Star to Ron for "operations against hostile forces." As my worst fears vanished, I couldn't have been more relieved and more proud of him at that moment.

I immediately wrote Ron to tell him that his medal had been sent to me. In a return letter, he modestly said it didn't mean all that much, that "every-body" gets one over there. He even added, "with that medal and a quarter, I could buy a cup of coffee."

Regardless, within a day I had assembled something of a shrine to him in my small apartment. The plaque, the medal itself, and several photos of him were proudly displayed on a tiny used end table in the only available corner of my living/bedroom. I was almost at the point of inviting select friends over, just so they could see it and I could exercise my bragging rights. But, I decided to forgo that idea in order to keep the secret of living alone. Besides, I knew Ron was too modest to have strangers looking at his medal and pictures.

Then, just before he was due to return from his combat tour, I received a letter in which he said he had "some bad news and some good news" for me. The bad news was that he had decided to extend his tour in Vietnam for another six months. He knew I wouldn't like this, but asked me to understand. He went on to say that the "good news" was twofold.

First, by extending his tour, he would receive a two thousand dollar bonus. The bonus, he said, could be used to buy me a car, since using my motorcycle wasn't safe during the Wisconsin winters. Secondly, he said he could be guaranteed a stateside assignment after the extension in Vietnam was completed. He said he would try for Fort Sheridan, Illinois, or some-place else in the Midwest so he could be closer to me.

I wrote back to him that the idea of him buying me a car was nice, but I didn't want him to feel obligated to do that, especially if it meant risking his life for another six months in Vietnam. I did like the idea of him being stationed closer to me in the States, and readily told him so. But, since I knew he didn't particularly like being stationed here compared to over-seas, I reassured him I could continue taking care of myself. I said I would support him, no matter what his decision was, just like he had always done for me.

Of course, he opted to say in Vietnam. By this time, I was more comfortable with him being there, since he had made it through his first year unscathed. He even survived the notorious Tet Offensive in early 1968, although at one point during that time, I didn't receive a letter from him for nearly three weeks. But I also had not received any *official* notifications of any kind from the government, so I convinced myself everything was okay with him. I assumed he was just a little *busier* during that time.

On a gloomy gray day in early November 1968, I stopped after work to check my mailbox before climbing the stairs to my apartment. I was disappointed in not finding a letter from Ron telling me when he was coming home. While I was on the third step from the top, I looked at the alcove outside my apartment door, and there he stood! He was in full military uniform, holding a flight bag and smiling. "I lost my key somewhere in Nam, hope you have yours!" he said smugly as I tripped up the last few steps to shake his hand.

All was well in my world again!

It was nice having to sleep on the floor again, while Ron slept on the sofa. But, after only a few nights into his thirty-day leave, I noticed a distinct difference in his sleeping habits. His nights were much more restless than they were before he went to Vietnam. Now sometimes he would mumble things in his sleep, but nothing I could understand. A couple of times I was awakened by the smell of cigarette smoke and would open one eye to see him sitting upright and just staring out the window at nothing in particular. These things happened long after his ten-thousand-mile jet lag had worn off. He never spoke about specific experiences in Vietnam, and I knew never to ask about his time there or about what was causing his sleep disturbances.

I was just glad he was back safely from the war zone. Each week, about three to four hundred of his fellow soldiers were coming back in coffins. I made no excuses for being glad that my brother, my mentor, and my hero had come home alive from his time in Vietnam.

Chapter 4

Coming of Age

"Wake up, boy, we're coming into Laredo!"

I was conscious of a fly buzzing just above my sweaty closed eyelids. Ron reached one arm over the back of the driver's seat and was shaking me. "Time to wake up, we're here!" He had been driving for so long, that at first I couldn't remember where "here" meant. But any place had to be an improvement over the black vinyl oven I had been sporadically napping in these past few hours of our long trek from Fort Hood, Texas, to the border town of Laredo.

Ron was now stationed at Fort Hood in central Texas. He called it just a long stateside R&R after having spent eighteen months in Vietnam. He had wanted a duty assignment at Fort Sheridan, Illinois, just outside of Chicago, so he could be closer to me in Wisconsin. But, according to the Army, the closest they could get him to the upper Midwest was Texas. Ron dismissed this as "Army logic."

I had planned to travel to Washington, D.C., with my high school class during the four-day Easter weekend that year. This was considered to be *the* big event of my high school career. Traveling to the nation's capital was a major lifetime event for many of the students at Ripon High. However, somehow I felt the anticipation of making this class trip waned in comparison to the possibility of taking an adventure to a Mexican border town with Ron.

Just two weeks before the class trip, I checked the mailbox outside my quaint little hole-in-the-wall apartment and found a letter from Ron in a business-size envelope. He wrote at least once a week, but always mailed his letters in the standard small envelopes. When I opened this larger envelope, I immediately saw the reason for the change. Inside was a brightly colored American Airlines folder, containing a round-trip ticket from Milwaukee to Dallas, made out in my name, for the upcoming long Easter weekend. Also, there was a Greyhound bus ticket from Dallas to Killeen, Texas, which I knew was the closest town to Fort Hood. Attached to the tickets was a brief note in Ron's handwriting:

Tom:
Hope you didn't have any plans for Easter. I arranged some time off, and thought you could get away from Wisconsin and fly down here. We can drive down to Mexico, if you like. Will call this Sunday morning to work out the details.
Love, Ron

The class trip had diminished to nothing by the time I finished reading Ron's note! Three or four days just kickin' around with him while on furlough in Texas and Mexico! A class trip to *anywhere* would have been dull in comparison. Whatever Ron had in mind for us, I knew would be far from dull. So I eagerly accepted his offer when he called the next Sunday to finalize the arrangements.

❈   ❈   ❈

I shooed away the annoying fly from my face and pulled myself up to lean on the back of the front seat. It was late afternoon, and hot and dusty. "Age of Aquarius" was playing on the radio of Ron's 1966 black Chevy Impala. The station crackled with static, and the song was intermittently interrupted by a few words of Spanish interference.

Looking out the window, I assumed the heat had gone to Ron's brain. Just a minute before he said "we were coming into Laredo," but all I saw was a lot of nothing.

The terrain along the side of the highway was desolate—sand, rocks, and sagebrush. The land was also slightly contoured with dry, rolling hills. As the car came to the top of one of these grades, Ron suddenly said, "There's Laredo, boy." I saw it as soon as he did and felt only relief at the fact that our long drive would be coming to an end.

What we saw, of course, was the American Laredo, the city north of the Rio Grande River. We actually were en route to Nuevo Laredo on the Mexican side. It was there that a guy could "have a good time," according to Ron. Since he had been there a few times before, I figured he knew what he was talking about; but then, I always figured he did.

Ron told me that the last time he was in Nuevo Laredo he had left a star sapphire ring with a Mexican madam named Celia, for safekeeping. He'd bought the ring in Malaysia when he was on R&R from Vietnam. It was valued at over a thousand dollars.

I would question the sanity of anyone else leaving such a valuable item with a foreign "lady of the evening," but not Ron. He told me he had his reasons, and I'm sure he did. He said he knew he would get it back on this visit. Somehow I knew he would.

We drove through the streets of Laredo as I thought of the song that country singer Marty Robbins had made famous. We wound around some side streets, finally pulling the dusty Chevy into an equally dusty little parking lot surrounded by a twelve-foot-high hurricane fence. There were a half-dozen other cars already parked inside, all bearing American license plates.

Down a slight embankment beside the parking lot was the almost stagnant Rio Grande, with Nuevo Laredo on the far side. A large, modern four-lane bridge, connecting the two cities and countries, was just downstream about a hundred yards.

"We'll leave the car here on the American side," Ron explained. "I know the guy who runs this lot, and basically can trust him. We'll walk across the bridge into Mexico. At least this way the car stands a better chance of not getting stripped or ripped off."

Just then the old attendant came walking up to us from under a small tree where he had been enjoying a siesta. He was dingy looking and had a zigzag scar on the right side of his forehead. He seemed to recognize Ron and offered a half-toothed smile. Both hands were extended as he approached, the right clasped Ron's in an overly friendly handshake, and the other received the crisp ten-dollar greenback Ron was handing him.

"Keep our car here until tomorrow night," Ron said in more of a business tone than a friendly one. "And, amigo . . . make sure none of your grease-backed friends uses it for a taxi. I checked the odometer this time," he growled intimidatingly at the old man.

"Si, señor," was the attendant's only reply, as half of his smile disappeared, like he had just remembered this particular gringo was no easy mark.

With that taken care of, Ron and I set out to cross the bridge over the Rio Grande into Mexico, and the experiences that lay beyond.

Ron always believed in traveling light, so we were—just the clothes we were wearing and our wallets. Most of our money was dispersed among different pants pockets, and I even had some in the bottom of one of my socks. Two gringos from the States can't be too careful when going to a rough border town for a good time, now can they?

On the topic of being careful, just as we stepped onto the bridge sidewalk, Ron nonchalantly asked, "Do you have your protection with you?"

I was surprised at this question, since he knew I was carrying a .32 caliber automatic holstered inside my waistband under the fatigue shirt he loaned to me. He had given it to me to carry before starting the drive to Laredo. He also carried a .38 revolver in a leg holster wrapped around his left calf. Both of the weapons were, of course, simply a precautionary measure.

"You know I've got the automatic you gave me," I said quietly so no one else would hear.

"I don't mean *that* kind of protection," Ron said impatiently. "Do you have any rubbers with you? I don't want you taking any border rot back to your girlfriends in Wisconsin."

Oh, *that's* what he means, I realized, rather embarrassed. "Of course I've got some," I answered in my best man-of-the-world tone. I thought about the same single Trojan I had been sitting on in my wallet for at least the last year—just in case I ever needed it. I wasn't sure what condition it was in, but it was "lubricated with a receptacle tip" and had been "hermetically sealed" at the factory. The last time I pulled out the foil package to show a friend, most of the printing had been worn off. So, that being the case, I figured that the product inside the foil was probably dried and cracked resembling a thin potato chip. Some protection for me here in Mexico! "Have you got yours with you?" I asked Ron in as an adult manner as I could muster.

"Never use 'em anymore. Remember, I've been all over the world these past ten years. Got immune to most of that crap years ago."

Wow, was all I could think. My mind was racing with anticipation now that I knew for sure what Ron had in mind for the next twenty-four hours!

We dropped our coins in the turnstile halfway across the bridge, showed our IDs, and we were there! I was in Mexico, and was looking forward to whatever the evening could offer us two men of the world. Well, maybe one and a half, as I reconsidered my status.

Ron walked along the dirty little sidewalk with a smooth, determined, yet casual stride.

His eyes darted randomly from side to side, taking everything in, but obviously looking for something in particular. I stayed close by his side, but a bit behind him. I certainly didn't want to get lost in a foreign country, especially since I didn't speak more than a handful of Spanish words.

As we walked along, by then on a back street, I noticed Mexico wasn't brightly colored like the travel brochures depicted. Instead, it was all quite drab. The late afternoon sun was already retreating below the horizon, spilling evenly colored long shadows on the narrow streets. This effect made the streets and buildings blend together, devoid of all contrasts, that is, if there were any distinguishing hues to begin with. The streets and crumbling sidewalks were a chalky gray-blue that molded into the bases of the likewise crumbling stucco buildings of the same shade.

Even the local people milling about seemed to be of the same color, wearing drab, colorless ponchos, loose-fitting shirts, and sombreros. Their teeth and skin did nothing to enhance any contrast either. Along this back street, far from the more familiar paths paved with American tourists' dollars, Mexico was definitely not "bright."

We finally stopped at a tiny intersection in the maze of small buildings. "Fourth street from the bridge," Ron said soberly, mostly to himself. "Now two blocks west, and it should be on the left side of that street."

I didn't want to interrupt his train of thought regarding the directions as we turned and began walking west, so I said nothing. But something inside of me was burning to know what the "it" was. I guessed I would find out when we got there.

As we rounded the corner of the street two blocks from where Ron last spoke, he uttered a satisfied, "Good, that's it."

The "it" was the front of a run-down cantina just down the street. "Emilio's" was spelled in half-worn letters on the front just above the open-air entrance.

I couldn't believe that Ron had purposely walked with me to this place. Surely, I thought, there must be better places in Mexico to show me than "Emilio's Cantina." It looked as though Emilio's only clientele were a few of the locals.

Walking through the open front door was like walking into a darker shade of drab. The meager appearance of a half-dozen wooden spindle-legged tables and chairs in the small room did nothing to break the interior's monotony. An old man was asleep and snoring with his head down on a table in the far corner. On the opposite side of the room there were a few stools in front of a well-worn wooden bar. A large cracked mirror and faded Mexican flag hung on the wall behind the bar. A chipped bust of the Virgin Mary with a glass-beaded rosary draped around the neck was on top of a cabinet in front of the mirror. A couple of faded *Playboy* foldouts hung on a far wall. The whole scene was a strange collage of nationalism, religion, and sin, I thought to myself.

"Emilio!" Ron called out in the direction of a small doorway leading into a room behind the bar.

A rather robust, impoverished-looking Mexican I figured to be Emilio waddled in from the back room, obviously just awakened from an overly long siesta. He gripped a well-used copy of some girlie magazine in his left hand.

"Wake up you goddamned spic, I'm back!" Ron half-hollered in a friendly, but commanding tone.

"Ah, Señor Reilly. Good to see you again," Emilio responded. "I see you brought a gringo friend with you this time—thought you always come here alone."

"This time is special, Emilio. Meet my brother, Tom," Ron said proudly, but protectively.

"Ah, Señor Tómas," smiled Emilio as he directed his attention to me. His smile became wider as he offered his fat, burly hand across the bar to me. As I looked into his face, I couldn't help but notice that his right eye seemed to be lifelessly peering off into space over my left shoulder, and was a duller shade of brown than the one that was looking directly at me. I also noticed that Emilio carried a spare meal or two in his rotting teeth. When he clutched my hand while shaking it, I couldn't help but wonder where that sweaty hand had been a few minutes earlier. Great acquaintances this brother of mine makes around the world, I thought.

Just then Ron leaned over the bar and stuck a folded twenty-dollar bill into Emilio's dirty shirt pocket, at the same time mumbling something in his ear.

Emilio looked at Ron, still bearing his wide grin, dropped my hand, patted his pocket, and said, "I will see what I can do for you, Señor Reilly." Then he waddled back into the dingy little room behind the bar.

Ron stepped behind the bar and helped himself to two bottles of Mexican beer, a brand that was unfamiliar to me. He opened them with a bottle opener mounted on the edge of the bar and handed one to me with a satisfied demeanor.

"What's going on, Ron?" I asked, no longer able to quell my burning curiosity.

"Just trust me, boy. Emilio is taking care of the arrangements. You want to celebrate Easter weekend, don't you?"

"Sure do, this just seems a little strange, that's all," I said, immediately wishing I hadn't.

"Trust me, boy."

I was just forcing down the second to last swallow of the bad-tasting beer when Emilio reemerged from the back room.

"Come with me, my friends," Emilio said with a sly grin.

Ron beckoned me with a quick movement of his head, and I followed them as we stepped behind the bar and out through a back door of the shabby little hole-in-the-wall cantina.

We stepped into the narrow alley, now illuminated only by faint street-lights on the bordering streets. In the near darkness I could make out what seemed to be a 1950 Ford. It was black, beat-up, and equipped with an old external sun visor that extended out over the entire windshield.

An unshaven, cutthroat-looking local was leaning across the front fender of the driver's side, chewing on a toothpick. I didn't see anyone else in the front seat, so I assumed he was the driver. I was right. When Ron and I walked towards the car, the man jumped into action, hurrying to the rear door of the passenger side, which he opened chauffeur-style. Ron and I got into the backseat, as our driver fumbled in the darkness for the keys.

"Here amigo, gracias," Ron said to our silent driver, handing him what I thought was a five-dollar bill.

"Muchas gracias," were the first words the driver had said since we first encountered him. He hurried back around to the other side of the car, got in, and we quickly drove off, squealing fan belt and all.

Ron, sensing I was feeling somewhat bewildered, said, "Don't worry, boy. We're going for a little ride that will take about thirty minutes." I was reassured knowing Ron was my guide and had obviously been here before.

All the car windows were heavily tinted, making it difficult to see where we were going from the backseat. Intermittent glows and flashes of light indicated we were still driving through town.

The aroma inside the car was sickening—a musty mixture of cigar smoke, stale beer, and dried vomit. I tried to breathe in short breaths so as not to inhale too much of the putrid air, but it didn't work. I thought to myself that a person might be able to get used to this stench in a week or two, but not in the half-hour jaunt we would be taking through the streets of Nuevo Laredo.

I attempted to take my mind off the smell by trying to identify sounds outside the car. Even though my hearing seemed more acute what with my vision being reduced, the bad muffler and shrieking fan belt on the old piece of junk served to camouflage most exterior noises.

After several sharp turns around city corners during the earlier part of the trip, our route straightened out onto a main road in the country, and our speed accelerated accordingly. Suddenly, the car slowed and negotiated a right turn over some extremely rough road. Another hundred yards or so, another slow turn, and the car came to a stop.

Ron, who had been quiet throughout most of the ride, except to curse the driver's ability occasionally, said, "We're here."

Our driver got out, came around the car, and opened the back door on my side.

At first, all I saw in the darkness was an old adobe wall about twenty feet high. Emerging from the car, I could see more of the wall, which ran about forty yards to the front of the car and disappeared into the darkness behind us. It would have seemed as though we were out in the middle of nowhere, except for the fact that the sky was glowing from different colored lights, and muffled sounds of music and laughter were coming from whatever was happening on the other side of that adobe barrier.

Ron paid the driver, who quickly drove off, leaving us standing there.

I could tell that Ron had been holding something back from me ever since we crossed the Rio Grande and headed for Emilio's. I was even more aware now that he had some ominous surprise in store for me.

"Let's walk around the corner," he said with an air of anticipation.

We walked towards the nearest end of the wall and turned the corner. There was a huge wooden double gate that appeared to be the entrance of whatever we were about to visit. We walked to a small door adjacent to the gate. I suddenly realized that we were about to enter some sort of old Mexican fort, which, by the looks of it, was probably more than a century old.

Ron stepped to the smaller wooden door, opened it, and motioned me through with a sweeping arm gesture, a half-bow, and a smile. "Welcome to Boys' Town, boy. At least that's what some call it."

Boys' Town, I thought to myself. *I've heard of that. That's a place in the Midwest for wayward boys run by a Catholic priest. They've got one here in Mexico, too?* After all, I thought, *this is Easter weekend, maybe Ron knew some of the kids here and wants us to visit them.* It struck me that the Catholics down here must celebrate Easter much more festively than those in the States because the music got much louder and the lights much brighter as I walked through the entrance.

I was in awe!

It took less than half a blink of an eye to realize that what I was walking into was *not* the same sort of Boys' Town I was familiar with! My curious and youthful senses were met with an immediate and overly inviting array of lust, desire, and sin.

My initial focus from just inside this red light district took in the brightly colored neon signs spelling out words like *Girls, Manhattan Club, Girls, Schlitz, Girls, Sunset Strip, Girls, Girls, Girls!* However, once I got past that visual assault, I could also see the far less inviting side streets, where the glittering commercialism was replaced by random piles of garbage and small streams of raw sewage.

My inquisitive gaze also took in the people: people moving about, people standing, people sitting along the streets, people who were talking, laughing, singing, and yelling in Spanish.

I became conscious of Ron tugging on my arm, half-breaking me out of my spellbound state. "Wait right here while I register us gringos with the local policía," he said, pulling out his wallet as he entered a small room just inside the main gate.

The room had an official-looking governmental emblem over the door. The bottom corner of the emblem was missing, probably a foreboding of the kind of local policía that operated within these walls.

While standing outside the small police station, one of the people in my view caught my eye. She was a young Mexican girl, about my age or a little younger, leaning seductively against the outer wall of the next building. She wore a white peasant-type blouse, which complemented her red, full skirt. Even though her skin was dark, it contrasted vividly with her long, straight black hair. She was looking in my direction. When our eyes met, she smiled widely, her teeth adding an even more striking contrast to her face. Her eyes were dark and sparkled in the flashing neon lights.

She glanced away, looking nowhere in particular, then slowly, almost seductively, ran one hand from just under her chin, down her throat, to about midway on her chest. This gesture appeared to be a reaction to her sudden realization that it was a hot night. Still not looking at me, she slowly slipped her fingers under the elastic edge of the neck of her blouse, sliding it down over first one shoulder, then the other. As she finished with her left shoulder, which was closest to me, she demurely looked back into my eyes.

This young girl was incredibly alluring, and I wondered what she was doing there. I forced a nervous smile through my drying mouth, subconsciously hoping it would take Ron all night to do whatever he had to do inside the police station. Actually, I had already forgotten that he was gone. I also had forgotten about all the bustle that was going on in the streets around me. Everything else was a dull haze compared to the distraction of this beautiful Mexican girl who was filling my senses. In response to my smile, she stood up straight, clasped her hands in front of her skirt, and shyly began walking towards me in a sort of schoolgirl fashion. *Ron, don't come back now, not yet anyway,* I thought to myself.

She continued slowly towards me, smiling, and becoming more beautiful with each step. My knees were turning to mush. My throat got drier with each step she took in my direction.

She stopped right in front of me, less than an arm's length away. My nose took in the heady aroma of her perfume; my eyes took in her soft features, her bronze shoulders, the enticing view of cleavage hinting at what was just below the elastic of her blouse. *Ron, I don't even want to see you until tomorrow!*

"My name is Maria," she said in the softest broken English I had ever heard.

Another nervous half-smile and slight nod of acknowledgment was all I could muster as I groped for the right words to use.

"I like you. You GI?"

"No. . . no . . . no, I'm not," was all I could force out.

"No care. I fuck you five dollar American; ten dollar all night."

Confusion! Utter confusion! This fair young Mexican girl was a hooker! I couldn't believe it. "Ah . . . no . . . ah, no thanks." Where the hell was Ron when I needed him, goddamn it!

"Get outta here, you greedy little slut!" Ron was back! "Get out of here, bitch!" he barked again, as the girl stomped off in a manner that was in total contrast to her earlier approach. "What are you trying to do, boy? Get tapped out before we even get into some serious drinking tonight? The night's still young!"

"I just thought I'd check out the local going rates, since I was waiting here all night for you," I said, forcing myself into my best man-of-the-world persona.

"Well, now you know, boy, now you know. But we'll do better later on at Celia's Blue Room."

We sauntered down the main street as if at a carnival, complete with sideshows and people in pursuit of a good time. The glaring difference from the carnivals back home was the lack of children.

After passing several clubs, Ron and I entered one named The Eldorado. At least this one had a Spanish name, unlike the others, which were cheap knockoffs of familiar American watering holes. We sat at the bar and ordered two tequilas. The club was dark, with thick red velour curtains in the foyer just inside the door. A small raised platform in a back corner was the stage for a dancing Mexican woman, wearing only a sequined G-string. She had to be in her forties, but had a body that looked not a day over fifty. She seemed to be entranced in her own world, as she gyrated out of beat with the jukebox music.

A second female, obviously a hooker, sat at the far end of the bar, shooting a phony smile in our direction. A hint of a gold tooth winked ever so often in the dim lighting. She could have been the older sister of the exotic dancer. Ron politely shook his head at her, and she apparently decided to forgo the added effort of coming down to our end of the bar.

The bartender brought us each a small bottle of tequila and set a saltshaker between us. I found the saltshaker odd, as I was certain we hadn't ordered any food yet.

Ron paid the bartender, picked up the saltshaker, sprinkled some on the side of the big knuckle of his index finger, licked it off, and hurriedly took a long swig of tequila. He repeated the salt trick and pushed the shaker over to me. Although I really didn't understand the purpose of this ritual, I decided to take my turn anyway.

I sprinkled a small amount of salt on my finger just as Ron had, then quickly raised it to my mouth. I vowed right then and there never again to inhale through my nose while attempting to lick salt from my finger. Despite what fell on the floor, what went down my shirt, and what got into my nostrils, I managed to taste a few grains, which I washed down with a drink of tequila. I hated the taste of tequila and decided to have beer the next time. Besides, drinking tequila involved way too much effort and coordination.

Ron decided there was no action in The Eldorado club, so we left and eventually headed to Celia's Blue Room, which Ron said was a "classier" place near the rear of this walled-in city of sin.

Back along the main street, the carnival atmosphere was thriving. A young girl, no more than sixteen and wearing heavy makeup, came running up to Ron and grabbed his arm. At the same time, she pulled down half her blouse exposing a small breast with a tiny brown nipple. "You like me, gringo?" she asked smiling.

Ron shrugged her away, telling her to go find her mother.

"Bastard!" the young Lolita hollered, running off behind an adobe building.

Similar offers were made at least two more times before we finally arrived at Celia's Blue Room. One of the prostitutes even grabbed Ron's crotch and offered her experienced wares for only a few pesos. Ron was a little irritated by her bold approach, but seemed to take it in stride. It was the right thing to do, considering the locale we were visiting.

From the outside, Celia's Blue Room looked just like all the rest of the squat little adobe dens of the devil. It did appear, however, to be slightly larger than the other lounges. And there were two small windows on either side of the solid oak door, which were adorned with royal blue velour curtains. The main difference was that Celia's actually *had* a door, while most of the other hooker bars only had heavy curtains strung across their main entrances. Above the door and windows was a large blue neon sign telling the world, or at least Boys' Town, the name of the establishment.

I followed Ron in and immediately noticed that the place was in fact a bit classier than the others. It was brighter inside. The rough-textured walls were painted a pleasing robin's egg blue, and the back half of the floor, where there were about six tables, was even covered with a cheap dark blue carpet.

Two of the tables were occupied with couples: one by a not-too-pretty Mexican señorita and what might have been her boyfriend, and the other by a cute Mexican girl and a young American GI. Three other girls sat conversing among themselves at the bar. All were wearing tight-fitting short dresses that were slit up one side to reveal ample views of their bronzed thighs. One of the three was strikingly pretty, while the other two I considered to be only average in the looks department.

Nearly everyone in the place was smoking. The blue-gray smoke was swirling in midair, surrounding everything with a hazy aura.

Ron walked up to the prettiest of the three girls at the bar and asked if Celia was in tonight. She smiled at Ron, and I was surprised when she didn't come on to him like all the girls we had encountered outside. She slid off her stool and went behind a draped partition into what was probably a small office at the end of the bar. She returned in a moment, and told Ron Celia would be right out.

The girl had no sooner finished saying it, when the curtains parted and a sturdy looking Mexican lady walked out with an inquisitive look on her face. She was striking and wore a low-cut, dark-flowered dress, which afforded an easy view of her abundant cleavage. Her impressive dark eyes matched her ebony hair, which was swept back in a stylish wave across her forehead.

She wore the dour expression of someone who is in charge and wondered why she had been summoned to the main bar area. But that expression disappeared as soon as her dark eyes focused on Ron. "Ron!" she yelled, breaking into a joyous welcome-home-type greeting. "So good to see you again!" she said, running across the room with outstretched arms. She was quite a sight, running in her high heels and a tight dress, with her half-bare chest jiggling. The thought struck me that Celia was the south-of-the-border counterpart of *Gunsmoke's* Miss Kitty.

Celia swung her arms around my brother in a near bear hug as he hugged her back—both in politeness and in self-defense. She also showered his cheek with big wet kisses, as he, with some embarrassment, tried to calm her exuberant greeting.

When he succeeded, he said, "Celia, I've come here for two reasons. The first is to pick up the ring I left the last time I was here, and the second is to introduce you to my brother Tom." With that, he half-turned towards me, put his hand on my shoulder, and said proudly, "Celia, this is Tom. Tom, meet the best goddamned Mexican madam in Boys' Town."

At that, Celia stepped around and looked me up and down. "So, you're the brother he always talks so much about? How do you keep your grades so high in school by sneaking down here with your brother when you should be back up north studying?"

My God, I thought, *this woman knows all about me! Ron really does talk to his friends about me!* I felt the red warmth of embarrassment riding up my neck.

"Since this is your first visit to my club, you will receive special treatment," Celia said with a friendly smile and a sparkle in her pitch-dark eyes. "Come sit at this table here, and I will get you your drinking pleasure and a special young friend. I have some jewelry business to discuss with your brother."

I glanced quickly at Ron for reassurance, and he gave me a barely noticeable nod of approval. He seemed to sincerely appreciate Celia's outward acceptance of his younger brother with quiet pride.

I followed Celia over to the table and sat down, my back against the wall. I didn't want to miss anything that might happen. Ron said he'd be back in a few minutes, then he and Celia headed towards her office. Celia stopped at the end of the bar and said something to the bartender, who simply nodded in response and walked to the middle of the bar.

A minute later, the bartender walked over to my table and set a bottle of Carta Blanca beer down in front of me. He also set a dark mixed drink across the table from me, as if serving an invisible customer. I reached in my pocket and pulled out a small wad of money.

"No señor, no money," the bartender said gesturing with his hand that he didn't want me to pay. "Señorita Celia said no money," he added.

So that's what Celia had meant by "special treatment."

I only had a minute to wonder who the mixed drink was for, when a short, petite girl of about seventeen came out of the office and walked over to my table. The midnight blue miniskirt she wore accentuated her soft, full figure. She wore her hair pulled up in a large flowered barrette. She was not exactly pretty, but was sort of cute and natural looking—a real contrast to all the other females we had encountered since entering Boys' Town.

She smiled with what looked like a trace of shyness as she approached my table. In almost perfect English, she introduced herself as Anita, then asked if she could sit down.

I nodded and reached over to pull out a chair for her. "My name is Tom, I'm here with my brother."

"I know, Celia told me," she said, sparking my curiosity.

"Do you work here?" I asked.

"Oh, no. I just come to visit my Aunt Celia once in a while. Mostly just on holiday weekends like this."

I wasn't sure if I should believe her, but she did seem to be different from the other women, in both demeanor and physical appearance.

Just about then, Ron and Celia came back into the room, ordered drinks at the bar, and joined Anita and me at the table. I noticed a star sapphire on Ron's left ring finger.

The bartender followed them over and served Ron a bottle of beer, and Celia a shot glass of something with a murky-looking chaser.

"I see you've met my niece," Celia said. By that time I believed Anita really was her niece, and not just another hooker. I also got the feeling that Celia saw great things in her niece's future—things like marrying this young gringo and having lots of little babies, all north of the Rio Grande.

The evening wore on at the Blue Room, and fortunately the local Carta Blanca beer was surprisingly mild and didn't do a lot of damage to a novice drinker like me. Anita was quiet and polite. Celia, on the other hand, was open and loud enough for the four of us. After about two hours of complaining about her business dilemmas and her ex-husband's atrocities, Celia began nuzzling up to Ron. I knew that Ron's only weakness was women, especially the buxom type like Celia, so I realized it was just a matter of time before he surrendered to her obvious charms.

No sooner had that thought crossed my mind, than Ron leaned over to me and spoke in a whisper, "Celia and I have some more business to discuss in her room next door. You gonna be okay for an hour or so?"

He made it clear by the tone of his voice just what sort of "business" he was going to discuss. He also made it clear that if I didn't want him to leave me alone in the bar, he would put off his romp with Celia until another time.

"Sure, oh, sure, I'll stay here and talk with Anita for a while," I said.

"Okay, boy, but if we somehow get separated tonight, meet me back at the car across the river at noon tomorrow."

"Gotcha, just have a good time, I'll be all right," I said.

Ron winked at me and got up from the table with Celia. He patted me on the shoulder, which made me feel like I was an adult like him and not just his kid brother.

As they turned to leave, Ron glanced back and said over his shoulder, "Don't forget your protection." I answered with a slight nod and a smile meant to reassure him.

Wow! I was actually here on my own in this so-called Boys' Town! I immediately inventoried my situation. I was in a hooker bar and only slightly tipsy from the beer at that point. I had a girl at my table to talk to. I had plenty of cash to get me through the night, and I had double protection: a concealed .32 caliber pistol under my shirt, and hopefully, a *useful* Trojan in my wallet. But what was more, I had my brother's confidence that I could survive on my own in this strange environment, even if only for an hour or so. With all these plusses, I had it made!

Just as I was feeling smug and worldly—and planning my next move with quiet little Anita—she spoke up. "It was nice to be in your company tonight, Señor Tom, but I must go now. I have to sing at the early Easter mass in the morning. Do you want to come to church with me at seven o'clock tomorrow?"

"Ah, no . . . no, I don't think I can make it, Anita," I said, realizing I was just losing one of my plusses. But after all, I rationalized, Anita probably was not the right type of girl for me here in Boys' Town. She was quiet, not all that pretty, and probably still a virgin. A definite contrast to all the available lusty harlots.

"Gee, Anita, that's too bad you have to go, but I do understand. It was nice meeting you," I said, already thinking ahead to my next prospect. As she got up to leave, I said, "Hope to see you the next time I'm here."

She smiled and said, "That would be nice," then left.

I sat at the table alone for the next few minutes, both to finish my beer and to give Anita time to leave. The single girls that had decorated the bar when we first arrived were no longer there. Two were busy entertaining what looked like a couple of locals, and the third had apparently left.

I decided to do some sight-seeing on my own out in the streets. I went over to the bar and left a message with the bartender that I would stop back in about an hour in case Ron was looking for me. Then I walked out into the stagnant sin-filled air of a Saturday night in Boys' Town.

My immediate intention was to wander around the old fort's interior, stopping along the way to pursue anything of interest. Somehow I knew there would be something of interest, which probably wouldn't require much pursuing on my part.

I was becoming accustomed to the atmosphere. I accepted what my senses were perceiving with more familiarity than I had during my first mystified walk with Ron only hours earlier. I still got a few come-on looks from the street whores, but shrugged them off with a staged indifference, not unlike that of my brother. I was a quick study when it came to learning things from Ron, which worked well in this situation.

A short way down the main street, I crossed over to the other side, where a noisy crowd had gathered between two buildings. As I approached, I saw a crude fence made of wooden slats placed in sort of a circle. The area was lit by torches and by the glow of the nearby neon beer signs. The crowd was cheering wildly, and several locals were waving fistfuls of money.

I wound through some of the people in the crowd until I could see what they were all cheering about. Two roosters were fighting in the dirt inside the small corral. I watched for a few minutes until deciding the stench of body odor from the spectators was greater than my interest in watching the cockfight.

As I was easing out of the crowd, a burly Mexican with bad teeth tapped me on the shoulder. "Hey, gringo, don't you want to stay and watch the donkey show?"

I didn't think the small enclosure was large enough for two donkeys to fight like the roosters were doing, so I asked him, "What donkey show?"

He was laughing furiously by then. "Señor, for only two pesos you can watch Juanita and her loving donkey. They will be here in just ten minutes."

I knew what kind of show he meant and decided to decline such a once-in-a-lifetime attraction. I wandered back into the street, then, deciding to leave the main artery, walked down one of the side streets. One particular lane was much quieter, with fewer people and even fewer neon lights. Except for the occasional hooker in a doorway here and there, you could almost characterize the street as *quaint*—if that was a word ever used in Boys' Town.

Even the hookers along this street were different, or one might say of somewhat lesser quality than those on the main streets. One obese hustler winked at me as I walked by, imploring me to sample her undoubtedly well-experienced wares for "one dollar." Not to overuse the old saying, but she would have had to pay *me!*

About halfway down this "quaint" street was a small bar similar to the ones on the main drag. It had a Carta Blanca sign flashing in a small front window, and unlike the more popular bars, this one seemed quiet, more in keeping with a side street. I decided to stop in for another beer, hoping half-heartedly to find some beautiful young local whore that I could fall in love with for an hour or so. I wanted to show Ron I could handle myself alone and get some results in the process.

The bar was really small inside. For some reason, it reminded me of the inside of the old school bus I used to ride when I lived on the farm. As my eyes became more accustomed to the dim light, I realized it *was* an old school bus. Some ingenious, and obviously cheap, property owner had taken an old bus, gutted it, cut it in half, and attached the back half to an adobe front wall. Add a front door, a window with a beer sign, a short bar in the rear, a few chairs and tables, and voilà—a nightclub is born!

Even though there wasn't a person in it, this bar intrigued me so much that I decided to stay and idle away the next half hour before going back to check on Ron. I chose a table in the front corner under the beer sign flashing in the window.

The bartender, a small wormy looking fellow, was sweeping up some broken glass near the bar. Someone must have dropped a bottle. When I sat down, he came over to my table clutching the broom in his hands so hard it was shaking. He seemed uncommonly nervous as he asked what I wanted to drink.

"Just a beer, Carta Blanca beer, amigo, and make sure it's cold," I said. I was amazed at how worldly I was becoming.

He hurried back behind the bar to get the beer. As he was bending down, fumbling for a bottle, a piece of glass the size of a pie tin fell out of the mirror behind him, shattering on the floor. The barkeep peered at me just over the bar's edge, then brought my beer over, set it down, and hurried out the front door.

Strange combination for a bartender: sort of paranoid, but trusting enough to leave me alone in his establishment. So I decided to enjoy myself, just sitting there sipping a bottle of beer in a school-bus-turned-tavern. Suddenly, before my second swallow of beer, the front door burst open, and two Mexican policemen entered. One leveled a double-barreled, sawed-off shotgun at my navel, while the other brandished an automatic pistol on a lanyard aimed directly at my forehead.

Instinct took over, and I decided not to move, not even to sweat, for fear of being cut in half by the shotgun, or having my cranium decorate the wall behind me. I didn't have to move. Before I knew what was happening, the larger of the two cops holstered his pistol, grabbed me out of my chair, and literally threw me against the wall. He must have done this a lot, because after bouncing off the wall, I slammed into it again, with my arms and legs spread in the classic search position. He certainly was good at this work, and seemed to enjoy it. He quickly patted down my sides and legs, coming up with a slight, but very painful, fist in my crotch. Meanwhile, his partner was standing to the side, grinning and toying with both hammers of the shotgun, which was now pointed towards my left ear.

Then came the handcuffs—first one arm pulled back, then the other, as he banged my head against the metal wall. He was so close to me, the combined smell of sweat-soaked clothes, hot bad breath, and mildewed leather from the gun belts was putrid enough to make me gag. However, I was fully aware that gagging probably wasn't advisable at the time, and I decided it also wasn't in my immediate best interest to ask what the hell this was all about. It was apparent the Mexican cops were in control of everything.

Then the big guy spun me around, hooked his log of an arm through mine, and dragged me out the door. Hard steel poking me in the back served as a harsh reminder to be mindful that the second shotgun-toting cop was not far behind, as together they pushed me through the establishment's door.

My mind was racing. *This can't be happening! This has to be a movie set I happened to walk in to. That's it! Any moment now, the director of some B movie is going to holler "cut," and they'll realize I'm the wrong guy!* But, as I took a very heavy bounce off the front door casing, which was only meant for one person to go through at a time, I didn't see any lights, cameras, or director as we emerged from the bar.

There was only the spineless bartender—the little bastard was still holding his broom as he stood just outside the bar watching the action. He was smiling and nodding his head at the same time talking excitedly to my captors. I somehow knew that bartender was responsible for what was happening to me. He apparently had gone for the police after serving me my beer. But why? I wondered, trying to keep just ahead of the shotgun as I was being dragged down the street. I hadn't done anything. It couldn't be because I was underage. I was eighteen, but who checked IDs in foreign countries, especially in Boys' Town?

We rounded the corner connecting the quiet side street with the busier main street. Our little spectacle didn't really attract a lot of attention, thank God, but there were a few snickers directed at me from some of the idle Mexicans standing along the street. My guards were obviously enjoying any notoriety they were gaining by dragging their hardened criminal—and an American at that—through town.

As we passed in front of Celia's Blue Room, I decided it was time to make a futile call for help. "Ron!" I hollered as loud as I could, hoping my scared voice would carry over the commotion of music, laughter, and other bar noises. "Ro . . . ," I began to yell again, when I felt a blow to the back of my head, and all I saw was a quick flash of white light before everything became dark, quiet, and peaceful.

❋   ❋   ❋

Something was causing me pain. This time, something hard was throbbing in my lower back. Segments of thoughts about a shotgun butt were flashing in my mind. Everything was still dark and quiet, but something was hurting my back.

I moved my left arm and hand towards the pain, and it was then I realized I was lying on my back. But, there was still something causing a pounding pain through my lower back. My hand went underneath me as I lifted up slightly and touched a hard object. It was my pistol! I half-consciously began removing it, as it was still in the holster under my waistband, when I heard voices—strange voices speaking Spanish. I quickly took my hand off the gun. I forced an eye open slightly and saw a yellowish, bare lightbulb staring back at me against a background of cracked plaster. Flies, the size of black olives, were buzzing around the lightbulb.

I heard the voices again and changed my labored focus by turning my head slightly to the side where I could see some indistinguishable people seated in a row a few feet away. But, as I moved my head, I felt a sharp pain at the base of my skull. Great, now I had a pain in my head as well as one in my back. With my right hand, I felt what I was lying on, trying to determine whether it was some sort of table that I could fall off. I didn't want any more pain at that point. But I wasn't on a table; I was lying on a dirt floor. So far, all I knew was that I was lying flat on my back on a dirt floor, under a fly-laden bare bulb, in the company of some Spanish-speaking guys who sat a few feet to my right.

Despite the pain in my head, I decided to slowly turn to my left to see what delights awaited me in that direction. Bars! I was sorry I had taken the effort to look. Dark, dirty, steel bars, an inch thick, and half a foot apart were anchored in the dirt floor. A closer look told me they went from floor to ceiling.

Great! I thought. *I'm in a jail cell!*

Then the thought segments began forming a clearer memory. I recalled how I had been accosted and dragged off to jail for reasons I still didn't know. I couldn't remember anything that had happened after I had been hit on the back of the head—probably by the cop's shotgun butt—while passing Celia's Blue Room.

But what was I doing in jail with my pistol?

I decided to leave the gun holstered under my shirt for the time being, at least until I could get a handle on my immediate situation. I raised up on one elbow and looked around. I found myself in a large bullpen cell, with three concrete walls and a fourth made of bars and one lightbulb hanging from the ceiling over the dirt floor.

Suddenly I realized I was in the company of about fifteen other prisoners, all either lying down or seated against the cell walls. Not one of my fellow inmates looked like the sort you'd want to start an intelligent conversation with, even if they did speak the same language. It occurred to me that a prudent person wouldn't even want to be in the same hemisphere with any of them, let alone locked in the same jail cell.

As I looked at some of their faces, I decided I was most likely in the company of murderers, rapists, robbers, and other assorted thugs from northern Mexico.

I was the only "Anglo" in the bunch. And the way a couple of them were grinning at me, I felt as if I was a new delicacy imported into this part of the world just for them. I wasn't so naïve I didn't know what happens to new, young prisoners in a place like that.

I inched back closer to the bars and hoped this would be a very temporary situation. Ron would certainly come looking for me. But what if he had fallen peacefully asleep for the night in Celia's arms?

I tried to check my watch to see what time it was, but my watch was gone. I quickly reached behind for my wallet. Also gone! Great! They take away my watch and wallet, but leave my pistol and holster on me. I guessed the burly—and probably inadequately trained—local cops simply missed the weapon during their search.

I felt a distinct need to relieve myself of the several beers I had drunk earlier. The only toilet facility in the cell was a beat-up old bucket situated in the back corner farthest from me—at least that's what I figured the bucket was for. Several flies were buzzing around it, and every so often an overpowering smell of urine wafted from that direction.

I decided not to use the bucket and backed up closer to the bars, careful not to reveal my pistol. I could only imagine the chaos that would ensue if my fellow prisoners discovered a sophisticated weapon in the cell with them.

Even though I was armed, I completely eliminated any thought of using the gun to make an escape. I reserved that option for a more serious situation—like if they were going to hang me or imprison me for life. Surely, whatever this was about would be resolved before matters got that serious . . .

Outside the cell was a hallway with a formidable-looking iron door at the end. Every now and then a guard would press his face to the small observation window in the door to check on the prisoners. I assumed the main office of the police station was on the other side of the door.

Some of the other prisoners began babbling among themselves. I was relieved that they didn't seem to be talking about me, although I had no way of knowing for sure. So, I decided to stay on the dirt floor with my back up against the bars and wait it out. I tried to keep my mind off my bladder by concentrating on my headache and future freedom.

Time seems to pass much slower when there is no way to keep track of it. After what seemed like hours, but was probably in fact only about thirty minutes, I heard some muffled angry shouting on the other side of the iron door. It subsided briefly, then began rising again to an even louder crescendo.

It was Ron's voice! Thank God! I didn't have to decide whether or not I wanted to be blindfolded in front of a firing squad. I knew he wouldn't let me down! Hopefully he'd have me out of here in a few minutes, unless of course, he was also being arrested. I tried not to think about that.

"That's my brother out there," I shouted, "he came to . . ." my voice trailed off when I realized that not one of the other prisoners could understand a word I was saying. Nor did they care. But I sure got their attention for a moment.

I heard a key in the iron door, then it opened. A jailer, an official-looking officer-type, and Ron walked through the door together. Ron wasn't wearing a shirt, as he apparently had just left Celia's bedroom.

I jumped to my feet, hardly noticing my headache. "What is going on Ron? Why did they arrest me?" I asked him excitedly.

"It's all bullshit! I'll explain later," he said, as the jailer opened the cell door. "Come on, let's just get you out of here, boy!"

I was relieved to know he was here to help me and not under arrest as well.

As I passed through the main office, a second guard placed my wallet on the counter. Ron insisted that I check the contents and count the money. Surprisingly it was all there. But my watch was nowhere in sight. Even though it was only a twenty-dollar Timex, it was important to me because it had been a gift from Ron. "Everything's here, except my wristwatch."

"Which one of you assholes has my brother's watch?" Ron roared at the officer in charge.

The former shotgun-toting cop was leaning against the far wall of the main office. The officer in charge shouted something at him in a flurry of Spanish, and the cop reached into his trouser pocket and pulled out my watch.

Ron started towards him, but was restrained by the officer, who hurried over and grabbed the watch out of the cop's hand. He brought it back and handed it to me. "My apology, amigo. My compadre thought your watch was evidence."

"Let's get out of here!" Ron said a little calmer now that I had all my property.

As we walked back to Celia's to get his shirt, he explained the whole incident to me—the way it had been explained to him.

It seems that two American GIs had been in the school bus bar just before I wandered in. They began quarreling, which culminated in a drunken brawl. The fight scared off the few customers in the establishment, and the GIs fled when they realized their fighting broke a bottle of whiskey and the large mirror behind the bar. One of the Americans wore an army fatigue shirt. A few minutes after the GIs left, I wandered into the same bar—a young American wearing a similar shirt. To the Mexican bartender, all American GIs looked alike. With this as a basis, he decided I was one of the troublemakers who had come back for more. Hence, the police, etc., etc., etc.

Ron went on to explain that the bartender at the Blue Room had caught a glimpse of the police dragging what he thought was a young gringo off to jail. He also saw the prisoner get a blow to the back of the head with a shotgun butt, just as he hollered something in front of the Blue Room.

Apparently the bartender wasn't sure who the police had in custody and hesitated about disturbing Ron and Celia. Finally, after an hour passed and I hadn't returned, he decided to tell Ron what he'd seen.

Ron said he had jumped into his pants and shoes and run down to the police station near the front gate of Boys' Town. He told me he'd spent a night or two in foreign jails around the world and immediately offered them fifty dollars "bail" to get me out and forget about the incident.

I stammered that he shouldn't have paid anything because I was innocent, but he just smiled and said, "They've got different laws and procedures down here, boy. Just be glad you're out and forget it."

Well, I knew I would never forget *that* experience.

It was only about one o'clock in the morning, and Ron said there was still time to salvage the night and "have a good time."

After he got his shirt and socks from Celia's, we hit several of the bars along the main street. We'd go in, have a beer, and see what they had to offer in the way of entertainment.

By the third or fourth such stop, all the bars and hookers started to look alike to me. I was getting drunker by the minute. By the fifth or sixth bar, I was in no shape to tell if it was the third or ninth, nor did I really care. I do remember Ron sort of guiding—rather dragging—me somewhere. Or, was it one of the ladies of the evening dragging me?

I also remember revisiting the police station and signing something in the company of others. And then there was a ride in someone's car to some unknown place. There was also laughing, and hugging, and carrying on. I must have really been having a great time. But, where, and with whom?

* * *

Then there was quiet and mostly darkness again. My head was throbbing, and I had the sensation of lying on my back. This time I felt my left arm outstretched, and I couldn't move it. *Am I back in jail again?* I wondered. Only this time it was worse—my arm was pinned down. But I wasn't on a dirt floor; I was lying on something much softer.

My head was throbbing so badly, it hurt even to open my eyelids halfway. I looked to my left and saw what appeared to be a dark curtain, with splintered rays of bright sunlight streaming through small rips in the material. Then, to my surprise, I noticed why I couldn't move my arm. I was lying naked in bed with a female, who was also stretched out naked and asleep on my arm. She was on her side with her back facing me. As she slept, her long black hair cascaded over her back and my upper arm. The bedsheet was draped over her lower body, from her buttocks down. From the position she was in, it was apparent she had quite the hourglass figure.

It was literally too painful to search my memory for details of this girl, or what may have transpired earlier. I just relaxed, laid my head back on the pillow, and stared at the ceiling, trying to figure out my next move. I sensed I was in some third-rate hotel room; it was too dark to make out much of the surroundings, but I was conscious of another bed off to my right. The dark blankets were pulled up, and I wasn't sure if anyone occupied it. If someone did, I was sure it would be Ron and possibly a female companion.

As I lay there, my young male ego found its way to my throbbing head. *Not bad for an eighteen-year-old kid from Wisconsin,* I mused to myself. And on Easter Sunday at that! I feared I would surely go to Hell.

As I was slowly trying to work my left arm out from under my raven-haired bedmate, she began to move and turned towards me. She started to nuzzle up to my side, opened her eyes, and looked at me with a confused expression; then she relaxed and smiled, showing a row of perfect white teeth. She was about my age. Then I recognized her! It was Maria, the gorgeous hooker I had encountered just inside the main gate when I first arrived at Boys' Town. She allowed me to remove my arm and flex it, as she coyly pulled the sheet up to her neck in order to cover herself more.

"How did we get here? Where are we?" I asked.

"The man with you, señor. He checked us out at the Policía. Told me to take you here. This is a hotel in Nuevo Laredo."

Maria asked with a smile if I had enjoyed. Small pieces of what seemed far away, erotic dreams floated through my mind. They must have been real, and not dreams . . . I assured her I had indeed enjoyed being with her, confessing only to myself that I couldn't remember a damned thing!

"Good señor, me too," she said.

"Ron," I hollered in the direction of the other double bed. My eyes were now more used to the dim light, and I could make out for certain that someone was under the covers in the second bed. "Ron . . ." I tried again. There was no answer or movement under the covers.

So I got out of bed by slithering out the foot end, found my shorts along the way, and put them on. It was warm in the room, and the floor felt musty and damp on my feet. I walked over to the other bed and gently shook the totally covered form that was under the blanket.

I was answered by a man's guttural groan.

"Ron, wake up, it's late. We'll have to check out of here soon."

Another groan, then the form turned over and pulled the covers down to reveal a face. To my astonishment for the second time that short morning, I realized the covered body was not Ron, but some mean-looking Mexican guy who appeared to be about forty years old. Then, another sleepy señorita looked out from under the blanket beside him, apparently awakened by the commotion.

The man, still half asleep, began grumbling something at me in Spanish. I looked back at Maria for translation.

"He wants to know who you are and why you wake him up," Maria said, trying not to laugh.

"Where's my brother?" I demanded.

"He didn't come to this hotel," Maria answered, turning a little indignant. Apparently she remembered Ron cursing at her the night before.

This whole situation was a little too much for me to handle with a hangover on Easter morning. I hurried into the grimy little bathroom to relieve myself. While doing so, I got a sudden bolt of fright. I hadn't used my protection, I was sure of that. I rushed back into the bedroom and found my pants, checking for my wallet. When I found it, I discovered it still contained nearly all of my cash, except for about twenty dollars. But my worst fear was confirmed—there hidden away in its secret compartment was the unused condom, neat and safe in its worn hermetically sealed foil package.

I rushed back into the bathroom and turned on the water in the tiny shower stall. I took off my shorts, got in the shower, and nearly boiled myself for the next ten minutes, until the hot water ran out. I used so much soap that I was sure I was turning certain parts of my anatomy into raw hamburger. I finished the ritual with a small prayer, hoping that nothing would develop over the next two weeks.

When I came out of the shower and into the bedroom, the other three were asleep again. Being careful not to touch anything in my now near-sterile condition, I quietly found all my clothes, got dressed, and left.

Emerging from the dark room to the street was like walking into a brightly lit oven. From what I could tell, I was on a small side street, still on the Mexican side of Laredo. I walked to the nearest street with traffic, found a passerby, who, when asked, struggled in English to give me directions to the river and the bridge leading back to the American side.

I discovered I was only a few blocks from the bridge Ron and I had crossed when we came to Laredo. That seemed like a week ago instead of just a day.

At the bridge, a customs agent stopped me and searched my pockets and socks for contraband. I heaved a sigh of relief when he didn't find my gun either. It was still inside my waistband holster in the middle of my back. By then it was a little after eleven, as I hurried across the bridge, wanting nothing more than to return to the U.S.A.

I located the fenced car lot on the American side, and it looked as though Ron's car had survived with all its parts. At least, all the wheels, hubcaps, and bumpers were still there. The attendant said Ron had not come back yet, so I found a shady spot where I could see the bridge and sat down to wait.

Finally, at about five to twelve, I saw Ron walking casually across the bridge from the Mexican side. He was smoking a cigarette and stopped once to look down into the slow-moving water. I watched him traverse the expansive bridge, thinking how much he meant to me. As he approached the sidewalk up the bank leading to the car lot, I got up and walked down to meet him.

He saw me coming and smiled. When we met, he matter-of-factly inquired how long I had been waiting for him.

"Oh, I just got here a few minutes ago," I said.

"Well, let me ask you this, boy. Did you enjoy yourself in Mexico?" he asked, with a sparkle in his eye.

"Yes I did," I said philosophically. "I'm sure it beat the class trip to Washington, D.C."

"I'm sure it did, Tom," he said putting a hand on my shoulder as we walked towards the car. "I'm sure it did, and you probably learned more, too!"

Chapter 5

The Notification

Strange, somehow, that the sun seems hotter when you're closer to it. Ninety-three million miles from earth to sun, yet being only twenty feet closer on my perch atop a painter's ladder feels as if I'm a stone's throw from the sun's corona. July in central Wisconsin is hot and humid, and painting just under the eaves of an old two-story house while in the bright sunshine is enough to make one's blood run hotter and cause one's brain to sizzle.

I knew the working conditions of our agreement would not be easy. This whole escapade was Dr. Statler's idea. He was motivated by both compassion and a desire to teach me the value of investment coupled with plain hard work. I had worked part-time through high school in his veterinary hospital doing everything from cleaning kennels to assisting with delicate surgery on dogs, cats, cows, and even a canary. However, he saw brighter things in my future. It was his idea to buy the old house in sleepy little Montello. He provided a few thousand dollars for paint and remodeling supplies, and I put in three sweat-filled summer months of amateur labor, so "we" could turn around and sell the house for a handsome profit. This presumed profit would then be split evenly between us. In the most sincere sense of the phrase, "it was an offer I just couldn't refuse." I would be making some "big" money without investing any of my own funds. That appealed to me, snce I didn't have any extra money to invest. I had just spent all I had completing my freshman year at the University of Wisconsin, just as Ron had wished. I also had no place to live once I moved out of the dorm at the end of the spring semester. This shabby old house was no palace, but then I had never lived in a palace, anyway. At least it would be good shelter, after I fixed the leaky roof. In addition, Dr. Statler said he would pay me twenty bucks a week for food and miscellaneous personal spending. Since about the only entertainment in Montello was a movie theater that was open only on weekends and a drive-in root beer stand, I felt his offer would be more than enough to cover my food and "entertainment."

In addition to giving me a place to live and a chance to earn some money for my remaining three years of college, this old house project also afforded me time to relax and think.

By that time, at age nineteen, I was feeling quite satisfied with the way my life was turning out. I considered my teenage years to have been successful. Living on my own, working my various part-time jobs, and keeping my grades up in school, all combined to give me a great sense of accomplishment.

But more importantly, I was fulfilling the master plan that Ron had set for me years earlier while I was still on the farm. None of my accomplishments to date, including finishing my first year of college at the UW's Madison campus, would have come to fruition without his constant support and encouragement. I could tell he was extremely proud of me as I completed my spring semester and planned to return for the upcoming fall year. I got the sense that he felt he had accomplished his mission of setting me on the right course to lead a productive life.

Seeing that my grades were all right at the end of the fall semester in December, Ron informed me he was once again going to try to get reassigned to his old combat unit in Vietnam. Being stationed at Fort Hood, Texas, was not his idea of serving as a soldier while there was a war going on. However, he was frustrated with all the Army's red tape he had to deal with in getting reassigned. So frustrated that he even had me send a letter to then-Senator William Proxmire of Wisconsin requesting his reassignment to Vietnam. The letter seemed to help his cause, because in a few weeks he had his orders to return to the war zone. He left in early April 1970 for another tour in Vietnam. Combined with his previous extended tour of eighteen months, this assignment would give him a total of two and a half years there.

Ron took the last two weeks of March as leave before reporting to Vietnam. He stayed about ten days of that time with me in my college dorm room. He even attended some of my larger lecture classes with me, and every night we would go out for dinner and a few beers in Madison. He was quite popular with my dorm mates, who thought he was a pretty "cool dude," even if he was a Vietnam vet on his way back to a "totally wrong war."

Spending this time together in Madison was like coming full circle for Ron and me. I didn't know which of us was prouder to be walking the same campus sidewalks that we had toured together seven years earlier.

❈ ❈ ❈

I guess it was because I was thinking about how to keep the beads of perspiration from blurring my vision, while at the same time listening to Paul McCartney's "Long and Winding Road" on the radio, that I didn't hear the car drive up in the gravel driveway below. But just as I reached down to put my brush into the paint can that dangled from the top rung of the ladder, I caught a glimpse of a thin cloud of dust around the car that just stopped. It was two o'clock on a Saturday afternoon, and I wasn't expecting any visitors until at least Monday, when Dr. Statler said he'd drop by. I had been partially conscious of local cars and pickup trucks going past the house all day long, but figured none had a reason to stop.

In a few moments, I would be wishing that this car hadn't stopped either.

The car was like none I'd ever seen around town before. It was drab and plain and had no chrome and no wheel covers. It had some very unfancy white lettering and numbers on the driver's side door. My first thought was that it was a squad car without emergency lights on the top, but I knew what most of the local police cars looked like. This one was olive drab. Suddenly I realized why it looked so plain and official—it was a military sedan, just like I had seen while visiting Ron at Fort Hood a year earlier.

I couldn't see the driver's face from where I stood on the ladder, but I could see that he was wearing a khaki summer Army uniform. Then I saw the apex of some gold and dark green stripes on the sleeve. A sergeant. Ron was a sergeant! He had been wearing the same uniform when he left for Vietnam just four months earlier. I had just received a letter from him that morning. What was he doing here? I could hardly back down the ladder fast enough. My heart was pounding so fast I thought it would shake the paint can right off the ladder. As I scurried down, almost reaching the ground, I looked over my shoulder and saw the driver's door opening. I yelled to him, "Sure know how to make a guy's day, don't you?" while jumping off the third rung onto the lawn. I turned towards the car, grinning, waiting to see that old familiar easygoing smile on Ron's face. He was just getting out of the car, adjusting his service hat. I ran towards him; in just a second, he would stand upright and stretch out his hand to shake mine.

His right arm extended in the gesture of the handshake. I began reaching for his hand and looked up into his face. Under the dark bill of the service hat there was no smile. I froze in the dusty gravel driveway with my outstretched arm dropping as if in slow motion. It wasn't Ron. He wore a khaki Sergeant First Class uniform like Ron's, but this man's name tag read "Nelson." A split second glance to the other side of the man's chest revealed he wore two rows of campaign ribbons, including Vietnam service ribbons, just like Ron did.

The sergeant stepped closer to me, his right arm and hand still outstretched. Now I could see his eyes. An uncomfortable pain was present in those eyes. He took my hand, clasping it in a slow handshake and asked with a cold quiver in his voice, if I was Tom Reilly.

My entire world just collapsed around me at the sound of his voice and that painful, anguished look in his eyes. The heart-pounding exhilaration I had experienced just a few seconds before evaporated. My knees weakened, and my hand fell from his. I stumbled the few steps over and leaned on the front fender of the sedan. Joyful thoughts were quickly replaced by the worst sorrow I knew I would ever experience in my life. I turned away from the sergeant as I fought back tears. He softly cleared his throat and said with an even greater quiver in his voice that he had some "pretty bad news" for me. There were a few seconds of silence during which the sergeant stepped closer and firmly clutched my shoulder from behind. I sensed he couldn't say anymore just then, nor did he have to. All I could feel at that moment was a sense of betrayal.

"Oh God!" my brain screamed, "If you really do exist, why is this soldier back from Vietnam, standing here wearing the same uniform as my brother? Why can't it be Ron clasping my shoulder, like he's done before? Oh God, don't you know how much I worshipped my brother?" Even at that horrible moment, I knew nobody could ever answer those questions.

Deciding to pull myself together and act like a man, just as Ron would have wanted me to in front of one of his peers, I clumsily swallowed and gulped half a breath of air. Then I turned to the sergeant, looked into his reddened eyes, and asked, "How did it happen?"

He looked so relieved when he realized that he didn't have to verbalize what he had come to tell me. We both knew why he was there that sunny Saturday afternoon. He didn't have to say the words, and I didn't have to hear them: The brother I loved so much was dead halfway around the world.

As he fumbled in his uniform pocket and removed a yellow piece of paper, the sergeant told me he didn't have many details.

He handed me the paper, and I slowly unfolded it. It was a telegram from the Defense Department addressed to "Tom Reilly, Next of Kin." It read: *"The Department of Defense regrets to inform you that your brother SFC Ronald H. Reilly died as a result of non-hostile causes in the Republic of Vietnam on 16 July 1970 at approximately 0825 hrs. Stop."*

Of all the things I've read, no sentence will ever have a greater impact on my life. I had just lost forever my brother, my mentor, and my hero.

�֎ �֎ ✖

The hills of the Bay Area were sprinkled with lights as the TWA 707 dropped out of the clouds on its final approach to San Francisco International Airport. The flight from Milwaukee had been a long one, four hours, to be exact. It had departed when the sun was low in the west, and because of the time difference, was now arriving on the coast just after it disappeared below the horizon. Strange how when you chase the sun, time seems to slow down. How I wished I could have chased it to the west far enough and fast enough to slow down time and actually reverse it by eight days. It was eight days since Ron had died in Vietnam, ten thousand miles farther west.

Now here I was traveling to San Francisco, or more precisely, to Oakland Army Base, to meet his casket and escort him the final way home, back to the green fields of Wisconsin.

This wasn't my first trip to San Francisco. I had flown there once to meet Ron under much happier circumstances. About two years earlier, he had sent a money order and instructions to use it to buy a ticket to San Francisco, so I could spend a long weekend with him while he was there on furlough. I knew San Francisco was one of Ron's favorite cities besides Madison, and I felt honored he wanted to show it off to his kid brother.

The lights of the cities surrounding San Francisco Bay twinkled out my window as the big jet bounced down on the runway before taxiing to the terminal. I could feel the bittersweet sensations of sorrow and loneliness creeping through my body, remembering that Ron had met me at the same airport. Now, a different sergeant would be waiting for me at the gate; he didn't know me, and I didn't know him. Sergeant Janssen was his name. I talked with him twice on the telephone long-distance from Wisconsin. He was the Army's official escort for Ron's body once it arrived back in the States. He was charged with acting as liaison among the government, the family, and the local funeral officials in handling all details of the burial. From talking with him on the phone, I got the idea that he was older and more compassionate than what an Army sergeant is generally thought to be. But this was his job, which apparently he had done many times before, and even if he hadn't been compassionate to start with, his difficult work had molded him that way out of necessity.

The first time I spoke with him was to gain information regarding the details and procedures for shipping Ron's body from Vietnam. He explained that his body would come directly from Vietnam to the Oakland Army Base across the bay from San Francisco before being shipped home to Wisconsin. The second time I spoke with him was about two hours later to tell him I was coming to escort the casket from California to Wisconsin with him. He tried to talk me out of it, saying it would be too difficult for me emotionally and that it wasn't necessary. When I told him it *was* necessary, he relented and said he would meet me at the San Francisco airport. I wired him what flight I would be on the next day.

As I made my way off the plane and into the gate area, I saw Sergeant Janssen immediately. He was standing well to the rear of a small crowd of excited friends and relatives who were gathered to welcome the other passengers from the flight. He was in a full dress green uniform, proudly displaying the bright gold stripes on his sleeves, signifying his rank of Sergeant First Class. Every time I saw those stripes I felt a twinge of heartache and pride, knowing that my brother had worked nine years to wear that same insignia of rank.

Sergeant Janssen was older, as I had expected, probably in his mid-forties. Standing there in the airport, he reminded me of a minister waiting at the door of his church after a Sunday sermon. He looked very calm. From the half-smile on his face and the distinct wrinkles around his eyes, I got the sense he cared for people and was, indeed, compassionate. The smile revealed his hope for humanity; the wrinkles revealed the pain he felt about what reality too often does to humanity.

Perhaps he recognized the sorrow on my young face. At any rate, he knew I was the passenger he was there to meet. We walked towards each other and shook hands warmly.

"How was your flight, Tom?" he asked.

"It was fine, just long," I said.

"Well, I'll drive you over to Oakland Army Base, where I've arranged a private room for you tonight at the BOQ, ah, that's the Bachelor Officers' Quarters; it's about a thirty-minute ride at this time of day. As I told you on the phone, your brother's casket arrived this morning."

"Will I be able to see him tonight?"

"No, that won't be practical due to security tonight. After breakfast tomorrow, I'll take you to the arrivals warehouse, and then the casket will be brought back here to SFO by Army hearse for the flight home to Milwaukee. I've made all the arrangements."

By now, we were walking through the airport to where Sergeant Janssen said he had parked his car. As we walked, I had a million questions, but tried to only ask the most important ones, not wanting to look like a dummy to one of Ron's Army peers, even though I knew they had probably never met.

"What happens when we get to Milwaukee?"

"I've made arrangements with the funeral home in Brandon, and a representative will meet us at the Milwaukee airport with one of their hearses and an extra car to drive us up to Brandon. It's about fifty or sixty miles, isn't it?"

"Yeah, that's right, I guess," I answered. I was thoroughly impressed with the efficient, yet compassionate, way Sergeant Janssen was in control of things.

"Do you do this for a job? I mean, escorting bodies and making all the arrangements?" I asked as we got into an Army sedan that was parked just outside the terminal building in a space marked "Military Parking Only."

"Unfortunately, I've done this more times than anyone, including me, would ever want."

As we were leaving the airport and entering the freeway heading towards San Francisco, I couldn't help but ask him the next question. "Did you know my brother?"

"No, but I feel like I know him now," he said, a hint of a soft smile crossing his lips as he looked into my eyes.

As we drove north from the airport on Highway 101, we crossed an open part of San Francisco Bay. Off to the front right, about a mile away, I could see the bright lights of Candlestick Park. It was about 9:30 on a late July evening. The Giants must have been playing a night game. Sergeant Janssen confirmed that they were when he said he hoped we could get past the stadium before the game was over so we could miss the traffic.

The sight of that stadium tugged harshly at my heart. The last time I had been on that stretch of freeway was two years earlier, and Ron had been the driver. I remembered him pointing out Candlestick Park to me and saying it was too bad the Giants were playing out of town that weekend, or we could have gone to a game Saturday afternoon. Now, the sight of those stadium lights only served to make me fight back tears—tears I knew Sergeant Janssen couldn't completely understand, because he didn't know the history Ron and I shared. The result of this personal flashback was silence in the car, as the sergeant drove into the ever more congested parts of San Francisco towards the Bay Bridge, which connected San Francisco with Oakland and the East Bay suburbs.

As we approached the lower level of the huge double-decker bridge, I had another important question to ask him. "Do you have any more details of how Ron died?"

"No, I'm afraid I don't, Tom. I tried to get more information when I knew you were coming out to meet your brother's body, but I couldn't find out anything more, I'm sorry. All I know now is what you probably know, that he didn't die as a result of hostile action. The only statement they're giving out at this time is 'unknown causes.'"

There were too many unanswered questions, but I decided they would have to be answered at a later time. Right now, I had a brother to take home and bury, and that's all that concerned me just then.

"Look, Tom, there's Alcatraz Island over there on the left," Sergeant Janssen said, probably sensing my disappointment at his not being able to provide any further details of Ron's death.

"Yes, I see it. I was here about two years ago with Ron. He was on leave, and I spent the weekend here in San Francisco with him. He was coming back from his first tour in Vietnam and on his way to Fort Hood."

"Is that so? I was in Vietnam about that time. Do you remember what unit he was with then?"

"He was with the 25th Infantry Division at Cu Chi in Tay Ninh Province. Fourth Battalion, 9th Infantry, I think," I proudly rattled off.

"No kidding, I was with the 25th too, but in a different battalion. Do you know the nickname for the 25th Division?"

"*Tropic Lightning.* And the motto of the 9th Infantry was '*Keep up the Fire.*' Ron received the Bronze Star while serving with that unit." The admiration for my older brother was obvious.

"Sounds like you and Ron were pretty close."

"Yeah, you could say that," I said, knowing I could have talked for hours to the sergeant about our relationship, but thought it better not to.

Besides we had crossed the long bridge by this time, and were taking one of the first exits for the Army base.

Sergeant Janssen took me directly to the BOQ, which was near the administration building and the post's main flagpole. After getting me signed into an austere, yet comfortable-looking, private room with a shower, he bade me good night and said he would meet me for breakfast at 7:00 A.M. at the BOQ's front entrance.

I was exhausted. It was only ten o'clock, but my Midwestern body clock was already on midnight. I unpacked my shaving kit, hung up my one change of clothes for the return trip, and went to bed. Before drifting off to sleep, I set the alarm clock for 6:00 A.M.

It turned out I didn't need the clock; the two-hour time difference made me wake up without it by about five o'clock. As I lay awake in bed, it wasn't long before a bugler—or, at least a recording of a bugler—blew reveille into a loudspeaker.

As planned, I met Sergeant Janssen for breakfast at 7:00. We ate in the base's main mess hall. At first I was concerned I would stand out too much in my civilian clothes, but when we entered, I saw several other civilians, probably government workers, eating there as well. Sergeant Janssen gave a voucher of some sort to one of the servers behind the counter, who simply nodded and handed me a plastic tray. The natural momentum of the others in line kept me and Sergeant Janssen shuffling along until our trays were filled with assorted breakfast foods. After we got our coffee at the end of the food line, he directed me to a corner table, which was more private than the long, plastic-covered benches where most of the enlisted men ate.

We exchanged the typical morning small talk, then he said he had found out one more piece of information regarding Ron, but it was only a small piece. "I checked the manifest this morning, and it says your brother's body is 'viewable.'" He saw the look of confusion on my face. "Well, some bodies coming from Vietnam are listed as 'nonviewable.' Those are the ones that, well, let me say, the government thinks is best that the families don't see. The caskets can only be opened by funeral directors for professional reasons. They aren't supposed to let the families see in the casket, because the condition of the body would be too much of a shock for a loved one. It depends on how the person died."

"I understand. This means that I can actually see him—he's not mangled or anything like that?"

"Yes, it means you will be able to see him, but not until after the casket arrives at the funeral home in Brandon, is uncrated, and the funeral director checks it all out."

"*Uncrated?*" I asked.

"Yes, the casket is a standard military issue of very good quality, but it's currently in a large wooden shipping crate to protect it until it arrives at the funeral home. This is the part that most official next of kin and families don't see. But, because you're here while the body is still in transit, I just wanted to explain that to you."

I was glad that he did explain it. I had been expecting to see a flag-draped coffin; it would have been a shock to see just a wooden crate.

After we finished breakfast, I rode with Sergeant Janssen past a row of several old single-story warehouses farther back into the base. We parked in front of one of the warehouses that had large doors opened in the center. Three hearses, all the typical Army olive drab, were backed up to the building. The one closest to the main entrance had its rear doors open, and a driver in Army fatigues stood near the back.

Sergeant Janssen and I walked passed the row of hearses and into the building. I didn't know exactly what to expect, but I was confident the sergeant had matters well in hand. My heart was racing. I had this feeling of meeting Ron inside that building—that he would come walking out of the interior. After all, I hadn't seen him in nearly four months. And the Giants were playing at home this weekend . . .

"Wait here, Tom, I'll be back in a few minutes," Sergeant Janssen said, breaking me out of my daydreaming. My thoughts were probably some sort of defense mechanism, since I knew the awful reality.

I became aware that just inside the main entrance where I was asked to wait, there were two walls resembling large bulletin boards, each displaying several even rows of framed 8" x 11" black picture frames. Each frame contained a close-up of a soldier in uniform, with a name and date engraved on a small plaque beneath it. The word *posthumous* was also engraved under most of the dates. Above the top row of photos, on both sides, in large letters were the words *Medal of Honor Recipients*. In smaller letters beneath them was a sign reading "Dedication, Honor, Sacrifice."

I realized I was looking at a hall of bravery—knowing that most of the men in those photos had died for their country, and had also returned to this very building in crates before their bodies were sent home to their families throughout America. Many of the dates were within the last few years.

I felt both honored and saddened as I stared into those framed faces, knowing that I didn't have exclusive rights to the pain I felt regarding Ron's death. It was something I shared with the kid brothers and other family members of the hundred or so soldiers honored on that warehouse wall, as well as thousands of others throughout the country. Looking at the eyes of those framed faces, I knew there was no glamour or heroics remaining, only pain and a sense of finality for them and their loved ones.

Just then the sergeant returned from the interior of the warehouse carrying a large gray envelope about a half inch thick. Behind him, two soldiers were slowly pushing a waist-high metal cart on wheels.

Then I saw it, the large crate Sergeant Janssen had told me to expect. It was made of plain, raw unfinished wood with several metal handles screwed along the sides. The shape and size of the crate left no doubt as to its contents.

As my eyes took in the sight of that crate, my heart stopped.

The two soldiers pushed the cart slowly towards me with solemn respect. At the moment I thought it a bit strange because they hadn't known the person inside, but I appreciated their consideration anyway.

They stopped the crate in front of Sergeant Janssen and me. I noticed a large, plastic shipping envelope was glued to the side of the crate. Behind the clear plastic was a one-page typewritten form. Across the top of the form, in large one-inch stenciled letters, was the word *VIEWABLE*. Also stenciled on the edge of the crate itself, above the form, was the word *HEAD*.

Sergeant Janssen placed his hand on my shoulder, and we walked the few steps over to the wooden box. My knees were shaking, and I was fighting back tears, but losing the battle with each wobbly step.

He removed some paperwork from the envelope he was holding and compared it to the form attached to the crate. He began to lay the forms on the top of the crate as he removed a pen from the breast pocket of his Class A dress uniform. He hesitated, then, apparently out of respect for my presence, he beckoned one of the soldiers over, turned the soldier around so that his back faced him, and placed the forms on the soldier's back to sign them.

I stepped up to the crate and touched it for a moment, staring at the word *HEAD*. I knew my hand was only a few inches away from Ron's face. I read the typed words on the form attached to the crate. Among the jargon of military abbreviations and destination instructions, one line stood out all too clearly: *"Deceased: SFC Ronald H. Reilly,"* with his Social Security number following his name.

Yes, Ron, I've come to meet you once again, I thought to myself. Only this time it was under the most horrible circumstances a kid brother could imagine.

That plain wooden box bearing his name and the more haunting words *HEAD* and *VIEWABLE* finally made his death all too real and irrevocable. Sergeant Janssen and the soldiers gave me a silent moment, as I touched the crate. Even though they did this on a routine basis, it was *not* routine for a next of kin to be involved at this point. I was fully aware of that and was determined not to interfere with their duties.

"Are you okay, Tom?" Sergeant Janssen softly asked, patting me lightly on the back.

"Yeah, ah, yes," was all I could answer, still fighting back tears.

"If it's okay with you, we can load Ron into the hearse now," the sergeant said softly.

A slight nod from me was followed by a more authoritative nod by Sergeant Janssen to the two soldiers. As I stepped back, the three of them gently rolled the carted crate out the front entrance, and to the hearse.

I couldn't help but think that Ron was making his final exit from a military building, while the eyes of the hundred or so Medal of Honor winners witnessed it from their photographs. Perhaps that was the purpose of those pictures lining each side of the lobby—to give a silent salute to all the dead soldiers leaving their final government building.

Using the metal handles on the sides of the crate, Sergeant Janssen, both warehouse soldiers, and the hearse driver, gently lifted the box into the back of the vehicle. Sergeant Janssen, by himself, pushed it in the last couple of feet, as the bottom engaged the rollers on the floor of the hearse.

After closing and securing the back door, the driver, along with one of the warehouse soldiers, got into the front of the hearse, while the sergeant and I got into his Army sedan.

Sergeant Janssen drove slowly, following the hearse as it drove back through the main part of the Army base. Just as we were exiting the main gate, an MP stationed at the front gate noticed the hearse approaching his post. He immediately came to attention and raised his right hand in a rigid salute, holding it until the hearse passed him, then slowly lowered his hand as our car went by.

I knew enough about the Army to know that this was simply a show of respect from the MP. There were no officer markings on the front of the hearse or on our sedan, meaning a salute was not required by regulations. I wondered how many times a day Vietnam had caused the front gate MPs to make similar salutes to passing hearses.

Our two-vehicle procession pulled out into the busy traffic and merged into the lane entering the Bay Bridge. By now, it was near the end of the morning rush hour, but the top deck of the bridge was still congested and moving slowly.

Sergeant Janssen had to concentrate on traffic and staying behind the hearse, so there was practically no conversation, except for his comments about the traffic. I didn't mind. The westbound upper deck of the Bay Bridge affords a passenger sweeping views of San Francisco, its bay, Alcatraz Island, and even the Golden Gate Bridge in the distance. I couldn't stop thinking of how much I had enjoyed seeing all this for the first time with Ron just two years earlier. It seemed unfair, beyond comprehension, that now I was looking out on these sun-drenched sights with Ron only a few yards ahead of me in the other vehicle. But now he couldn't enjoy those sights with me, nor would he ever again. He was just thirty-two. What a terrible waste.

The San Francisco end of the Bay Bridge connects to Highway 101, where we proceeded south another dozen miles to the airport. Here the traffic became lighter, and soon we were close to the airport, passing Candlestick Park again.

Ron and I wouldn't be making a ball game today, or ever. In a few hours, I would have him back home in the quiet of central Wisconsin, away from San Francisco and the rest of the world he had set out to be a part of more than ten years earlier.

Sergeant Janssen and I would be flying back to Milwaukee with Ron's body on TWA. As we entered San Francisco airport, we followed the Army hearse to a big white building near the front of the complex. The red letters over the several warehouse doors indicated it was the "TWA Cargo" building.

From our sedan, we watched while the hearse backed up to an overhead door on the far end of the building. Sergeant Janssen explained that the crated coffin was, in fact, to be handled as *airfreight*. We watched for a moment or two until the building door was opened by a TWA worker in coveralls, who spoke briefly to the hearse driver. Then the worker went back into the warehouse, returning a minute later with another worker and a metal baggage cart about eight feet long. Soon the TWA workers, along with the Army driver and his assistant, were carefully unloading the crate from the hearse and placing it on the cart. When finished, the TWA employees pulled heavy curtains across the open sides of the cart, concealing the crate from view.

Seemingly satisfied with these arrangements, the sergeant then drove us over to the main terminal, where we checked in at the TWA counter for our flight.

"They'll take good care of him," Sergeant Janssen reassured me as we walked to the departure gate. He must have sensed my uneasiness in relinquishing the crate to more strangers. I told him I wasn't worried, even though I did feel some anxiety over having to let Ron out of my sight. But it was the only practical thing to do.

We arrived at our gate early, and there were only a few other people present. I wandered over to the glass wall of windows and looked out over the white-and-red passenger jet that would soon be carrying all three of us back to the Midwest. The baggage handlers and other ground crew were busy preparing for the flight. As I watched, I caught sight of another TWA employee approaching on a small tractor that was pulling a single baggage cart with drawn curtains. He was heading towards our plane.

I went over to Sergeant Janssen, who was seated in the gate area reading a newspaper. I told him I thought they were bringing Ron's body over to the plane. He seemed to sense the anxiousness in my announcement.

"Let me see if we can go down to the tarmac," he said and then went and spoke briefly to the gate attendant. The attendant looked across the room at me for a second, then nodded to Sergeant Janssen. Both men beckoned me over to a door that opened onto some stairs leading down to ground level.

Upon seeing us, a ground crew employee, seeming to be in charge, walked over and met Sergeant Janssen and me at the base of the stairs; after all, this was an unusual place for nonairport personnel to be. I sensed that Sergeant Janssen's uniform would be of some benefit in the situation even before he explained our purpose.

"Hello," he said to the employee, "this is Tom Reilly. He's a passenger with me on this flight. His deceased brother will also be flying with us today."

That was all he had to say. Apparently this employee, whose name was Chuck, according to his work shirt, had been made aware of any *special cargo* beforehand. Chuck looked at me, offered brief condolences, then asked, "Would you like to help us load your brother into the plane?"

I was amazed that I would be allowed to become so involved with this process! "Yes, I would really appreciate that," I said, looking at Sergeant Janssen for his approval, which he conveyed with a smile and gentle nod.

Chuck led the sergeant and me around to the right side of the enormous jet to where a couple of his crew were loading suitcases and small boxes onto a conveyor belt that extended up through the open cargo door into the belly of the aircraft. It was noisy with all the equipment and pumps whirring away.

Chuck said a few undistinguishable words to the two baggage handlers, who immediately stopped what they were loading. He then motioned for the tractor driver, who had been waiting with his single cart several yards off to the side, to drive it into position near the conveyor. When the cart was in place, Chuck called me over and pulled back the curtains, revealing the shipping crate.

Chuck, the two other baggage handlers, and I carefully turned the crate ninety degrees on the bed of the cart and took up positions at each of the four metal handles. Chuck directed me to take the handle closest to the *HEAD* stencil.

With a nod from Chuck, the four of us lifted the crate, carried it a few steps, and gently placed it on the conveyor. I couldn't believe how heavy the wooden box was. All four sets of hands then guided the crate, as the mechanical conveyor belt took over the work and lifted it into the cargo hold of the plane, where two other employees guided it off the conveyor.

Chuck switched off the conveyor, jumped up on it, and to my surprise, turned and reached out his hand to me. I took it, and he helped me walk up the conveyor belt into the plane. In a second I was inside the cavernous belly, a place where I guessed few people had ever been, except for certain airport employees. A lot of baggage, boxes, and orange canvas bags marked "U.S. Mail" were stacked just to the left of the door. I followed the lead of the employees as we moved Ron's crate to a section just to the right, towards the front of the plane. There were several other smaller boxes of freight already there to one side. The crate holding the casket was moved to the opposite side, and the two employees secured the crate to the wall with straps.

Chuck explained to me that nothing would be placed on top of the crate, nor would any other freight or baggage be stacked in a way that could possibly fall on it during flight. Then he led me back out of the plane and took me back to Sergeant Janssen, who had been standing nearby while the loading had transpired.

I couldn't believe I had been allowed to do all this, and I sincerely thanked Chuck and the other workers before going back up the stairs to the boarding area with Sergeant Janssen.

✳ ✳ ✳

The flight from San Francisco to Milwaukee was uneventful. Sergeant Janssen was apparently an avid reader, because except for some occasional small talk, he kept his head buried in a book for most of the four-hour return flight. I surmised this was for a good reason. First, his job was stressful enough, constantly dealing with funeral arrangements and bereaved relatives, so his flight time was probably good for his personal relaxation and inner peace. Books were a good way for him to escape the reality of his job. Secondly, he was not used to having a next of kin travel with him. Yet, he was compassionate enough to know that I needed my space to dwell on my private thoughts as well. His reading for most of the flight helped both of us.

With the two-hour time change, it was already late afternoon when we landed at Milwaukee's General Billy Mitchell Field, the city's main airport. As Sergeant Janssen had previously arranged, we were met at the gate by a driver from the local funeral home in Brandon. After a brief, and almost too professional an offering of his condolences, he informed us that his partner was with their hearse at TWA's cargo facility, a short distance from the passenger terminal.

On the walk through the terminal, the driver, named Robert, eagerly told Sergeant Janssen that this would be the first full military funeral he could remember in tiny little Brandon. He said news of the upcoming funeral had already spread throughout the town's population of eight hundred. Apparently, recognizing that, although this might be an exciting event for the funeral directors, it wasn't for me, Sergeant Janssen kept Robert's professional enthusiasm in check by simply asking if all of his previously sent instructions were being followed by the funeral home.

"Yes, sir! We're all set!" Robert proclaimed.

The three of us arrived at the cargo pickup building just as Robert's partner and a few TWA employees loaded the crate bearing Ron's casket into the shiny black hearse. Before the back door was closed, Sergeant Janssen dutifully walked over and checked the paperwork by peering through a side window of the hearse. Obviously, after coming this far, he wanted to make sure the right body had been loaded.

Robert ushered Sergeant Janssen and me to an equally shiny black Cadillac parked near the hearse. While his assistant drove the hearse, Robert would drive us the sixty or so miles from Milwaukee to Brandon.

Robert, taking a cue from Sergeant Janssen, didn't talk much, as we traveled north on U.S. Highway 41, then cut over onto State Highway 49, which took us through Waupun and eventually to Brandon where we arrived about 8:00 P.M.

I was familiar with the route from my early childhood. My dad, Ron, and I would sometimes drive the same way to Milwaukee to a Braves baseball game. One time Ron even caught a foul ball that was hit into the stands just above first base. After the game, Ron waited near the players' locker room, and was able to get the great Warren Spahn, who was pitching that day, to autograph the ball. Ron said he told Mr. Spahn it was for "his kid brother," who was a big fan.

We met briefly that evening with one of the funeral home's owners. He, Robert, and Sergeant Janssen spent some time making all the arrangements for the next two days. There would be a military burial detachment, consisting of an officer, a color guard, a firing squad, and a bugler to blow taps, arriving the next evening from Fort Sheridan, Illinois. In all, there would be thirteen men, and they would be billeted overnight twenty miles away in Fond du Lac, a city that had the closest hotel large enough to handle that many in one party.

Sergeant Janssen and the funeral director delicately asked if I wanted the casket open or closed for the viewing scheduled for the next evening. I didn't know until they told me that making such a decision was one of the obligations of the official "next of kin." That is, if the option was available. I was reminded that I did have that option, since the shipping documents had been stamped *VIEWABLE*.

Since this was new territory for me, I tried to think what Ron would like if he were alive. I caught myself thinking that that was a stupid thought, since if he could make that decision, he wouldn't be in a casket! My mind raced back to each of my parent's funerals. Each had lain in state, in an open casket at the very same funeral home twelve years earlier. I could still see all the relatives and friends attending each wake, walking up close and peering inside the casket for several seconds, some feeling it necessary to utter comments.

I made the decision with little effort. "Ron was a very private person. I think he would want a closed casket service, and that's what I also want for him. But *I* need to see him," I announced to the funeral director.

I *had* to verify, at least for myself, that it was really Ron in that box. I had heard a story of a family who had lost a loved one in Vietnam, who had been shipped back home in a *NONVIEWABLE* casket. Since no one had viewed the remains before burial, some of the relatives later convinced themselves that their loved one was still alive, and being held as a POW in North Vietnam. I couldn't risk such uncertainty.

"Very well," the funeral director said, "the wake begins at 10:00 A.M. tomorrow. You can come in for a private viewing at 9:30 if you like."

I agreed and drove back to my temporary quarters in Montello. Sergeant Janssen, using a car offered to him by the funeral home, left for his hotel in Fond du Lac. It had been a long and emotional day. It seemed like I woke up a week ago in the BOQ in Oakland, California, rather than just that morning.

�֍ ✶ ✶

I arrived at the funeral home shortly after nine the next morning, after a restless night of nothing more than short, interrupted naps. I walked into the empty foyer of the well-kept Victorian two-story house. There was no one around, so I stepped into the main room, which I knew all too well from experience, was where the casket would be displayed for the wake. There it was. The casket itself was not visible, because it was completely draped by an American flag. The red, white, and blue colors never before looked so vivid to me. A large lit candle, encased by burgundy-colored glass, was atop a tall brass floor stand near the foot of the casket. A dark-colored kneeling bench had been placed in front of the casket at the head end. I was amazed to see that several flower arrangements had arrived and had been placed around the casket. About fifty metal folding chairs, with padded seats, were lined up in perfect rows a few feet from the alcove that contained the casket and flowers. A center aisle, leading up to the casket, divided the chairs into two sections. I was very impressed with the care that had been taken and work that had been done by the funeral home staff.

I was compelled to walk forward and kneel on the velvet-covered praying bench in front of the flag-draped casket. I reached out and placed my hand on the flag above where I thought my brother's chest might be. It was my way of touching the heart that had touched mine for as long as I could remember.

I don't know how long I knelt there, not really praying to the crucifix on the wall above the casket, but just being close to the brother I adored. I knew I would miss him deeply for as long as I lived, and I was so thankful he had been there to get me at least this far in life.

Suddenly, I sensed a presence behind me in the room and turned to see the funeral director standing quietly at the back. He walked towards me, using smooth, flowing movements I figured they must teach in mortician school.

"Are you ready to see your brother, Tom?" he asked.

"Yes, that would be good, at least before anyone else gets here," I said, standing up.

With that, the funeral director moved the prayer bench out of the way and gently began to fold the blue and white-star portion of the flag back from the head end of the casket. It was then I got my first actual look at the casket that had been inside the rough wooden shipping crate. It was gray metal, with grooved handrails along the side—*simple, but nice looking, as far as caskets go,* I thought.

The funeral director folded the flag back far enough to expose the edge of the lid, then reached under the front flange and unscrewed something. As he did this, he glanced back at me and slowly opened the lid of the casket.

My heart was pounding with a myriad of emotions.

He stepped back out of the way, and I cautiously stepped up to the side of the casket. There was the person I loved most in the world, possibly the *only* person with whom I ever shared a deep bond. Ron was lying in the casket in a green Class A dress uniform. Each button was carefully in place. His black name tag, with engraved white letters spelling REILLY, was above the pocket on his right chest. In the same location on his left chest were his two rows of campaign ribbons and medals. Rather than being arranged in the familiar civilian "pose" of arms across the chest and hands folded, Ron's body had been positioned at military attention, only lying down. His arms and hands were extended straight down at his sides. His hands were in white gloves with the fingers extended and joined. His face gave the impression of restful sleep. A piece of clear glass covered the open half of the casket, about an inch above his face, serving as an airtight seal. Upon seeing this, my first impulse was to tell the funeral director that Ron couldn't breathe under that glass. Then reality hit me in the face—Ron wasn't breathing anyway. I knew those eyes would never again open, nor would his mouth ever again speak another word, or smile at me. His hand would never again shake mine. Yes, unfortunately, this was Ron in the casket; my painful mission to verify it was him had been regrettably successful. I vowed to him right then and there, as he lay motionless, that after the funeral I was determined to find out how and why he died, no matter what it took.

I stood at the side of the open casket for several minutes, not verbally, but in my thoughts, telling Ron how important he had been to me. How I wished I could have prevented his death in some way. I also vowed that I would carry on, get my college degree as he had wanted, and make something of my life. As I stood there, I silently dedicated the rest of my life to him.

I became conscious of a hand on my shoulder. I turned so that my very reddened eyes met the only slightly reddened eyes of Sergeant Janssen. My only thought at seeing him was, *he does this for a living?*

�֎   �֎   ✖

It seemed like the entire town of Brandon wandered in and out of the funeral home during the course of that day. They came not only to pay their respects, but also to satisfy some sort of curiosity regarding Brandon's connection to a distant war they knew only through their TV sets. I was glad that I'd made the decision to have a closed casket. I wouldn't want Ron to be the object of curiosity.

Distant relatives also came—many aunts and uncles, as well as great-aunts and great-uncles, who came from as far away as Chicago. The last time I had seen those people was twelve years earlier, when they had made the same pilgrimage for my parents' funerals. I couldn't count the number of times that day I heard someone say, "Oh, there's little Tommy, the last time I saw you, you were only this tall!" Of course I was only *that* tall then, I was only seven years old. Now I was nineteen, for Christ's sake!

I left the funeral home several times that day and walked aimlessly around the streets of Brandon, trying not to be noticed. I wandered past the corner tavern, where I lived in the upstairs apartment with my family from the time I was born until I was about five. I walked down a deserted street to the old canning factory at the edge of town, behind the funeral home. At one point, I found myself sitting on the edge of the bandstand in the middle of Brandon's small municipal park. My dad had helped build that bandstand just before he died in 1958. From there, I could look in one direction and see the lumberyard, where he had worked one of his two jobs—the one he loved, as a carpenter. In the other direction I could see the corner grocery store, now a sporting goods store, where Ron had worked part-time in high school.

Reflecting on all these rather simple landmarks made me feel better about bringing Ron home from the more complicated world to be buried just outside Brandon. He really could have peace here.

I returned to the funeral home about six that evening. Sergeant Janssen was still at his duty station in the lobby, exchanging small talk with some of the townspeople as they dropped in for short visits. He had been doing this most of the day. He felt it was his duty to represent the Army, and he did it well.

It was about this time that another Army sedan, followed by two similarly painted passenger vans, pulled up and parked in one of the funeral home's two long driveways. Sergeant Janssen noticed the activity and excused himself to go out to meet the procession. It was the burial detachment from Fort Sheridan.

An officer and driver got out of the car and met Sergeant Janssen on the lawn. After exchanging salutes, they engaged in conversation. The officer, I was surprised to see, was a major, signified by the gold oak leaf clusters on his epaulets, and the "scrambled eggs" on the bill of his service hat. Ron would be impressed, a field-grade officer was in charge of his burial detachment.

While they were talking on the lawn, the other personnel exited the two vans. I could tell by their actions that their three-hour drive had been a long one. Many were tightening their neckties and putting on and buttoning their dress green jackets. They were also putting on their very shiny, dark-colored helmet liners that bore their unit's insignia. The group of enlisted men milled around near the driveway, until the officer and Sergeant Janssen walked over and quietly ordered them to "fall in" and come to attention. By this time, a dozen or so townspeople were watching this, the largest regular Army group ever to assemble in Brandon.

While the officer talked to his men, Sergeant Janssen ushered the mourners and me back into the funeral home, and asked us all to be seated in the main room in front of Ron's flag-draped casket. I'm sure everyone in the room wondered what was going on, including me.

Within about a minute, we heard several sharp, loud voice commands from out on the lawn. A few seconds later, the officer entered the lobby and with very stiff, deliberate steps, strode down the center aisle between the chairs, approaching Ron's casket. When he was a few feet in front of it, he stopped and snapped his heels together, coming to attention. Still facing the casket, he very slowly bent his right arm at the elbow, fingers extended and joined, and gave a perfect salute to the casket. After holding the salute for several seconds, he just as slowly lowered his arm to his side and smartly did an about face, so that he now faced me. He looked directly into my eyes and saluted *me*.

I wasn't prepared for such a show of respect, first to Ron and then to me. All I could do was slowly nod an acknowledgment to the major's salute. He also nodded, continuing to look into my eyes as he dropped the salute, and then, taking strict military movements, he took up a position near and at a right angle to the casket.

After he took his place, each of the other twelve enlisted men, individually, took a turn walking through the center of the room, snapping to attention in front of the casket and executing similar slow-motion salutes. When done with his salute, each man remained at attention, did a stiff half-column right, and marched out the side door of the funeral home. When the last man exited the room, the major turned for one more salute to the casket and then, as smartly as he had entered, he left the room through the same side door.

Everyone in that room was stunned by the display of military ceremony and respect that was paid to just one man. But after all, he was a fellow soldier. It didn't matter that they had never met him.

I was extremely proud and grateful for the professional regard these men had shown my brother and me. I leaned over to Sergeant Janssen and expressed those thoughts, telling him I wanted to go outside to thank them. He told me they were already heading for their hotel and that I could speak to them after the service the next morning.

I drove back to Montello that night, thinking about how those soldiers were helping me get through this nightmare. I knew I would never forget the respect they had shown my brother that day. I was bursting with pride, and I knew Ron would be too—although taking it in stride, as was his manner.

Ron's funeral was set for the next morning at 10:00 A.M. The mass would be held at tiny St. Mary's Church, about four miles outside of Brandon, in Springvale Township. Ron would be buried in the family plot adjacent to the church. The land for the church and cemetery had been donated by our great-grandfather. It was actually the highest and driest land on the farm, which was located just across the road from the church. My father and his brothers were the last Reillys to work on the farm. Now, four generations of Reillys would be buried in the small cemetery set amidst the green fields and gravel roads of rural Fond du Lac County.

One time, when he was home on leave, Ron and I visited our parents' graves in St. Mary's cemetery. They were situated in a back corner near three enormous evergreen trees. In what I considered a strange premonition, Ron walked over and stood beneath the evergreens and said, "If the worst happens to me, boy, bring me back here." I could only nod that I would. Ron never again mentioned that subject to me, nor did I ever bring it up. I never forgot his personal request. So when the funeral director asked me where I wanted Ron's gravesite, my answer had been immediate and without reservation. It had nothing to do with where *I* wanted the grave, it had been Ron's choice. I silently thanked him for relieving me of making that important decision.

Shortly before ten, the burial detachment arrived to transport Ron's casket to St. Mary's. With solemn military dignity, the honor guard of six enlisted pallbearers accompanied by the officer, moved the casket from the funeral home to the private hearse waiting outside. The long procession of cars with headlights on moved slowly through the few streets of Brandon, and out into the open countryside en route to the church. I rode with Sergeant Janssen and the major in a black Cadillac directly behind the hearse.

While the somber procession moved through Brandon, I was amazed to see two old men from the town standing along the sidewalk wearing tattered blue Veterans of Foreign Wars garrison hats. Both did the best they could to stand at attention, and with arms and hands bent by time, came to a salute as the hearse passed them. Sergeant Janssen and the major crisply returned the salutes of these old warriors that I never knew existed in innocent little Brandon. It was just one of many touching moments I experienced during those sad days.

Upon arriving at the church, the honor guard had great difficulty trying to position the flag-draped casket in the front of the congregation near the altar. They had to leave it in one of the two aisles. The tiny wooden church had been built to accommodate only about fifty people, and the space inside was quite small and cramped. Funerals were usually not held at this location for that reason. That day, there were more than a hundred people in attendance, so half had to endure the mass outside, in the heat of late July. When the priest saw the crowd, he suggested performing a more abbreviated *low* funeral mass, and I agreed, much to the relief of the congregation.

When the mass concluded, the honor guard, once again in perfect unison, carried the casket to the open grave under the evergreens. Already in position at the rear of the cemetery was a seven-man firing squad. Sunlight was glistening off their shiny helmets; their white-gloved hands were a vivid contrast to their dark green uniforms and the rifles they held across their chests at port arms.

The priest offered a blessing to Ron at the graveside, sprinkling holy water over the flag, which still covered the casket.

Upon the major's terse command, the honor guard, now on both sides and facing the casket, snapped a salute and held it. Suddenly, from the far back corner of the cemetery came the mournful sounds of the bugler playing taps. Once taps have been played for a loved one, a person never forgets the rush of emotions those notes evoke. As I listened, I knew I had just become part of that special fraternity of mourners.

As the last note trailed off over the neighboring trees and cornfields, another verbal command was heard near the firing squad. In perfect unison, the seven soldiers in the back of the cemetery aimed their rifles in the air and fired three abrupt volleys before returning to order arms and attention.

The reports of the rifles seemed to interfere with the peaceful rural setting for a few seconds, causing birds to fly from trees, and a chill to penetrate my whole body.

With a brief command at the gravesite, the honor guard began folding the flag that had been covering the casket. This was done, once again, with ceremonial precision and dignity. Once folded, the honor guard sergeant presented it to the major, who inspected it. Assured it was properly folded, the officer walked over where I was standing, came to attention, and holding the flag with both hands, presented it to me. While doing so he said, "On behalf of the President and government of the United States, please accept this flag in recognition of your loved one's faithful service." Then, he took one step back and saluted the flag one final time as I held it.

Yes, Ron, I pledge all my energy to find out why you are being laid to rest here today, I thought to myself as I accepted the flag.

Chapter 6

Saigon–Arrival and Deportation

My frustration with the Army's red tape steadily increased during the weeks following Ron's funeral. As many times as I tried, I couldn't get any answers from the Army officials or civilian bureaucrats at the Department of Defense in Washington, D.C., regarding the details of Ron's death. I thought this rather strange, since the military and the Pentagon were used to dealing with the families of casualties. With no small measure of perseverance, I did find out that a military medical staff in Vietnam had performed an autopsy, however, the results were not yet available.

Up to that point in my life, Ron had been my whole world. Now that he was gone and I wasn't being told why, I began to suspect that maybe he had been murdered either by civilians or even others in the military.

I had always known Ron was a very worldly guy, living much of his life "on the edge." The short time I spent with him in Laredo showed me that his life and travels had brought him into contact with some pretty unsavory people around the world. Perhaps he had gotten involved with similar types in the underbelly of Saigon, where, I knew from his letters, he spent a lot of time. Even though he was a pretty capable guy and could handle himself, just maybe he had gotten in over his head.

Just the thought of something like that conjured up all kinds of scenarios in the mind of a grieving brother and next of kin who had just lost most of his reason to live. And with each scenario I envisioned came a desire to seek revenge on anyone who might have contributed to Ron's death.

But whether he died under suspicious circumstances or of natural causes, I decided there was only one way for me to find out the truth. *I had to travel to Vietnam.*

Then one day, about a month after the funeral, I received a business envelope in the mail from Servicemens' Group Life Insurance of Newark, New Jersey. The envelope had been forwarded from my last official mailing address at the UW dormitory in Madison. Inside was a check made payable to me as beneficiary in the amount of fifteen thousand dollars and a copy of the form Ron had signed making me sole beneficiary. An accompanying letter informed me this was the standard life insurance for servicemen.

I rushed the check over to a local bank, and, after verifying its authenticity, opened a new account with it. The funds would be ready for withdrawal in ten days, if necessary.

I did find it necessary to make a withdrawal after the check cleared.

I went to the only travel agency in Ripon and requested information about a round-trip ticket from Chicago to Saigon. The elderly travel agent, after his initial shock at my intended destination, had to do some inquiries, but eventually located a seat on a Pan Am 'Round-the-World Clipper flight, departing San Francisco with stops in Honolulu, Guam, and Manila. I could take a Greyhound bus from Ripon to Chicago, then a flight from Chicago that would connect to the clipper in San Francisco.

The round-trip ticket in coach class would cost fourteen hundred dollars. I went to the bank, withdrew the money, and instructed the travel agent to book the flight, which would be leaving in ten days. This ignited a flurry of objections from him, insisting I "couldn't" just fly to Saigon as a lone teenager. He informed me I needed a passport, immunization shots, and permission (but from whom, he wasn't sure). Basically, he was trying to talk me out of going.

But, I had made up my mind. I already had a passport, because Ron had suggested I get one while I was in high school, in case he wanted me to meet him anywhere in the world. And I assured the travel agent I would get whatever shots were required by the World Health Organization.

I conceded the "permission" part could be problematic. The travel agent suggested I check with the State Department to see if any particular forms or visas were needed for an American civilian to visit South Vietnam. I took his advice and anonymously called the State Department in Washington, D.C., the next day. It took more than an hour on the phone and being transferred to a half-dozen variously titled bureaucrats before I talked to one who could "almost" answer my questions regarding entry into South Vietnam by a U.S. civilian. The reason he could "almost" answer my questions was because my situation didn't really apply to any procedures currently identified in the government manuals. The career bureaucrat on the other end of the phone could tell me what I needed if I were in the military, or if I were working for a U.S. company in Vietnam contracted by our government or by the South Vietnamese government, or if I were a member of the clergy on missionary work. But, he said he couldn't find anything regarding the entry of a civilian traveling there alone for personal reasons.

The bureaucrat strongly suggested that I not go, then put me on hold for about five minutes, apparently giving him time to explain my situation to his supervisor.

Before too long, the supervisor got on the phone and sternly lectured me about how a nineteen-year-old civilian has no business going to Vietnam for "frivolous reasons." This then turned into a heated debate, with me yelling at him about judging my reason for going, and him yelling back, demanding my name and address. He was not getting either one from me!

Finally, I calmly asked this man if he could *stop me* from traveling to South Vietnam.

"Well, ah, no . . . as long as you have a valid passport," he answered.

That was a good enough answer for me. I immediately called the travel agent back and told him to book my flight, the one departing in ten days, if possible. He reluctantly said he would.

Next were the immunizations. I visited a local doctor, who took a day to research what shots I needed for traveling to that part of the world. Just listening to the list of requirements made my arms hurt: typhoid, cholera, tetanus, hepatitis, and malaria. To make matters worse, some of them required two or three injections over a period of weeks. And, if that wasn't bad enough, he also informed me not all of the shots would be administered to my arms. The good doctor advised me which ones I should get first, so the pain in my butt would be gone before sitting on a plane for thirty-two hours.

Yet another complication was that the fact that the malaria shot was only administered at the University Hospital in Madison, seventy miles away, and required a sixty- to ninety-day period before it took effect.

The doctor and his staff also tried talking me out of going, because it was impossible to get all the immunizations completed in the short time that I had before my scheduled departure. Time constraints aside, they also thought I was totally insane.

I appreciated their advice, but I didn't follow it. I ordered the shots, and for the next week, at least one of my arms and one of my ass cheeks was in constant pain. The cholera shots also made me feverish and nauseated for a couple of days. And, if some of them didn't have time to take effect before I arrived in Vietnam, then I would just have to take my chances.

There was one other very important thing I had to do before leaving. With Ron's death and all the unrest taking place on college campuses, including mine, I decided to put my education on hold and enlist in the Army. The Army was offering a "Delayed Entry Program" for enlistees. This meant that one could take their entrance physical, and if one passed it, could take the oath of service, but have up to ninety days to report for duty.

Ron always told me that those who enlisted had more benefits than draftees. One such benefit was that as an enlistee, I could choose a job in the Army, rather than the Army choosing one for me. And, as long as I qualified for it, I could have it guaranteed in writing before actually enlisting. Enlistees had a better chance of securing their first or second choice of duty locations as well. Draftees were usually sent anywhere the military needed them. And now, due to Ron's death in Vietnam, I knew I wouldn't *have* to be assigned to a war zone unless I volunteered.

All of this was confirmed, in writing, by the recruiting sergeant in the nearby city of Fond du Lac.

So, the week before I was scheduled to leave for Vietnam as a civilian, I took a bus to Milwaukee, passed my physical exam, and took the oath of service. I was given a wallet-size card guaranteeing me a Military Occupational Specialty (MOS) of 95B, also known as Military Police. My reporting date for basic training was set for October 15, my twentieth birthday, leaving plenty of time for my trip to Vietnam before I had to report.

On the bus ride back from the Milwaukee enlistment center, I made a silent pledge to Ron that I would finish college and get a degree after my three-year enlistment was up. I also felt comfortable that he would understand this was something I had to do at this time, because without his rudder I was beginning to feel a little lost for the first time in my life.

For the next few days, I concentrated on preparations for my trip to Vietnam. "First things first," as the saying goes. I decided I needed to travel light, because I had no idea what was in store for me, or how I would get around once I got to Vietnam. I settled on one suitcase and a small Army surplus rucksack. The rucksack had several outer pockets that would come in handy, and also had shoulder straps, allowing me the use of both hands, if needed. Since I planned to keep the rucksack with me at all times, I packed the all-important personal items, such as my shaving kit, a change of socks and underwear, and all my travel documents. A full change of clothing including shirts, pants, more underwear, and shoes, would go into the suitcase. The idea behind these logistics was that I could "stash" the larger suitcase at a hotel or some military unit and just carry my more portable rucksack.

I also needed to fit two cameras into the rucksack: a small Kodak Instamatic for slides and prints, a Polaroid Land Camera for instant shots, and extra film for both.

Because the thought Ron's death could possibly have been a result of foul play and I felt a need for revenge, I also considered taking along a gun and ammunition. But after checking with the airlines about regulations concerning transporting such a weapon, and since I was a minor to boot, I quickly nixed the idea. I didn't want to take the chance of smuggling one on board in my luggage either. Besides, since I was going to an active war zone, I figured if I really needed a gun, I could probably obtain one somewhere once I got to Vietnam.

A big decision for me was how much of Ron's personal information I should take. About two weeks after his funeral, I received a sturdy cardboard box from the Army. The box was only about four cubic feet in size, but held the entire contents of Ron's life, including one complete change of civilian clothes and shoes, a few Army fatigue shirts with his name sewn on the chest pocket, a shaving kit, a Seiko watch, sunglasses, and a shoebox filled with photographs, small notebooks, and a stack of nearly all the letters I had sent him over the last couple of years. There was also a small brown bag containing nine medium-size nails. I had no idea why he had these, unless they were used to hang pictures on the wall of his barracks.

I was totally amazed that the sum total of a man's life could fit so compactly into such a small box. But Ron always said he liked to travel light, and since the Army provided most of his living essentials, I figured he didn't have much use for material things.

His notebooks were the most important part of his personal effects in terms of my mission to Vietnam. I figured they could possibly be of some help in determining how he died, since they contained names of people and places in Vietnam, Malaysia, and other parts of Asia where he occasionally traveled while on R&R. I highlighted the name of the *"Long Hotel—Tu Du St.—Saigon,"* and decided I would make it my first destination upon arriving in Vietnam. I could work my way to his field unit from there.

✳ ✳ ✳

A loud whining roar jarred me out the uncomfortable half-sleep that I had been restlessly not enjoying during the last phase of my thirty-two-hour ordeal of crossing the Pacific. I took a groggy look out the cabin's window and saw a green-and-tan camouflage-painted jet fighter that appeared to be drag racing our passenger jet about a quarter-mile off the wing. Fortunately, the fighter bore the markings of the United States Air Force. A quick look across the cabin showed that a second jet fighter was just off our starboard wing as well. Both planes kept an even pace with our jet. A comforting feeling, I thought, me and the other passengers were being given a multimillion-dollar military escort through the air space approaching Vietnam.

For about the first time since leaving the last refueling stop in Manila, I sat upright in my window seat, trying to get a first glimpse of the country that had torn America apart by taking so many lives from so many families during much of the past decade.

Our 707 had already begun its descent into Saigon's Tan Son Nhut airport, when the first hint of something other than the monotonous ocean became visible. A deep green outline, bordered by a thin white line, could be seen in the early morning sunshine. The green had to be the Vietnamese coastline. As we approached closer and lower, the white line became the border of the surf washing ashore.

Closer and closer we approached. Small huts were visible on the farmland below. The land itself was divided into small parcels that crisscrossed the entire area. The neatly arranged squares of land were shining, reflecting light, as if they were mirrors lying flat on the ground. I realized that these were irrigated rice paddies—those ominous booby-trapped pieces of real estate common to Vietnam, where so many men had died so violently.

The lumbering Pan Am jet banked slowly to the north, still descending. When it leveled off, what looked like a large city could be seen just ahead.

Deplaning instructions were being given to the passengers in English, French, and an Asian dialect. It seemed strange for such a huge jet to be nearly empty, except for about a dozen passengers. Of that dozen, only two of us, a middle-aged Filipino businessman and me, were getting off in Saigon. The others were continuing on to Bombay, India, after refueling in Saigon. Most of the other passengers, a mixture of Asians and Filipinos, appeared to be quite nervous. I'm sure the poor bastards didn't relish the thought of coming close to the ground in war-torn Saigon, let alone sitting on the runway for the thirty minutes it would take to refuel.

I heard the landing gear being lowered, as we were in our final approach to the airfield. Both jet fighter planes were slowing and still abreast of us. They didn't put their wheels down, so I assumed they would soar off again as soon as we were close to touchdown.

From an altitude of about two thousand feet or so and closing, a new feature came clearly into focus on the flat countryside as we approached Saigon. Ugly, brown circles dotted the ground, some small, some large. Many were big enough to park a semi rig across their diameters. Shell holes! Hundreds of them could be seen as far as the horizon. Some overlapped each other. Some had metal or wooden debris in or near them. A few were surrounded by mangled and disabled vehicles.

My God, I thought, *I am in a combat zone!* The scarring on the farmland just outside of Saigon was the result not only of past months and years of rocket and mortar attacks, but also of "current" shellings. How frightening it must have been for the local farmers to work in their fields!

In another minute the plane touched down, bounced, and touched down again. Both fighters had disappeared by the time we were on the ground. Several olive drab helicopter gun ships were circling both sides of the main runway. Isolated, sandbagged bunkers and trench fortifications were sprinkled along the runway as well, with others near the terminal. Everything about this airfield looked military. I was sure our big, shiny white-and-light blue Pan Am 707 looked out of place.

We slowed to a near stop at one end of the field, turned, and began taxiing to the terminal. Two Army jeeps, with mounted machine guns manned by South Vietnamese troops, escorted the plane across the tarmac towards a line of large bunkers and fences that I assumed was the terminal.

The other passenger who was deplaning and I were told we would be given a military escort from the plane's door to the terminal. We were also advised to leave the jet without delay and walk quickly until we were safely inside the building.

I dislodged my rucksack from under the seat in front of me, grasped it tightly, and made my way almost too easily to the jet's open exit door. The other passenger stood in front of me. Both of us stepped out onto the top step of the portable steps and waited a few seconds for the squad of South Vietnamese soldiers to form a loose circle at the bottom of the steps.

During that brief period, I took my first breath of the musty Vietnamese air. It was humid, hot, and weighted with a dankness aroused by the suffering of a country at war. My first instinct was not to breathe it in, but, of course, that was impossible, and the air forced its way into my nose, mouth, and lungs, forcing out the breath of peace. I couldn't help but think that Ron's last breath had been consumed by such an undesirable vapor.

Next, I was gently pushed from behind as one of the Filipino stewardesses urged me and the other passenger to hurry down the steps. We did so; I tried not to start getting paranoid yet, but was still feeling quite vulnerable to a sniper's bullet as I hurried down the steps behind my fellow passenger.

Upon reaching the bottom, we were surrounded by five or six of the South Vietnamese infantrymen. On a quick command, our circle of armed protection, with us two civilians in the center, began walking the hundred yards from the plane to the sandbagged terminal.

I felt a little less vulnerable, but a lot more ridiculous in the escort situation. That is, until I looked over the shoulder of one of the guards and sighted a large shell hole not thirty feet from where we walked. Of course, I questioned how all this extra human flesh would protect me from a mortar or grenade. I tried not to think about it and just kept walking.

Now the air was not only musty, but it was also permeated with the foul smell of sweat-soaked kapok. Obviously, our guards did not get a clean change of uniform every day, nor would that have helped in the intense heat and humidity of Southeast Asia.

Mr. Midwestern College Boy had to wear a long-sleeve shirt, dress slacks, and a corduroy sport jacket, no less. Halfway to the building I knew I was overdressed, at least in terms of the *amount* of clothing I was wearing. In the heat and humidity, the corduroy jacket gave the effect of walking into a Turkish bath in a heavy bathrobe. Since I planned to spend two to four weeks in this little cesspool, I decided I wouldn't let the weather bother me too much. After all, I figured that in an hour I would have the distinct honor of smelling like all the other guys in town.

Just inside the fortified building, the light grew dimmer and the air danker. Everything about the interior decor looked semiofficial, including the Vietnamese immigration agent seated behind a well-worn mahogany counter. He rifled through the passport and other papers of the passenger in front of me. Without uttering a word, he firmly stamped a page of his passport, gave a brief nod of his head, and motioned the passenger out through a side doorway.

I stepped up to the counter, and very businesslike, handed the official my American passport when he put out his hand, which seemed like a very familiar gesture for him. He paged through it, stopping to turn it sideways and compared the picture to me. I attempted to strike the same pose so there would be no doubt I was the same guy as in the photo. Still expressionless, the old agent thumbed through the rest of the pages, glanced at me, and then looked over the last few pages again. I thought maybe he was surprised to see a new U.S. passport with no other stamps in it. But something told me this wrinkled little man in front of me didn't get surprised by much. I realized he was looking for something in my passport that he couldn't find.

I was starting to get nervous, when he interrupted my apprehensive thoughts by his first words to me in slow, but understandable English. "Where is your visa to enter the Republic of Vietnam? What is your business here?"

What had been hot sweat a minute ago turned to ice on my forehead. "Sir, I didn't think I needed a visa, I'm here on pleasure. All I need is my passport." I didn't want to reveal my true mission, and wanted to keep everything at this point as unofficial as possible.

"Pleasure?" he stood up and shouted, "What American comes to my country for pleasure? You need reason to come here. You need visa for reason before you come."

I couldn't believe this was happening. A fourteen hundred-dollar ticket, thirty-two grueling hours in the air and layovers, and this arrogant shithead was telling me I need a visa to enter! Five hundred thousand Americans in this godforsaken country, most wishing they were somewhere else, and this guy won't let me in. Then it dawned on me: I had never really thought I'd end up at the *civilian* part of Tan Son Nhut airport, but rather at the U.S. military base there. I just naturally thought I would be greeted by American military officials who would be sympathetic to my cause, once I explained it!

Then I remembered something Ron taught me about some foreign officials and decided to try it. I quickly took a twenty-dollar bill out of my wallet and placed it under my passport. He looked like a bribable government official to me.

He wasn't. He flew into a rage of Vietnamese curses, shoving my passport and the twenty back at me. "You are under arrest!" he shouted. "*You must take the next flight out of this airport!*"

What goddamned luck! An honest official in Saigon, and I had to find him!

He calmed down a little and explained that the "next flight" meant any commercial flight out of the country to *any* destination, at my expense. If

I wanted to gain entry back into South Vietnam, I would have to apply for, and be issued a visa for a specific reason at a South Vietnamese embassy in some other country. By this time, I noticed that my original Pan Am flight was already taxiing for takeoff, so that option was out. He added that the next civilian flight left for Rangoon in five hours. Some consolation, I thought. Until that time, he told me I would be held in a vacant hangar under armed guard.

The offical shouted a flurry of irritating instructions in singsong Vietnamese to some armed guards, who were standing nearby, and they roughly escorted me through a dark corridor and into a huge empty room. This section of the terminal looked unused. The roof was of curved corrugated steel. Near one corner of the roof was a large, gaping hole with jagged and rusty edges, which was covered by a dingy Army green tarpaulin.

My guards amused themselves by walking around me, pointing their American M-16 rifles at me, acting as if the outcome of the war depended on how well they guarded me.

I'm sure I posed a formidable threat to the five of them. Here I was, sitting on my luggage in the middle of a deserted hangar, unarmed, and hardly able to hold my head up after a day and a half of flying across the Pacific. My mental and physical resistance was so low right then, that I doubted I could have even removed my drenched corduroy jacket without help.

The first hour in the hangar passed slowly with a lot of unnecessary tension on the part of the guards. During the second hour, I realized that they were getting paid for working, not me, so I decided to close my eyes and get some desperately needed sleep. That was much easier thought than done. The floor was hard concrete, and my suitcase and rucksack didn't make good pillows. Every few minutes I would open my eyes to see at least one rifle pointed at my head. I didn't know what the immigration official had told these guys, but it was either a lie, or they were really overreacting to a simple deportation.

Then I heard a noisy door open at one end of my overgrown Quonset hut "jail cell," and I watched as three men entered. The newcomers were dressed in baggy uniforms that were different from the ones my guards wore. One had a pearl-handled six-gun strapped to his waist and hanging low. Another had a large hunting knife in a sheath across his chest. The third appeared to be unarmed.

This is it, I thought! This was probably the interrogation squad coming to get some answers out of me. But I didn't have any answers. I couldn't even imagine what sort of questions they would ask. Maybe they weren't going to question me at all. Maybe they were just going to show what happens to people who don't get their passports in order. Maybe . . .

When they got closer and walked into better light, I could see these guys were Americans. The baggy uniforms they wore were combat flight coveralls. The most clean-cut of the three was a sandy-haired man who looked to be about forty years old, bearing the gold oak leaf insignia of a major on his collar. He walked closer to where I was sitting and made a complete circle around me without uttering a word. When he came back in front of me, he spoke. "What the hell are you, boy, a hijacker?" he asked in a slow Floridian drawl.

I told him I wasn't and quickly explained my predicament to him and his men. I learned that his name was Major Hawkins and he flew C-130 cargo flights in and out of Vietnam. He also said he had a flight going to Bangkok, Thailand, in an hour and I was welcome to come along. Hawkins said I could stay there for a few days and obtain my visa through the South Vietnamese consulate there. He added, while winking at his two crewmen, that a young guy like me could really enjoy a few days in Bangkok anyway.

This sounded like a great offer to me, and I immediately took him up on it. I never thought I'd ever go to Bangkok, but then again, it couldn't be any worse than Rangoon.

The major then went to clear it with the immigration agent. When he returned in a few minutes, he said something to my guards in broken Vietnamese, and they left. Judging by their expressions, I think all five of them were disappointed that I hadn't tried to escape.

The two men with the major each picked up a piece of my luggage, and I walked out of my "prison" with them. As we walked from the South Vietnamese portion of the Tan Son Nhut airport to the sprawling American part, complete with the traditional red- and white-checkered water towers, I told Major Hawkins why I had come to Vietnam. He was visibly moved and sympathetic to my mission.

The longer we walked, the more aware I was of the sun and intense heat. I began feeling strange. My feet seemed heavier with every step and my head felt lighter. Everything seemed so hazy and far away. The next thing I realized, Major Hawkins and one of his guys were easing me to the ground. Hawkins reached into a small zippered pocket on his sleeve and took out two small white pills that looked like aspirins. He forced them into my mouth and pushed a canteen of cool water to my lips. He kept telling me to swallow the pills and drink a little water. I managed to do so, and as I sat resting, he explained to me the pills were salt tablets, which would help protect against the heat's dehydrating effects. He handed me several more of the tablets and told me to take them every hour or so while I was outside until I got more used to the heat.

After resting a few more minutes, I felt sturdy enough to walk, and we made our way to an area of sandbagged trenches, where a half-dozen camouflage-painted C-130 cargo planes were anchored in a neat line. His plane was the first in line. Three more crew members were busy in and around the plane, including a lieutenant who didn't look much older than me. He introduced himself as Tim.

Hawkins asked Tim if the plane was ready to go, inquiring specifically about repair to one of the hydraulic lines. Tim told him he felt confident that they could make it to Bangkok and back without any problems. Hawkins explained why I would be tagging along to Thailand, and the seven of us boarded the plane. Hawkins and three of the crewmen took their places up front. Tim, another older sergeant, and I strapped ourselves into some very uncomfortable seats along the sides of the cargo hold.

The takeoff was smooth, and as we slowly gained altitude and banked to the west, I began to relax. I fashioned a sort of hard mattress out of some used cargo canvas near my seat and immediately fell asleep for the duration of the two-hour flight to Thailand. The fact that I was again with Americans helped me relax and gave me a sense of security.

I was cognizant of someone shaking me awake from my badly needed sleep. The C-130's crew chief was telling me we were in our landing approach to the Bangkok airport. I assured him I would prepare myself for landing, and he quickly returned to his position. From my position deep inside the dimly lit belly of the cargo plane, it was impossible to see outside. I put my trust in Major Hawkins that our destination was Bangkok and in the crew chief that we were arriving there. Hawkins brought the bulky green-and-brown plane down in a graceful landing and taxied off the main runway. When the plane came to a stop, the side door was opened from the inside by one of the crewmen, and I got my first glimpse of Thailand, a country I had never planned to visit.

About a hundred yards from where we were parked was the commercial terminal. The building was old and small, but neat in its general appearance. A small commuter-type plane was taking on a handful of passengers, and an Air India passenger jet was being refueled near the terminal. Outside the hurricane fence that surrounded the airport, was a curtain of lush trees of various shades of green.

Several things were notably different from the airport I had just left in Saigon. First, there were no sandbagged bunkers, and except for our aircraft and an Army truck, there were no signs of any military activity here. A short five hundred miles away, the United States was involved in a messy war, but here, in vivid contrast, peace still lived. Birds were singing in the trees, flowers grew just off the concrete runway, and there were no shell holes to be seen.

As I stepped off the plane, I was struck by another difference. Even though it was sunny and hot like it was in Saigon, here a gentle breeze was blowing, and the air smelled fresh and clean. The musty, mildewed stench of Saigon wasn't present here.

Since Major Hawkins and Tim had work to do, they pointed me towards Thai immigration and wished me luck. They also suggested that I stay at a newly completed hotel downtown call the Dusit Thani. I thanked them both for everything, picked up my luggage, and headed for the civilian terminal.

I went into the immigration and customs corridor for arriving passengers and was greeted by a cheerful, middle-aged, uniformed immigration official. He never stopped smiling, as he checked my passport and asked the necessary questions about why and how long I would be staying in Bangkok. He seemed excited to be talking to an American civilian and told me about his son, who was a student at UCLA. I almost expected him to ask me how the Dodgers were doing this year, the way he was carrying on. Fortunately, my passport was in order, and I didn't need a visa to visit Thailand for a few days. A customs official took a quick look inside my suitcase and rucksack and told me where I could get a taxi to take me downtown.

The interior of the terminal was small and moderately busy. In the place of the sandbags and soldiers of Saigon were brightly hued travel posters and large blooming plants. There was also a wall display, identifying some of Bangkok's more prominent hotels. Since the Dusit Thani had been recommended, I looked at it first, but before I was finished reading about "Bangkok's newest luxury hotel," I felt a gentle tap on my shoulder.

Turning around, I found myself looking into the smile of a Thai who looked to be about thirty years old. In very proper English, he said he had seen me reading the hotel's information and asked if I would like a ride to the Dusit Thani downtown. He quickly explained that he was a limousine driver for the hotel, as he picked up my luggage. The driver, who said I should call him Vic, short for Vicah, seemed sincerely friendly and didn't appear to be a hustler, so I decided to go along with him. Besides, I had never ridden in a limo before and couldn't be sure if the local cab drivers spoke English.

I was slightly disappointed when we walked out to the curb and I saw that Vic's car was not my idea of a limousine, but rather a shiny black late-model Mercedes. But it was fine, since I had never ridden in a Mercedes before, either.

It was several miles from the airport to the heart of Bangkok. For the first half of the trip, Vic and I made the usual small talk that would be expected between a local and a visitor to his city. He smiled broadly when we turned a corner and drove towards a newer-looking tall building, which Vic said was the hotel. From that moment until we arrived at the hotel, he fed me facts, figures, and words of praise about "his" new hotel, but since I was still tired and groggy from traveling, I really didn't pay much attention to him.

As we pulled up under the sprawling entrance awning, I was amazed at how luxurious this hotel really was. It could have been a good neighbor to the MGM Grand in Las Vegas. Vic gave me his card and wrote instructions on the back about how I could contact him at any time during my stay at the Dusit Thani. I had told him my purpose in coming to Bangkok, so he drew me a map of how to get to both the American and South Vietnamese consulates and said he would drive me whenever I was ready to go.

As I thanked him and handed him a healthy tip, he smiled again and said, "Mr. Reilly, should you desire certain female companionship while in Bangkok, call me, and I'll take you to only the highest class establishments. Do not take a taxi."

I thanked him but told him all I wanted to do in bed for the next twelve or so hours was sleep.

A maroon-suited bellboy carried my luggage into the main lobby to the registration desk. The lobby was pure elegance, complete with spiral staircases, full-sized fruit trees, and plush carpeting. I assumed a room would run around a hundred and fifty a night, and was later astounded to find out it cost only the equivalent of about thirty U.S. dollars. I had several thousand dollars in traveler's checks with me and figured the cost of a good room was worth it. I would have stayed at the Dusit Thani no matter what the price. After all, in a few days, I would be going back into a combat zone, where anything could happen.

After registering, I was shown to my seventh-floor room, which overlooked a tempting oyster-shaped swimming pool on the roof of the third-floor annex below. The room had all the luxuries of a five-star American hotel, including a king-size bed with satin sheets, four levels of air-conditioning (rare in that part of the world), and Muzak.

I stripped off my ripe corduroy jacket, turned the air up, closed the heavy drapes, and fell nearly unconscious on the bed. It was late afternoon; I wasn't sure what day it was or even exactly how many days it had been since I left Chicago, nor did I care at that particular moment.

A ringing noise jarred me out of my black sleep—a sleep that was as close to being in a coma as one can get. The ringing persisted, until I managed to collect my senses and realize it was the telephone, then muster the strength to crawl across the huge bed to the nightstand to answer it.

"Mr. Reilly, this is Vic. You want me to take you to Vietnamese consulate now? They close at six o'clock."

I thought I had only slept for about an hour and told him I would go the next day after getting some sleep. He quickly pointed out that it *was* the next day. It took me a moment or two to realize that I had been nearly unconscious for almost twenty hours! It was my personal way of dealing with jet lag and the visa problems I had encountered. I groggily told Vic I needed to shower and that he should drop by my room in an hour. I figured three-quarters of an hour in a hot, steamy shower would help me recover from such a long sleep.

An hour later, as I was toweling off, Vic knocked at the door. His outgoing demeanor was the same as it had been on the drive from the airport the day before. While I finished getting myself presentable for the Vietnamese bureaucrats, Vic sat in a chair, eloquently revealing his knowledge of American life and customs. As we made our way down the hall, onto the elevator, and to his car, he compared the California freeways to Bangkok's rather poor and overcrowded streets.

The South Vietnamese consulate was only a few minutes' drive from the hotel. Vic parked directly in front, getting out to move a rusty "No Parking" sign. The building was not as prestigious-looking as I would have expected. In fact, it was very plain—one would have a hard time distinguishing it from the other businesses along the same street. The outer walls of soft concrete were water-stained and mildewed, the results of many humid seasons and, apparently, very little national pride. The only unique external feature about this building was a small flagpole that protruded at an outward angle directly above the entrance. The flag itself was faded and hung sorrowfully limp. I recognized the yellow, green, and red colors to be those of the Republic of Vietnam.

Vic went inside with me, in case I needed any help with translation. The inside of the old building was as dreary as the outside. A middle-aged clerk, who was seated behind the main counter, was the only person in the outer office. He was methodically stamping official-looking documents with a round rubber stamp. The routine nature of his work led me to believe obtaining a visa might not be as difficult as I had feared. Perhaps all I needed was for him to stamp my passport.

I approached the counter and handed the clerk my American passport. I slowly and distinctly told him I needed a visa stamp for South Vietnam, emphasizing the "South." He paged through my passport without saying a word. After doing so, he looked at me without any expression and asked, in tentative English, what my business would be in the Republic of Vietnam. Not realizing I had to be on some official business to go there, I said I just wanted to visit his country. The clerk, still expressionless, turned and took my passport with him into an office towards the back of the room. It bothered me to have my passport out of my possession and in the control of a total stranger. I shot a nervous glance at Vic, who was not very reassuring, because he looked more nervous than I felt.

Soon after the clerk entered the smaller office, I heard an eruption of shouting in Vietnamese. The initial barrage was followed by a lower, staccato mumbling. Finally, the clerk came back into the main office without my passport, and sheepishly informed me that I would have to wait a few minutes.

To kill time, Vic and I strode towards a side window to watch the frustrated traffic outside, but before we got to the window, the smaller office door opened and a young Asian girl, who appeared to be in her early twenties, slowly walked out. She held the top of her plain gunnysack dress together with one hand and carried some official-looking form in the other. She walked straight out of the consulate building, never taking her eyes off the floor. As she passed, I noticed her forehead was wet from perspiration and several strands of her straight black bangs were matted to her skin. It also looked as though she had been crying. As she walked by, I could more closely observe the papers she carried. The top copy had a large red seal and a signature affixed to the top.

It didn't take me long to figure out that although the red stamp on the girl's paperwork was probably an official government seal, it had not likely been obtained through official procedures. Realizing that all one had to do was to offer "something of value," I quickly pulled out my wallet, which I knew contained about two hundred dollars in American and Thai money. Turning towards the window, I hastily pulled out all the money, except for fifty dollars in greenbacks. I put the wallet back and was just stashing the rest of the cash in my pants pockets, when a man came out of the same office. He, like the young girl, had small droplets of perspiration above his brow, which he dabbed at nervously with a well-used handkerchief.

The clerk nodded towards me, indicating that I was the next order of business. The man from the small office, who looked more like an Asian gangster than a government official, cleared his throat and inquired in distinctive English what my business was.

I walked towards him, stating, "All I need is a visa stamp to visit your country."

He looked a bit confused, but asked me to step inside the small office with him. Since he appeared to speak and understand English, I told Vic I would be back in a minute—at least I hoped I would.

As we entered, I noticed my passport was on top of his desk. We each took a seat on opposite sides of his desk.

"You are an American civilian?" he asked.

"Yes!"

"And you want to 'visit' my country?"

"Yes!"

"And what is the purpose of this visit?"

"Personal business," I said, hoping he wouldn't ask for details.

It worked.

"Do you know anything about my country?"

"I know there's a war going on there, and I also know there is a black market dealing in everything from cameras and guns to phony documents." I gave him a cold stare, emphasizing the words *phony documents.*

A slight sly smile of understanding shattered his arrogance, and at that point, I knew I had him. I also knew that the person sitting in front of me was definitely in business for himself, not for his government. "And, do you know what price some people pay for, how you say, phony documents?" he asked.

It was my turn to break into my own cunning grin. "I don't know what most people pay, but I do know that I would pay fifty dollars for a visa today."

"American dollars?"

"American," I answered, reaching for my wallet.

He almost drooled with greed as he watched the portraits of American presidents emerge from my wallet.

"How long do you need to stay in the Republic of Vietnam to attend to your 'personal' business?"

"Thirty days, sixty days, tops," I said.

"Okay. I will list you as freelance photographer. That way, no questions asked." He then hastily placed the cash in his top drawer with his left hand

and retrieved a round rubber stamp from the same drawer with his right. Seemed only fitting the one should replace the other. A quick stamping motion, date, and illegible initials, and I was on my way out of the consulate. Vic was waiting outside by the car. I felt smug about having obtained my visa in such an unethical, but effective manner. It was what I had come to Bangkok to do, and I had done it—simple as that. Ron would have been proud of my performance.

It was time to relax a little before figuring out how to get back to Vietnam in the morning.

Chapter 7

Escape from Bangkok

I had an elegant roast duck dinner that night in the windowed restaurant atop the Dusit Thani Hotel; it was my way of rewarding myself for a job well done on obtaining the visa.

The sun was a drowning fireball on the horizon, lighting a large margin of sky in a pastel orange glow. Below that margin, and below my restaurant window, was the busy city of Bangkok. The city, in contrast to the sky, was a grayish blue, speckled with twinkling lights and the motions of cars, mopeds, and every other form of motorized urban transportation you could imagine.

My thoughts were more involved with the sky. I realized I would be leaving this world of peace and returning to a country at war the next day. It occurred to me that maybe there was a reason, beyond my own simple comprehension, why I hadn't been allowed into Vietnam on the first try. Maybe I wasn't meant to go there. Moreover, maybe I should heed such an omen, but I figured I had managed to detour the system and get my visa, so at least I would be "officially" allowed into the country. I would just have to accept what fate had in store for me. Too much heavy thinking as the sun totally disappeared, and began to christen another night in Bangkok. So, I decided instead to enjoy some of that city's nightlife. After dinner, I freshened up in my room and headed down to the lobby.

The bell captain informed me that Vic had already gone home for the day, but had left his phone number in case I needed him. Electing not to bother Vic at home, I asked the bell captain if he could suggest any good bars. He told me most of the American soldiers and German tourists frequented New Petchabari Street in the Patpong District. That sounded like a good place to go, because I might be more apt to find someone I could communicate with, either in English or in German (if I could remember what I learned during my two years of labored high school study).

I left the lobby and hailed one of the cabs that was waiting under the opulent overhang. The cabbie couldn't speak English, but nodded his acknowledgment of my desired destination, when I said "New Petchabari Street." He drove through the busy Thai city on wide, multilane streets. After passing several intersections and making a few turns, he headed down a street heavily adorned with bright neon signs. The businesses along this street were illuminated more by their neon signs than by the streetlights. As we drove along, I noticed several Caucasian men mixed in with the Asians on the sidewalks. Their light hair and taller stature made them more noticeable. There was a lively and impatient atmosphere under the neon of this street.

"New Petchabari" was the only comment the cabbie made, as he pulled over to the curb in front of a nightclub, called of all things, "Whiskey-A-Go-Go."

I paid the cab fare and walked towards the entrance of the club, and suddenly I had the distinct feeling of déjà vu, involving "Boys' Town" on the other side of the world. The feeling went away as soon as I entered the establishment. It had a certain class that made Boys' Town in Nuevo Laredo look like it existed below the sewers.

This place had a live rock band playing on the stage in the back and a large, crowded dance floor with several tables and booths positioned around it. Although the nightclub was dark, it looked clean. A well-dressed, middle-aged Thai woman, probably the matriarch of the club, approached and welcomed me, in German, to the bar. I told her I spoke English, and her smile grew even wider, as she realized I was American. She showed me to a small table for two near the dance floor and took my drink order.

As my eyes became more accustomed to the subdued lighting, I began checking out the crowd on the dance floor. Of the thirty or more people dancing, I noticed there were only three or four males—most appearing to be from the West. The rest of the crowd, bobbing to the American rock music, consisted of pairs of young Thai girls, the majority of whom, I noticed, were very pretty and sexy. Several wore tight hip-hugger jeans or shorts, makeup, and a variety of colorful and revealing halter tops. As I took in the mass of bouncing braless breasts and sculptured derrieres, I noticed each girl wore a round metal button, like a campaign button, pinned near her waist. Each button bore a different number. A few of the girls looked my way and smiled, piquing my curiosity as to the meaning of the numbered buttons.

Just then a waiter brought my drink, and I asked him if he spoke English. He said he did and asked me if I had decided on a number yet. I must have looked a little confused, because he explained that many Thai girls like to date foreign men, and since there were more girls than men, the numbers were a way to help the men make a selection. Thinking back to Boys' Town, I clumsily asked what the charge was for a girl, to which the waiter indignantly replied there was no charge, since the girls were not prostitutes. A bit embarrassed, I asked him to come back in a few minutes so I could have some time to window shop.

My God, I could hardly believe it! I guessed the average age of the girls to be about twenty. As I studied them closer, I felt even more embarrassed about what I had asked the waiter, since most of the girls looked and acted more like college coeds than hookers.

My browsing eyes kept returning to number 23, who kept smiling coyly at me and dancing provocatively. She was, in my opinion, one of the lovelier girls in the place, which was saying something because I found Thai women in general to be unusually attractive. Something about their mix of European and Asian ancestry seemed to enhance their beauty. And number 23 was stunning in a very natural way, with her long black hair, skintight jeans, and petite figure.

When the waiter returned, I informed him of my choice. He went to her and whispered something in her ear, just as the band was finishing "Light My Fire" by Jim Morrison and The Doors.

She was smiling, yet showed just a hint of nervousness, as she walked over to my table and sat down. "My name is Lea, and I speak English," she said.

"My name is Tom. You are very pretty." She put me so at ease, I was amazed how easily my introduction came out. Then it was time for me to be awkward. "Do you work here?" I asked, trying to sound as if I didn't care if she was a prostitute.

She wasted no time correcting me, in a polite, but slightly awkward way. "Oh no, I do not work here like you think. I am a student here in Bangkok. I come here two nights each week to dance."

"Where do you go to school?"

"I study painting at the Academy of Fine Arts here in Bangkok," Lea said proudly. "Are you in Air Force here, Tom?"

"Ah, no, I'm a civilian, I'm not in the military." I said, not really wanting to explain my reason for being ten thousand miles from home.

Lea seemed to understand my reluctance to give her any details and tactfully retreated by asking if I would like to dance with her.

We spent most of the next two hours on the dance floor, alternating with rest stops at our table for drinks and small talk. Lea was filled with questions about the States and art, the latter of which I knew little about.

But, for one of the very first times since I had learned of Ron's death, I felt relaxed and was having an enjoyable time. The relaxation was no doubt promoted by the several scotch and waters I had put away. I felt Ron would be proud of me—his little brother sitting in a club in Thailand enjoying the nightlife. At least it was Bangkok nightlife—complete with American-style blue jeans, strobe lights, and music from Smokey Robinson to the Beach Boys. Except for the absence of nuns and the presence of the numbered buttons, this was almost like being at a CYO dance hosted by the Ripon Catholic Church twice a year. Almost.

Lea interrupted my smug thoughts, saying she had to leave so she could make it to her early classes in the morning. She thanked me for my company and said she would be back in three nights if I wanted to see her again. I told her I wouldn't be in her country in three days, but if I were to come back, I'd be sure to look her up.

She was obviously in a hurry, as she grabbed her purse, kissed me goodbye on the cheek, and said something about catching a late bus as she rushed out of the club. I sat at the table alone for another song or two, casually watching the blur of bodies on the dance floor. Deciding I had been in this place too long, I left enough money on the table for the drink tab and got up to leave.

By this time, the demon scotch was beginning to take a noticeable toll on me. My legs suddenly felt like they were made of silly putty, and my head seemed to float a few inches above the rest of my body. I somehow successfully maneuvered myself to the front door and out onto the sidewalk, where the cool night air came as a welcome friend.

New Petchabari Street was not as busy then as it had been earlier, but I was conscious of other people in the area. I had no idea where I was going, but decided to walk down the street, in hopes of finding an available taxi that could deliver me back to the Dusit Thani Hotel, and to the security of a bed that wasn't moving in circles, like my head was.

To help myself navigate, I thought it wise to stay as close as possible to the building fronts along the sidewalk. In my inebriated state, I assumed the buildings were at least in a straight line along the street. I negotiated maybe two blocks in this manner, when all of a sudden I noticed the number of neon lights had diminished somewhat and the street was darker. Even my steadfast guide of buildings had abruptly disappeared. Then I realized there was a large construction site where several buildings were being built. It was dark and vacant, and late at night. I decided I'd better turn around and go back up the street, where there was more activity and a greater chance of finding a cab.

Just as that thought was slowly making its way from my brain to my feet, I felt a thud where my left shoulder meets my neck. Startled, but still reacting slowly, I turned all the way around to see an equally startled Thai male, who looked to be in his early twenties, jump backwards. His right hand was moving up and down in my direction. The distant lights shimmered off the blade of a small knife he held in his hands. No one else was in sight. I stumbled backward a few steps, trying to put some distance between me and that blade. The Thai looked frightened, but he was apparently not frightened enough to stop coming at me. Just then, I remembered the four-inch switchblade Ron had given me. I had put it in my pants pocket, not in my wildest imagination ever expecting to use it as an actual weapon. But, as I backed up, my assailant kept coming. I clumsily pulled out the switchblade and clicked it open.

I thought now, surely the mugger would turn tail and run, and I really wouldn't have to prove that I was scared to death and didn't know the first thing about how to use a knife in a fight. But, he didn't run. Instead he looked even more determined. I just hoped I could stall him until I could get someone's attention, but the nearest people were at least a block away. I yelled for help anyway, hoping to scare this knife-wielding nut away from me.

Instead, he lunged at me, and we both fell to the pavement in a confused pile. I was on the bottom, desperately trying to get on top and gain control. I concentrated on keeping the menacing blade away from me, fearing that any second now, I would feel burning pain as it entered my flesh. I fought and struggled frantically to delay the inevitable for as long as possible.

Suddenly, my attacker screamed, his face, which was only inches from mine, contorted into a wince. This surprised me, and I stopped struggling slightly.

Now it was *he* who was frantically kicking and pushing me away from him. I heard what I thought was his knife fall onto the sidewalk, as he rolled free a few feet from me. He struggled to his feet, grasping his upper left arm. I didn't have the energy to get up, so instead, I scuttled backward away from him in a sitting position, holding my switchblade so tightly my hand hurt. The man faced me briefly, cried out something in garbled Thai, and then ran off down the street.

When he was out of sight, I was gasping for air and shaking so badly that I thought I should put my knife down on the pavement to avoid cutting myself. As I did, the blade brushed across one leg of the white pants I was wearing, leaving a dark smear. I looked closer at the smear and realized it was blood.

I picked up my knife and looked at it. There was blood on the blade. I wasn't feeling any pain, but because of the alcohol and the hysterical confusion, it took me several seconds to realize I must have stabbed my assailant before he had had a chance to stab me! I probably cut him on his left arm, the one he had been holding as he ran off into the night. I had no recollection of actually doing this, it must have just happened in the scuffle. I felt incredibly relieved that I had come out the victor in that life-threatening situation, though I felt bad that I had hurt someone that I didn't even know. I also didn't have any idea why he attacked me. But I didn't care about that right then; I was just so thankful I hadn't been hurt, as I sat there in a foreign country gulping in the fresh night air.

I was still trying to get my thoughts together when a uniformed man bent over me and shook my shoulder. The uniform distinguished him as a Thai policeman. He seemed to be checking to see if I was all right and looked genuinely concerned. He leaned over me and picked up the two knives, which were lying near me on the pavement. I hadn't even seen the second knife near me. He stared at them, a curious look on his face, straightened up, and helped me up with his free hand.

At first I thought he was taking me into custody, but he seemed too helpful to be a cop who was arresting someone. For a moment I decided he was on my side. He spoke a few short sentences in Thai, until he realized that I did not understand what he was saying.

The officer helped me down the sidewalk and around the corner to the next intersection. After the first few yards, I insisted I could walk just fine, even though I was a little shaken and still a tad bit wobbly from the drinks.

When we rounded the corner, I heard some authoritative shouting and saw two compact police sedans. Another Thai cop was yelling at a man in one of the cars, and yet another officer was talking to a short, older man dressed in a business suit, who was standing on the sidewalk.

As my escort and I neared the first squad car, I could see that it was my attacker who was seated inside. He was sobbing uncontrollably, and his arms were pulled back behind him. The entire left sleeve of his light blue shirt was stained with blood. Any doubts I might have had about where the blood on my knife had come from were immediately dispelled at the sight.

The officer who was talking to the man on the sidewalk noticed us approaching. He broke off their conversation, motioned to the business-man to wait, and walked over to me. He said something to the officer who had retrieved me, then turned to me and asked, "Sprechen Sie Deutsch?"

Realizing the uselessness of my sophomore German, I answered him in English, "No, I am American."

"Ah, English. I too speak English. Are you injured?" he asked as he examined my upper body with his eyes. Then quickly and with apparent concern, he leaned over and touched my pant leg where the blood was already beginning to dry.

"No, I'm not hurt, I think that's his blood," I said, pointing to my assailant in the police car.

The officer simply shrugged. "Are you American military?"

"No, I'm a civilian."

"Ah. May I see your identification card?"

"You mean my passport?"

"Ah, yes, your passport."

I handed him my passport, and as he scribbled down the pertinent infor-mation in his notebook, I suddenly got the chilling feeling that maybe they didn't understand the situation, and maybe *I* was the one in trouble here and being arrested. Maybe I would have to stand trial and spend time in a foreign prison after all. *Maybe I should run right now,* I thought. *No, maybe I should get my passport back first, then run; maybe, maybe . . .*

"Mr. 'Reely,' you need to come to bureau now with us."

I could feel the tingling in my legs, as my brain told them to run, all the while knowing it was too late to get away.

"The gentleman there," he pointed to the man on the sidewalk, "he told me he saw everything from across the street. He saw the suspect attack you. We need you to come to our bureau to make a statement."

Relief for the second time in the last few minutes! They did have it right!

I rode to the police station with the English-speaking cop and the wit-ness. Between quick bursts of Thai chatter, the officer explained that my assailant, after scuffling with me, had run down the street and around the corner. This certainly wasn't his lucky day, because, not only did he get cut on the arm, he also ran right into the Thai policemen, as they were return-ing to their parked car. The witness, who had chased after the suspect at a safe distance, quickly told the police what he had seen, and the assailant was immediately taken into custody.

The glimpse I had gotten of my wounded attacker, as he sat bound and sobbing in the patrol car, kept vividly flashing back into my mind's eye. I didn't realize it then, but that was the last time I would see him, despite the fact that the officials at the downtown Bangkok police station, or rather the "bureau," had other plans. After giving my statement, I was told the man was being charged with attempted murder, assault, and attempted robbery of a foreigner—an American, to be exact. The discouraging news, on a more personal front, was that I was being subpoenaed to attend his trial. It was quickly explained to me that I, being the victim and the most important witness in this case, would be able to provide conclusive testimony leading to my assailant's certain conviction. Apparently the fact that I was an American civilian brought more political importance to the case.

I told the authorities that since I had not been injured or had anything stolen, I just wanted to drop the matter and go on with my personal business. I assured them that I felt the poor bastard had paid enough, since he was the one who had been hurt and was made to suffer the ultimate criminals' penance of almost being caught in the act of his crime.

The officers in charge assured me that since I was a foreigner, the trial date could be set for thirty to forty days from now. Moreover, I would be required to foot the bill for this monthlong wait. Impossible! I protested that my personal business required that I leave Thailand the next day, and that having to wait for this trial was completely out of the question.

But they were adamant, saying I would simply have to postpone my plans in order to attend their trial. I sensed, watching the facial expressions of these high-ranking police officials, that the "trial" would end up as some sort of publicity circus for local government officials.

As things ended up, I was flatly told not to leave the country the next day as I had planned to do. My subpoena would be delivered to me at my hotel the next day, as soon as all the necessary formalities were met and signatures obtained. I was also asked to surrender my passport to the police, but I bluntly refused, taking it from my pocket and clenching it in both hands. I told them I would demand to see someone from the American Embassy if they physically attempted to take my passport from me. Any traveler in a foreign country quickly learns that without a passport, it is difficult, if not impossible, to travel between countries.

They obviously didn't want to deal with the American Embassy, and backed down, once again putting on friendly and sympathetic faces.

They told me that a police officer would drive me back to the Dusit Thani and that the entire matter could be discussed the next day. However, I was admonished not to leave the country, pending further work on the case.

It was just a little before six in the morning when the non-English-speaking policeman dropped me off at the main lobby of my hotel. It had been a long, long night without any sleep, but because of the unusual nature of the night's events, I felt weary and all keyed up at the same time. I still felt like I had been chasing the sun for the last few days and that my body and mind had not yet adjusted to the trans-Pacific jet lag. Simply put, my body hadn't the slightest notion of whether it was supposed to be tired or alert.

It was in this near-catatonic state that I walked into the Dusit Thani's lobby and took the elevator up to my room. The elevator seemed to take forever to reach my floor. All I could think about was how good it would feel to rest for a few blessed hours. I hoped the sleep would give me the presence of mind to figure some way out of my predicament. I simply couldn't hang around for a month, waiting for that poor bastard's trial. I had to get back into Vietnam, then back to the States, so I could report for basic training.

The elevator door opened on my floor. At this early hour, the hotel was deserted, as I walked to my room. When I rounded the hall corner, I surprised a Thai police officer, who had been lingering in the hallway near my door. When he saw me, he looked a bit nervous and quickly, but too nonchalantly, walked by me. Nothing was exchanged between us when we passed each other in the corridor, not even a nod or the slightest eye contact. As I put the key in the lock, I casually looked back at him. He was walking away and around the corner, glancing at a small piece of paper that was cupped in his right hand.

Even though the episode probably meant nothing, I was suspicious. I entered my room, and everything appeared to be normal, but, nevertheless, I spent the next ten minutes checking it out in detail—looking under and behind things in both the main room and the bathroom. I had no idea what I was looking for, nor did I think I would recognize "it" if it was right there in front of me. But at least I did feel better having checked. I had watched *I Spy* for years, and Robert Culp and Bill Cosby always checked out their rooms when they were suspicious. But they usually found "something," which only served to make me a little nervous when I didn't.

I did have a hunch that I wanted to pursue, even at the cost of not getting some much-needed sleep. I left the room and walked down the hall to the elevator. The same "hall monitor" was now seated on a stool at the far end of the adjoining corridor, with a full view of the elevator. Just as I thought! I was being watched. I took the elevator down to the main lobby. As I exited and walked across the lobby to the main entrance, I kept watch for "something." It didn't take me long to see it. A plainclothes "Joe Friday," with slightly oval eyes and a receding hairline, was seated in one of two plush chairs that faced the expansive main doors. His tactical position afforded a wide-angle view of the elevator, lobby, and front desk. "Sergeant Friday" even had the classic newspaper with him, but he seemed far more intent on reading my movements than the *Bangkok Times*.

I acted as if I didn't notice my newest voyeur and walked out the front door of the hotel. I stopped about ten feet outside, pretended I had forgotten something, turned quickly, and reentered the hotel lobby. Correct again! *I ought to be either a cop or a crook,* I thought to myself. "Sergeant Friday" was just sitting back down in his chair, the look on his face saying "Who me? I didn't move out of this chair to follow you."

While I was having a good time toying with my guards, I was struck by the very sobering realization that the local police had meant business when they told me not to leave the country. What was it about this guy they had arrested? He must have been on their Top Ten Most Wanted List, or something.

I didn't like the feeling of being imprisoned, even without bars. My only crime was that of circumstance. Why did that guy have to attack *me*? And even more ironically, I wondered why he had had to get caught. We were fellow prisoners; him in the city jail, and me in the whole damn country!

I was feeling sorry for myself, yet, in my state of exhaustion, desperately wanted to beat their system and leave the country. I didn't really care what fate would befall my ill-fated attacker. He was the last of my worries.

It was nearing seven o'clock in the morning, and I remembered Vic, my helpful hotel driver, would be coming to work soon. I decided I could forsake sleep a little longer, so I could tell Vic about my dilemma. He seemed to have a lot of connections. Maybe he had some pull at the police station. It was a long shot, but I had no other bets to place.

I sat on the far side of the lobby, across from "Sergeant Friday," who pretended to read and reread his newspaper. I had a sufficient view of the front-canopied driveway, where the cabs and limos pulled up.

After about twenty minutes, a hotel limousine drove up to the curb, and I recognized Vic behind the wheel. It felt like I was seeing an old and trusted friend, even though I barely knew him.

I hurried across the lobby, out the door, and quickly got into the backseat of his black car. Vic recognized me and started to smile, but I pretended not to know him and told him to drive away from the hotel.

Naturally, Vic was a bit confused, and he looked like his feelings had been hurt, but only after we reached the end of the Dusit Thani's long driveway and entered the traffic on the main street, did I apologize and explain what was happening. I looked back and saw a beige sedan leave the hotel drive-way, carrying two men in suits. They appeared to be following us.

Vic listened intently, and I could tell that he was sincerely concerned, which made me feel better, even if there was nothing he could do. He knew, too, that I wasn't exaggerating, because he had also noticed the beige car that remained one or two cars behind us as we cruised and talked.

"I know some people I think can help you," Vic said, when I finished my saga with an air of despair and fatigue.

"Are these people connected with the police or the U.S. Embassy?"

"No, no," he chuckled, "quite the opposite, but they help you."

"Why would they want to help me?"

"Money," was his one-word answer.

"How much money?" I asked, wondering if I could afford to get out of this mess. I was just beginning to realize that the people Vic referred to were not honest, and were not in good standing in the community. I was nervous about paying too much money to crooks, especially if it left me with too little cash to finish my mission in Vietnam.

"Not too much, I think," Vic said, almost as if he was reading my thoughts. "But now I'll take you back to hotel and you rest. Then we talk later today."

We were close to the Dusit Thani Hotel by this time, so Vic dropped me off at the main lobby doors with a reassuring nod.

We had apparently lost the beige car during the last bit of our drive, because it was no longer behind us as we pulled into the main hotel drive. But, if I had entertained thoughts of my surveillance being over, it was short-lived. As I disembarked from the elevator on my floor, I noticed that the uniformed cop was still at his post down the hallway. Seeing him made me all the more determined to at least investigate any options that Vic and his acquaintances had to offer. I hit the bed, exhausted, as soon as I entered my room.

�֍ �֍ ✖

The goddamned phone was ringing again! It seemed like every time I went to sleep in this hotel, I was jostled awake by that damn phone. I impatiently picked up the receiver before it could make that next horrible clang again.

"If you have eight hundred American dollars tonight, I have some friends that can get you to Saigon, but you must leave late tonight." I recognized Vic's voice, fully aware he was trying to keep the telephone information as brief and clandestine as possible.

"Ah, yeah, I have the money."

"You go tonight, late?"

"Sure, but how are you—"

"Not now, stay in your room, contact you later tonight," Vic told me in quick, short phrases.

Eight hundred dollars, I thought to myself, after hanging up the phone. It didn't take me long to decide that getting myself out of Thailand and back onto my original path was worth eight hundred dollars. I wondered if it would be dangerous. The tingling along my spine told me it probably was risky, but it was better than being forced to stay in a country where I really had nothing to do for the next thirty or so days. Yes! I quickly decided it was worth both the money and the risk.

Money here meant cash, American greenbacks. I checked my wallet and found that I still had about a hundred dollars' worth of "bahts," or Thai money, remaining from what I exchanged when I had checked in at the hotel. I had another two hundred dollars in American currency in a secret compartment in my shaving kit. That meant I still needed five hundred dollars. I had converted several thousand dollars from Ron's insurance settlement to traveler's checks, which were stashed in a half-dozen hiding places inside my rucksack and suitcase. I decided to cash six hundred dollars' worth at the hotel cashier. The extra hundred would come in handy for necessary incidentals, such as small bribes, during the pending excursion.

After locating the traveler's checks in my luggage, I left the room and took the elevator down to the front desk. I noticed that my "hall monitor" had apparently changed—the uniform was the same, but the face was different. This new guard still had a good view of the elevator, but he couldn't see my room around the corner. Also, "Sergeant Friday" had been replaced by a much younger plainclothes officer, who was seated in a different chair in the main lobby. Couldn't mistake him though. Out of the corner of my eye and in the wall mirror near the elevator, I could see him watching me intently then looking away when I happened to glance in his direction.

I didn't know what time it was when Vic called, but I noticed it was nearly dark outside. I must have slept most of the day again. The clock behind the cashier said it was eight-fifteen. I felt really rested, but keyed up about what would happen later. I was also ravenous.

While I was cashing the traveler's checks, I remembered that Vic told me to stay in my room so that I could be contacted. I rushed through the transaction and used additional traveler's checks to settle my room bill, hoping this wouldn't arouse suspicion in the surveillance team.

I hurried back to my room and ordered a large dinner from room service. As I lay on my bed listening to some Thai music on the radio, I wondered what method Vic or his so-called friends would use to contact me. My food arrived about half an hour later, but, given my heightened sense of suspense, I watched every move the server made, as he pushed the cart in and set up my meal. I kept waiting for him to give me some sort of clandestine sign or message. But if he did, he certainly was casual about it, and the message went unnoticed.

Before beginning my meal, I painstakingly checked under, around, and inside everything on the tray, including the tray itself, to see if a message had been left. I didn't find one.

As I was finishing dessert about fifteen minutes later, I heard two quick knocks at my door. My heart slammed against my chest, as I got up and went to answer it. Someone had slid a folded piece of paper under the door. I picked it up, then quietly opened the door just enough to look out into the hall. Whoever had left the note had vanished.

For a moment, I thought the paper in my hand might have been the subpoena the police said would be delivered, but it didn't look official enough. I hurriedly opened the paper and read the note, which had been handwritten in strange-looking English letters:

> Be ready with dollars and baggage at 0100. We get you from room. If OK, open, then close curtains 2 times now.

This was exhilarating! I sure wondered who these people were, but figured I'd find out at one o'clock in the morning.

I immediately went to the wide patio-style windows and slowly opened and closed the curtains twice, signifying it was a "go." I anticipated an interesting excursion.

Since I had several hours to kill before the early morning rendezvous, I decided to take a long shower. I had no idea how long it would be until the next shower, or even where it would be. Afterwards, I put on fresh clothes—dark-colored to aid in my nighttime escape—and then packed my bags very carefully. I also made sure both my passport and wallet were secured in button-down pockets and that wads of cash were strategically distributed inside my clothing and shoes.

By 11:00 P.M. I was ready to be smuggled out of Thailand, hopefully en route to Saigon. I felt well rested and well fed. I was clean, and my two bags were packed and waiting near the door. Now all I had to do was wait out the next two hours, a time period that I knew would be a real bitch to survive.

My head was once again filled with a kaleidoscope of thought fragments. How will they come for me? How many will there be? How will they get me past the cop in the hall? Is he one of them? How will I get out of Thailand? On and on the pieces bounced through my head, as I sat in a chair and listened to more music. Every few minutes I thought of some reason to check something in my luggage or pockets, just to make sure I was ready.

All of a sudden it was 12:55 A.M.

Once again, two sharp, quick knocks on the door penetrated the anxious atmosphere that permeated in my room. I hurried over to the door, trying to control my excitement. I had the feeling this wasn't happening to me, but instead I was watching it happen to someone else.

I opened the door a few inches without having any idea what or who would be on the other side. What I saw surprised me. A young Thai boy, who looked to be about twelve years old, stood there looking quite nervous. He wore a loose-fitting brown shirt, a ragged pair of black pants, and worn sandals. He kept glancing down the hall, as if watching for the guard. When he saw my eyes were focused on him, he quickly put his right index finger to his lips, indicating that I should be quiet.

My first thought was that the boy had the wrong room and was not connected to my escape. But his obvious display of nervousness made me believe that he was, in fact, part of this bizarre plot. I quickly let him into the room.

"Meester Reely?" was all he said.

"Yes, I—" He stopped me again, with his finger to his lips.

The slightly built boy went directly to my luggage and picked up the suitcase, struggling against the weight of it. I got the impression he wanted to leave the room immediately, with me following behind, carrying my rucksack. But, since it was obvious the suitcase was too heavy for him, I indicated that I would carry it. We traded and left the room in silence, quickly closing the door behind us. Instead of heading towards the elevator, which was my customary route away from the room, the boy led me in the opposite direction, down the hallway. I had wondered how my rescuers were going to get me past the cop stationed near the elevator, and now I knew. At the end of the hall was an emergency exit door fitted with a "crash bar" mechanism. When we got to the door, the boy reached a hand into his pants pocket and took out a key. He shot one hasty look back down the hall, then quietly disarmed and opened the emergency door. We quickly stepped through and found ourselves in a deserted stairway; I figured it was a combination utility and fire stairwell used mostly by hotel employees. I wondered if my escort was connected to the hotel staff, but at the same time, it didn't seem all that important if he was or not.

We quietly started down the partially lit steel staircase. Since we were seven floors up, my suitcase seemed to get much heavier by the time we were halfway down. My companion hadn't said a word beyond asking my name when we were back in the room. He appeared to be quite serious about his assignment. I had a hunch he didn't speak any English, and hoped he would take me to someone with whom I could communicate. I also hoped that someone would be a little older.

We got down to what must have been the ground floor, then exited the stairwell through an emergency door, similar to those I had seen on the stair landings of each floor. We walked through a short utility hallway, which had another, more formidable-looking metal door at the end.

The boy stopped at the door and listened intently for a few seconds, trying to hear something on the other side. Next, he gave the door three distinct knocks and listened again. I heard a key going into the lock from the other side, and suddenly the door opened.

A second Thai boy, probably about sixteen or seventeen, opened the door, which led outside. The younger boy and I went out through the door and found ourselves in an alley behind the hotel. Since it was about 1:00 A.M., it was dark, but there was enough illumination from nearby streetlights that I could see several garbage dumpsters to the left of the door and an old half-ton truck nearby. The truck had side racks on the bed, and a dark tarpaulin covered part of the cargo area. Inside were several crates and boxes that looked and smelled like they had been used to pack produce.

The older boy never spoke a word. They each took a piece of my luggage and hid it behind some boxes in the nose of the truck bed. Then they motioned for me to get in and sit near my bags. As soon as I was situated, they hastily pulled the tarp over me and the entire load. Then I heard them get into the cab and start the engine, and the truck began moving down the alley and out into the street. I had a feeling that a third conspirator had been waiting inside the cab and was now driving.

It was dark and smelly under the tarp, but I could catch glimpses of the streetlights where the tarpaulin sagged and buckled around the boxes near the tailgate. The combination of the old truck being badly in need of shocks and the apparent haste of the driver made for a jolting and ass-bruising ride through the streets of Bangkok.

We drove for about forty-five minutes, as I tried to protect various parts of my body from slamming against the hard boxes in the cargo bed. All the while I was very much aware of the fact that I was living a real adventure. Even though the boys were young, they seemed to know what they were doing. I realized I wasn't frightened at all, just excited, with my adrenaline at an all-time high. I wondered what would be in store for me next. Surely this truck wasn't going to drive me all the way to Saigon? Or was it? That would have meant an overland trip of five hundred miles through part of Thailand and all of Cambodia. I feared my flesh and bones would never withstand a journey of that length at the current rate of bruising.

The noise and lights outside the truck had decreased considerably, indicating we were probably leaving Bangkok and heading into the countryside. My escape truck had taken several different roads during the last twenty minutes or so—I bounced off the cab each time the truck downshifted and negotiated a turn. Finally, we slowed to a near crawl on a very bumpy road. Tree limbs would occasionally brush the sides or top of the truck.

I could hear the boys in the cab chattering in Thai. Then, suddenly we stopped, and the engine was shut off. I heard the voice of an older man talking to the driver, followed by footfalls making their way through underbrush and around to the tailgate. The tarp was pulled back, and a flashlight shot dim beams around the inside of the truck bed. Someone else jumped onto the truck bed and removed my luggage. I decided it was time to get out of the truck myself, and as my arms and legs fumbled in an effort to maneuver me to the back of the truck, I felt a hand grab my upper arm and guide me out. Soon I was standing on the ground behind the truck wondering where I'd be going next.

The adult, a Thai man probably in his fifties, walked up to me and shined the flashlight under my chin so he could see my face. He pointed to himself saying, "No English, no English," but then followed by asking "Eight hundred dollars American?" At least American money was universally understood, I thought to myself.

"Yes, I have the eight hundred," I said, reaching into my pants pocket and removing a wad of bills.

The man took it and counted it, cradling the flashlight under his arm at an angle that allowed him to see the denominations. As he was counting, I looked around, hoping to see Vic. But he wasn't there, and I was disappointed that I didn't get a chance to say thanks or good-bye.

As I surveyed these unfamiliar surroundings, I spotted a small single-engine airplane parked at the other end of the clearing we were standing in. So this was how I was getting out of Thailand and into Vietnam. Things were beginning to make some sense to me.

Even though my eyes were still not fully adjusted to the darkness, I made out the figure of another man walking under the wing of the plane—a Thai, of course, who could have been about thirty. He was peering under the wing, as if doing a preflight maintenance check. By the looks of the unnumbered plane, I guessed at least a week's worth of repairs would be in order. But a push on a flap and the tightening of a few bolts was all that was done before this second man turned away from the airplane and walked towards me, apparently satisfied the craft was flight-worthy.

As he got closer to the light of the old man's flashlight, I could make out that he was wearing a gun belt. He had an old, worn leather belt, with a full-flapped pistol holster on his right side and a sheathed machete dangling on his opposite hip. I could barely see the butt of a handgun under the top flap of the holster. Despite the weaponry, this fellow appeared to be good-natured as he joined our huddle, and I didn't feel any sense of threat from him.

A lot of Thai words were exchanged between my young escape accomplices and the two men waiting at the plane. The man with the gun seemed to ask a question of the old man, who, in turn, answered by grinning and displaying the wad of cash I had just given him.

With that, Mr. Gunslinger ordered the boys to load my luggage into the fuselage of the rickety plane. When they had done so, he looked at me, nodded with a sincere enough smile, and led me to the slightly rusting aircraft. The plane moaned as I placed all of my weight on the metal step just outside the door. I started to twist my body to the right, to climb up into the copilot seat, but my guide grabbed me, barked out something in Thai, and pushed me to the left, into a small, dark crawl space. I fumbled around until I felt my suitcase and rucksack, which were a few feet farther back in the interior of the fuselage. I lodged myself into the ninety-degree angle formed by the luggage and the interior wall of the plane. A large duffel bag was thrown in next, placed between the rear of the cockpit and me. I didn't care to know the bag's contents.

I heard the produce truck start up and drive away, as first Mr. Gunslinger, then the old man, climbed through the fuselage door and into the plane. The armed man turned out to be the pilot, and he crammed himself into the left seat. The older man secured the door in the dark, then moaned and groaned his way into the copilot's seat up front.

The pilot began flipping switches, one of which took several tries, with the encouragement of some obvious swearing and fist banging to negotiate its operation. The instrument panel lights somewhat illuminated the cockpit as the engine started to crank up. The plane became alive with new groans and squeaks, as the engine caused intense vibration.

We taxied for about thirty seconds, then turned and began accelerating down what I hoped was some semblance of a runway. I couldn't see where we were going out of the cockpit windows, because I was seated too low on the fuselage floor. All I could make out was darkness. Something told me that the pilot couldn't see outside any more than I could. It occurred to me that he had taken off from this clandestine airstrip many times before, since he seemed to be doing it in pure darkness without any kind of ground lights to guide him.

Suddenly, the rapidly accelerating bumpy ride on the runway disappeared, as the pilot pulled back on the joystick and we became airborne. The roughness we had experienced on the ground was replaced by severe vibrations that made it seem our flying machine might start breaking apart at any moment.

Just as I tried to crawl up and forward to peer out the cockpit windows, the plane sharply banked to the right, causing me to roll back down on my luggage and onto the fuselage floor in a heap. I did, however, catch a glimpse of city lights off in the distance. We appeared to be turning away from Bangkok.

At last, I was on my way back to Vietnam, complete with my officially stamped—and paid for—visa in my passport, allowing me to stay for at least sixty days. I wondered if we would land at Tan Son Nhut airport again, so I could see the same arrogant immigration bastard that I had previously encountered. No, I decided, I didn't want to see him again. I just wanted to get back into Vietnam so I could continue my quest, hopefully with no more major screwups.

Funny, I thought to myself, all the trouble and bullshit I'd gone through to get *into* Vietnam, when thousands of young American guys—most just a little older than me—were either trying to stay out of Vietnam, or were already there and just wanting to leave. But then again, my mission to Vietnam was not the same as theirs. I wondered if the average American soldier would understand why I *wanted* to enter Vietnam.

The vibrations abated somewhat as the light plane leveled off at a cruising altitude. From my low position behind the cockpit, all I could see through the windshield were sparkling stars above and to the front. The droning of the plane, combined with a sense of accomplishment over my escape from Bangkok, made me drowsy. I was aware that I was nodding off and didn't have any reason to fight it. I assumed I would be awakened when we began our final approach into Saigon, however long that would be from now.

✻ ✻ ✻

The sharp banking decent of the plane dislodged me out of my latest session of sporadic sleep. I convinced myself that I was awake, or at least that I should be, while scrambling up to look out of the cockpit window over the pilot's shoulder. What I saw was a hazy lightness on the horizon, indicating the night was in its last stages. Sharp, quick flashes of light, however, interrupted the left side of my view of the horizon. The flashes were low to the ground and seemed to quiver in the distance. Lightning, perhaps? Then I realized what it was.

Shell fire! Something in the distance was under some sort of bombardment. But how far? A mile? Ten miles? Twenty? Without anything to judge distance, except the blackness of the ground and the faint morning light on the horizon, I really couldn't tell. I did know that I was seeing my first glimpse of actual war, and we were coming in for a landing.

I assumed we were landing somewhere just outside of Saigon. When I tried to ask the pilot, he didn't answer, instead devoting all his time and energy to the mechanics of flying the airplane and finding a place to land in the semidarkness below. Besides, he spoke no English.

Just then, the copilot indicated with hand gestures that I should hold on tight to the back of his seat. I could see the outline of treetops speeding by the small plane, as we inched closer to the ground. Also out the window, I caught glimpses of what appeared to be a few torches on the ground, speeding past the cockpit.

The plane made a loud groaning noise, and we were bumping and skipping over the ground once again. In a few seconds, we coasted to a stop, still bumping our way over the rough terrain. The pilot spun the aircraft around and shut down the engine. The copilot kicked the fuselage door open and waved me out, with a hurried motion of his hand.

With the dark outline of trees smothering out the light from the predawn sky, it was even darker inside the plane than it had been, as I groped for my bags, grabbing my more important rucksack first, before exiting the aircraft.

From just outside of the plane I could see we were situated at the end of a long tree-lined clearing. A half-dozen burning torches on either side of the clearing marked the makeshift runway, on which we had landed. Even as I watched, the torches were snuffed out one by one down the field.

Three or four dark scurrying figures came running up, and completely ignoring my presence outside the plane, grabbed hold of the aircraft with the pilot and copilot, and manually pushed it into the darkness of the near-by trees.

As I watched, I wondered if I was supposed to help with the plane's disappearing act, but opted to stay and guard my bags instead. I heard muffled and distant shell fire that I assumed was part of the light display I had witnessed before landing. The grizzled pilot and a new character, dressed in a dark shirt, shorts, and open sandals, returned to where I waited. The pilot was handing the new person a small wad of money, while both babbled excitedly.

The new man just picked up my two bags and jerked his head, indicating for me to follow him. Oddly enough, I looked at my former pilot for his approval before following my new "friend." He nodded and waved with his arm for me to go ahead. Since the new man—who turned out to be a local farmer and part-time manager of this clandestine airstrip—looked like less of a cutthroat than the pilot, I felt more comfortable following him.

I followed my new contact, whose name I never did find out, down a small trail for about a quarter mile, until in the increasing light, I could make out a small thatched house. When I got close enough to see more than just an outline, I could see that it indeed had a thatched roof, but the exterior walls were made mostly of oddly pieced-together rusted sheet metal. The doorway was a single fabric curtain of a sun-bleached red-and-yellow floral pattern.

I was led in by the man, who placed my bags inside a large wooden crate in one corner of the only room and then motioned for me to sit on an upside-down, five-gallon can.

It was obvious this man spoke no English and had decided not to waste his native words on me, probably figuring I didn't speak his language, either. He went about moving some dishes around in a small cupboard, then went outside to an unlit campfire ring.

It was really beginning to get light by this time, and the birds were awakening the rest of the forest with their loud dawn calls. I watched from inside the hut as the man started a small fire and placed a pot on a metal cooking grill above it. I became increasingly aware that the local mosquitoes were getting in a frenzy over their newly imported delicacy—me. As I swatted one on my arm, I could feel another one on my neck, and so on. I was always just seconds too late to ward off the attacks.

When the man came back in, I decided it was time to break the ice and find out where I was, even though I assumed I was somewhere near Saigon in the Vietnamese countryside. I got his attention and pointed in the direction where I had heard the shell fire and had seen the light flashes on the morning horizon.

"Saigon? Is that Saigon over there?" I asked with exaggerated expressions and motions, hoping to overcome the language brick wall.

The man had a sort of quizzical look on his face. To me, it didn't seem like an unusual question at all. I sensed I had flown in an easterly, or at least southeasterly, direction from Bangkok. And my new contact certainly looked to be Vietnamese, judging by his facial features, betel-stained teeth, and clothing.

The man acknowledged me by shaking his head, pointing, and uttering short staccato syllables. He motioned for me to follow him down a small trail past his residence. Along the trail there was a thatched lean-to structure. When he took me around to the other side, I saw that the lean-to housed an old truck, which seemed to be at least thirty years old and appeared to be European—maybe French or German. The truck looked like it was at least kept in running condition, rather than being abandoned. There was a flatbed cargo section behind the cab with wooden sides about four feet high. A few crates were stored in the back, which was half-covered by a worn tarpaulin that stretched from the back of the cab. It reminded me of the produce truck that had smuggled me out of Bangkok only hours before.

My curiosity was growing. The man jumped up onto the truck bed, sat down and lodged himself between the cab and one of the larger crates, and pulled the tarp down over him, as if he were hiding. In a moment he jumped back into the unused portion of the cargo bed and said "Saigon," several times, emphasizing the first syllable.

By this time, the sun was just appearing over the eastern treetops. The man pointed to the rear, then pointed his finger and ran his hand in an arching movement through the sky until it appeared to pass down over the western trees. Next he pointed to me, cupped his hands, and then raised them to his face in a drinking gesture. After that, he placed both hands together and rested his face on them to indicate sleep.

Suddenly I understood! He was going to drive me to Saigon that night in the truck, after I'd eaten and slept. God, I was getting good at charades on this trip!

Then my friend, sensing that he was really communicating successfully with me, began kicking away the dead vegetation along the dirt trail. He squatted, looked around, and, with his finger, drew a foot-long line in the center of the cleared area. He marked an X far to the right side of the line. "Saigon, Saigon," he said, while pointing to the X. Then he placed a small dot with his fingertip just to the left of the centerline, pointing to what I assumed was our current location. "Cambodia, Cambodia," he said again, with strange accents on the syllables.

"Cambodia, here?" I asked, in some degree of confusion.

He nodded his head with a certain amount of excited satisfaction in realizing he could communicate with me. Then he got very serious, and with a small stick he had picked up, drew two little squiggly lines along either side of the centerline between what was obviously Cambodia and Vietnam.

"Ho Chi Minh," the little man said solemnly, as he moved the stick back and forth along the new lines. "Beaucoup VC, Number 10."

"The Ho Chi Minh Supply Trail?" I asked nervously.

He nodded with deadly seriousness as he drew a line from our dot in Cambodia, across to the X, indicating Saigon. This confirmed we would be crossing the infamous Ho Chi Minh Trail.

I knew from Ron, and accounts of the time, that this was a series of supply trails used at night by the Communist troops in North Vietnam to shuttle supplies to their forces in the south. According to those recent news reports, this part of Vietnam and Cambodia was considered safe haven for the North Vietnamese regulars and the Viet Cong; dangerous as hell for the Americans. Crossing this series of trails was precarious not only because of the Communist forces, but also because this area was frequently bombed at night by American B-52s and other aircraft.

Why I had been deposited here, in Cambodia, rather than just outside of Saigon, was an irritating mystery to me, especially now that I was faced with the prospect of being smuggled across the Ho Chi Minh Trail during its more active hours of darkness. However, I had no other options but to proceed with the bizarre and dangerous plan. I had come this far, and would continue to go as far as fate—and bribery—would allow.

Chapter 8

Crossing the Ho Chi Minh Trail

Fatigue was setting in again, owing to the lack of sleep and abundance of anxiety. I felt exhausted during my new friend's explanation of our present location, and at the realization that I would have to cross the Ho Chi Minh Trail later that night. He must have recognized the effects of the fatigue, because right after his cartography lesson in the dirt, he insisted I eat a bowl of rice and some foul-smelling fish soup. Then he led me back to his shack, where he laid out a woven straw bedroll and indicated with hand motions that I should sleep. When I lay down, he covered me with crude netting in an attempt to shield me from the mosquitoes and other assorted tropical pests.

I was barely conscious of lying down and trying to get comfortable, when I felt him shaking my shoulder, trying to get me coherent and mobilized again.

It was dark outside, but as I began moving around, I sensed it was still the early part of the night. I looked at my watch and confirmed my feeling—it was around 9:00. The combination of fatigue, humidity, and heat had teamed up, once again, to cause me to lose almost an entire day to sleep. It didn't matter anyway. The sparse surroundings that my Cambodian friend called home would have left me pretty unoccupied if I had, in fact, been awake all day. Besides, we had to cross the Ho Chi Minh Trail later that night, and, I hoped, get to Saigon before morning. I was becoming real accustomed to nocturnal travel.

My Cambodian host was much more solemn now than he had been earlier in the day. When I asked him, mostly through the use of sign language, if our excursion was still on for the night, he just nodded his head tersely and pointed to several large bags of what I assumed to be rice that were stacked on the ground behind his old flatbed truck. He indicated that he wanted me to help him load the bags, so I did.

After the rice sacks were loaded on the truck, my host jumped up onto the old floorboards and began arranging and rearranging the wooden crates and some metal five-gallon cans in the front half of the truck. I noticed most of the other containers bore an assortment of words and/or symbols in what I thought were Chinese, Vietnamese, and French. Nothing in English, which I thought was odd, but not totally surprising. It just seems that anywhere one travels in the world, English words can be seen somewhere. I got the feeling that the bags, cans, and crates on the back of the truck were more like props than actual cargo to be delivered. This thought was confirmed when the Cambodian motioned for me to jump up onto the truck bed and sit in a small enclosure, where he had created a nest for me among the wooden crates.

He rearranged the crates, then jumped down to ground level to check if I could be seen. He did this two or three times, until he was satisfied, then he had me get out of the truck while he lashed all the contents in place, leaving my hiding space intact.

The crates would form walls around me. He demonstrated that an old tarp would be pulled over the crates and truck sides to cover everything inside the truck bed, including me. The man even left room in my "nest" for my luggage. At least I could sit on my rucksack and lean on my suitcase with some degree of comfort, for what I assumed would be a long ride in the dark under the cover of the tarpaulin.

All these preparations were being made by the dim light of a kerosene lantern that was inside the hut a few feet from the truck. The night itself, along with the countryside, was nearly pitch black. It was as quiet as it was black. Every so often the screech of a bird or possibly a monkey penetrated the dark. It was eerie, so I concentrated on the familiar man-made things in the immediate illumination of the lantern. I was afraid if I broke that concentration I would begin to feel the black walls of the unfamiliar jungle start closing in on me. I was both afraid and anxious about what we might encounter later that night. I figured that, except for a few courageous

Green Berets and recon patrols, probably the closest any Americans had come to the trail was in a plane flying over the jungle during bombing runs. This was, by all accounts, "Charlie" country.

"What-ifs" started running through my mind:

What if my hiding place in the truck was discovered and I was taken prisoner?

What if the truck hit a mine, or even just had engine trouble?

What if my Cambodian "friend" turned out to be VC and turned me in out of a sense of patriotism, or more likely, to collect a reward?

That last "what-if" really bothered me and stayed in the forefront of my thoughts. But, as with all the other events of this ordeal, the only choice I had was to continue on and hope for the best.

The Cambodian and I ate another bowl of rice and drank some semi-sweet fruit juice from a can. Nothing was said during this meal, which only gave me time to worry about the last "what-if."

After we ate, we loaded my bags into the truck's hiding place, and then I got in, responding to the Cambodian's gestures. Then he covered the entire load—and me—with the tarp. Through a crack in the sideboards I could see the lantern go out in the shack. The Cambodian grabbed a small cloth sack filled with what I assumed were some meager provisions, stepped into the cab, and pounded twice on the back wall, as if to signal to me we were leaving. After a long cranking of the tired old engine, the truck started and we jolted forward.

As the truck shifted into second gear, so too did my fear of what might lie ahead.

Through the half-inch crack in the sideboards, I could catch only glimpses of vegetation along the crude road we were traveling. The dim headlights illuminated the edges of the road in gray-green tones, just enough for me to see that the underbrush was bordering the road's edge with no margin to spare. Occasionally branches would brush up against the sides or swipe down across the metal roof of the cab. Ruts and bumps were common, causing me to be jostled around with bruising regularity—more of what I had experienced riding in the vegetable truck out of Bangkok the night before.

My luggage was the softest thing in my three-foot-square enclosure. I sat on my rucksack and leaned against my suitcase as planned, wishing I had packed softer items. It seemed we were traveling no more than ten miles per hour. This was probably the maximum speed attainable on the road, which was more like a wide trail through the thick bush countryside of eastern Cambodia.

After about a half hour, the truck slowed and began a right-hand turn, severely rocking from side to side. All of a sudden I sensed that we had turned onto a real road, as the going became much smoother, a fact that my butt and shoulders greatly appreciated. I surmised by the sound the tires made that the road was a combination of old gravel and packed dirt. We also accelerated to what I guessed was about thirty-five miles per hour.

I discovered that if I rose up just a few inches, I could lift the tarp up a little with my head, which also lifted it off the large wooden crate that was between me and the back of the truck. When I did this, I could see just a hint of the road from the red glow of a single, dim taillight below the back bumper. This view confirmed that the road we had turned onto was of better quality and more traveled than the first rough trail leading from the Cambodian's house.

Just when I began wondering why we weren't encountering any other vehicles on this better road, I heard the loud noise of other engines. Rising up again, I could see that the road was vaguely illuminated by the dim headlights of approaching vehicles.

The driver slowed to a near crawl, inching over to the right side of the roadway, until the outer wheels were actually higher up on the earthen curb, obviously to allow the oncoming traffic more room.

I pushed myself back down into the blackness of my concealed nest to wait for the traffic to meet and pass us. I heard lumbering engines and smelled exhaust, as two large trucks made their way past, with only a few inches of clearance separating our vehicle from them.

A few seconds later, when I felt the trucks were safely by, I rose up and peered over the wooden crate again and saw the rear partition of two large canopied trucks disappearing down the road behind us. They were driving very close together in single file, but at a moderate speed. The trucks looked like military issue, but not U.S. military. I couldn't see clearly inside the open back of the last truck, but I thought it was carrying soldiers. Then, I told myself, I was only letting my mind wander; after all, I was still in Cambodia, not in war-torn Vietnam. As if it really mattered.

I felt us pull back squarely onto the road and resume our faster speed. During the next hour, we slowed a few times for no apparent reason, then continued along. We went up and down a couple of mild grades and negotiated a half-dozen left and right curves in the road. At one point we slowed to a near stop and turned left, apparently onto a new road.

Soon I could see the jiggling headlights from another vehicle following several hundred yards behind us. We slowed at least two more times, and I could hear the chattering of voices on my side of the truck. I assumed the voices came from groups of people using the road on foot. It was quite a busy thoroughfare for so late at night.

Suddenly we slowed in a series of short, jerky movements, as the dim headlights behind us crept up to a few feet from our rear. I sensed that we were waiting in some slow-moving line of vehicles. After a few minutes of this, I heard more voices outside the truck, this time, sounding more official, like the barking of orders. I heard a truck door somewhere in front of us open, then slam shut.

When we were at a complete stop, I heard footsteps and voices coming towards the front of our truck. A voice was raised, in what I thought was either Vietnamese or Cambodian, and simultaneously there were a few loud bangs on the front fender. The same voice shot a few quick questions at my driver, who was still in the cab just behind my back. He answered in what I thought was a calm voice. The next question was louder, and I heard the passenger door of the cab open. I could make out beams of light bouncing around inside the cab, apparently from a flashlight.

More orders were barked, and I heard the disconcerting crunch of hurried footsteps coming around both sides of the truck towards the back. The headlights of the vehicle behind us were shining directly into the bed of our truck. Beams of light and shadows were dispersed by the wooden crates and cans that concealed me.

At that point my heart was literally in my throat, as I crouched down as far as humanly possible. My breathing became rapid and, I feared, uncontrollable. My back and legs ached from the strain caused by the cramped fetal position I was in. Sweat was running off my forehead so freely that the salt was burning my eyes, causing me to blink. I had never been so frightened in all of my life.

Commands continued to be shouted outside, but everything was getting blurry to my senses. I thought I heard the click of the bolt from a rifle being readied. Next, I heard someone clamoring up on our truck's cargo bed. A few forceful steps closer, and the tarp was being pulled from the other side of my protective wooden crate. I knew this was the end of my trip—maybe even the end of my life.

My body trembled and I felt like I had to gasp just to pull half a breath of air into my lungs. I just wanted to stand up and throw the rest of the tarpaulin off me, so my would-be captor wouldn't find me hunched down, like the defenseless target I felt that I was. I fought back my fear as best I could. I knew fear could make me do something stupid, which could result in an even greater disaster.

The man on the back of the truck was so close I could smell his perspiration; I prayed he couldn't smell mine.

Twice, he kicked the wooden crate I crouched behind, and he moved the tarp that covered me slightly. My head was at a sideways angle down by my knees. From there I saw the beam from the flashlight split across the upper part of my hiding place. I thought about my suitcase next to me. Surely it would only be a second before I felt the bullets rip into my side, or at the very least, felt a hand grab me and pull me out of hiding.

Suddenly, everything went dark, as the tarp flapped back down over the crates. The footsteps stomped to the back of the truck and hit the ground. Words were again exchanged outside, and, miraculously we began to move forward.

I had no idea how the searcher missed me!

Still scared as hell, I quietly maneuvered around and peered through the crack in the sideboard. The outside of our truck was still illuminated by the headlights of the vehicle behind us. In that light, I could see several heavily armed Vietnamese soldiers. Their uniforms were a greenish tan, with red epaulets. Their helmets were flat and broad, some with netting bearing twigs and leaves. *NVA!*

My God! As I suspected, we were at a North Vietnamese Army checkpoint! I started trembling so hard I didn't dare touch the sideboards, for fear of shaking them and calling attention back to us.

But we had made it through, arousing only minor suspicion, and with no disastrous results. The rest of the night, or I should say early morning hours, were fairly uneventful after that. We passed other vehicles, some with their lights out, along the series of roads we traveled over the next couple of hours. I stayed safely secreted in my hiding place, except for the one time we stopped in the darkness, so the driver and I could relieve ourselves in the ditch. I was back in my hiding place under the tarp, before the zipper on my pants was completely up!

Soon we were on a good road, paved, except for occasional ruts and large holes that served as reminders of war—or whatever it was Vietnam was being called on U.S. campuses. We were able to make better progress now, only slowing occasionally to maneuver around large sections of road damage.

Through my peephole in the tarp, I could see that it was almost daylight, and I figured we must have been well inside Vietnam by that time. I could see by the faint light that the countryside we were traveling through was somewhat different than it had been in Cambodia. Instead of thick forests and jungle, this land was more barren and flat, with occasional patches of trees. I realized I was looking at my first Vietnamese rice paddies from ground level. My only other expeience of them had been as the ever-present backdrop on the *Evening News with Walter Cronkite*.

However, the predawn rice paddies were different than those on TV, because there were no black-pajama-clad people working in them yet; it was too early. Neither were there lines of GIs spread out and walking cautiously across them looking for mines. Also missing from the scene were the killing and wounding, which were so much a part of the news footage. Now the paddies were just peaceful little tracts of land bordered by earthen berms to contain the water.

As if in retaliation for that thought, the quiet of early dawn was ruptured by the loud, hollow sound of something approaching from overhead in front of the truck. The sound approached quickly, becoming more deafening by the second. The noise passed over us, and I could feel it reverberating in the bottom of my chest. I lifted the tarp up a bit and saw a wedge formation of four dark Huey helicopters flying directly over the road in the direction we had just come from. I could almost hear Walter Cronkite's voice, as the downward prop wash shook the tarp. This must be Vietnam.

At least those were Americans overhead, and we were headed in the direction from which they were coming. I finally decided to trust my driver, since he had had ample opportunity to turn me over to the "bad guys," if that had been his intention.

Seeing the American choppers fly over us gave me a real feeling of relief, which might seem odd, considering I was in the middle of the hottest combat zone in the world. But after the whole ordeal of getting kicked out of Vietnam, my eventful stay in Bangkok, and being smuggled back into this country, I sure as hell was glad to see Americans again! Suddenly a strange realization hit me: since I was entering Vietnam through the "back door," I didn't need the visa after all.

The more we traveled, the more traffic picked up on the road. More people seemed to be present along the road as we trudged along. At least twice more in the following half hour, I heard the distant rapid thudding of other helicopters in the not-too-distant sky. Even though I could only catch half-peeks through the crack in the sideboards and out the back of the truck, I could tell the scenery was changing again. It seemed like we were getting closer to a more built-up area—I caught glimpses of buildings and partial wire fences, and there were more people now than before.

At one point, we slowed and pulled way over on the right shoulder to allow a small convoy of jeeps and a few two-and-a-half-ton trucks to pass from the opposite direction. I could see out the back that these were American military vehicles, but they were manned by South Vietnamese soldiers.

Soon we were making turns on streets in what I supposed was a more urban area. The local people were coming alive with whatever they did to busy themselves so early in the morning. Traffic was actually beginning to be a problem. My driver kept slowing, speeding up for several hundred yards, and then slowing down again. Horns would toot every once in a while, and mopeds or scooters would buzz by in both directions.

Suddenly, we made a sharp right turn, then came to a jarring stop. My Cambodian driver turned off the engine, pounded twice on the back of the cab, and jumped out and began to stretch. I longed to do the same—I had been in my hiding place for about nine hours, with the exception of only one brief pit stop.

I heard him holler something in his native tongue, then he jumped up on the truck bed and pulled the tarpaulin back to expose me to the morning. "Saigon, Saigon," he said, grinning, no doubt proud of his accomplishment of having delivered me to my destination.

He motioned for me to stand up, which I did, slowly. I stretched and endured the pain. I felt so vulnerable standing up in the truck, as if I was on display, but nobody seemed to notice. I cut my stretching short, as the driver reached for my suitcase. He took it out of the cubbyhole, and I grabbed my rucksack, and we both made our way over the crates and cans to the back of the truck.

I was looking around and took in my new surroundings. If this was Saigon, I thought, the American involvement in this war had done nothing to help the local economy. We had turned off a main thoroughfare and parked just around the corner on a small side street. Some run-down shanties made of stucco, tar paper, and corrugated steel lined one side of the small street. Across the street, was a vacant dirt lot protected by a rusted hurricane fence.

Across the intersection on the main street was a line of connected shops, all run-down and seemingly all leaning slightly to the same side. Some of the shops were still closed, with their metal security grates pulled down across the fronts. The once brightly painted signs and backgrounds above the doors were now faded and chipped.

The street was already busy with mopeds, bicyclists, small delivery trucks, and some of the tiniest, ancient cars I had ever seen. Many were three-wheelers, about half the size of Volkswagen Beetles. An occasional ricksha would go trotting by, its barefoot driver running in short, measured strides. Some of the rickshas were powered by a bicycle-type affair and appeared to give a smoother ride. I later learned that these were called cyclos.

My Cambodian driver was lifting my bags off the back of the truck, when one of the three-wheeled, beat-up little contraptions, painted blue and yellow, pulled up behind us. A small sign in the windshield indicated this was a taxi.

The cabbie got out and jovially approached my Cambodian driver. After a brief period of chattering salutations, the cabbie came up to me smiling widely and reached out his hand to shake mine. "Where you want to go?"

What a relief, I thought. *This guy speaks English! First one in almost two days.*

"Is this Saigon?" I asked kind of sheepishly, not wanting to offend my truck driver, who had already announced that it was.

"Yes, yes, this is, ah, how you say, this is edge of Saigon. Where you go?"

I had studied a worn address book that I had received in Ron's personal effects before embarking on this adventure. In it there was mention of the Long Hotel, which was in the Tu Do Street district. I figured if it was good enough for my brother to stay there while on pass in Saigon, then it was good enough for me. Besides, it would give me a real special feeling to go to a place he had been to in this exotic part of the world.

"Long Hotel near Tu Do Street," I told the cabbie, with an air that suggested I knew where I was going.

"Tu Do Street, eh?" the cabbie grinned back to me. "Okay, is long way, but I take you there." He leaned a little closer, and, trying to be quieter, he asked, "You deserter or AWOL GI?"

"No, I'm civilian," I said with authority.

"Okay, we go now, but cost many Ps," he said, as he lifted my larger suitcase up onto the little triangular vehicle's roof and strapped it down. He threw my rucksack in the back passenger compartment, and I, too, climbed in after bidding a thankful farewell to my Cambodian truck driver.

We made a U-turn, almost in place, with the three-wheeler and got back into the main thoroughfare where the shops were. We headed east, so I figured we were going in the right direction. Suddenly, I realized I didn't have any Vietnamese currency on me, so I couldn't pay the cabbie when we got to the Long Hotel. "What time do the banks open here?" I asked him nervously.

"Why?" was his slightly confused, one-word answer.

"Because I don't have Vietnamese money to pay you."

"What kind money you have?" he asked with a surprising amount of interest. Surprising because I didn't think any money other than his native currency would be of any value to him.

"Well, uh," I didn't want him to know about all the American cash and traveler's checks I had concealed about my person, "I've only got *some* American money."

"Cash? Dollars? Greenbacks?" he asked excitedly, eyes sparkling with each word.

Upon seeing the cabbie's excitement, I remembered Ron telling me that U.S. currency was a big item on the black market in Saigon. So big, in fact, that U.S. servicemen in Vietnam were allowed no American dollars. All the troops were paid in "MPCs" (Military Pay Certificates), or as Ron called it, "Monopoly money." This was to keep the U.S. cash from finding its way into the black market, and eventually into Communist hands.

Not that I thought my cabbie was necessarily a Communist, but, judging by the gleam in his eyes and the fact that he was on the verge of salivating at the mere mention of dollars, he sure as hell had ties to the Saigon black market.

"How much greenbacks you have?" he pressed.

I knew I had about two hundred dollars hidden in various compartments of my wallet, along with a few bahts left over from Bangkok. My traveler's checks and more dollars were in my passport case. I pulled out my wallet and removed a twenty-dollar bill.

The cabdriver kept looking over his shoulder, and when he caught a glimpse of green, he immediately pulled over to the side of the boulevard, amid honking horns and shouts of presumed obscenities.

The cabbie twisted around in the tiny car to face me more directly. "You got twenty dollar. I give you thirty thousand P for that. That almost three times government rate. You got more?" he asked, reaching into his shirt pocket and pulling out a roll of unfamiliar currency that I figured must be piastres. He began counting his wad of cash, which was in large denominations.

Before taking the money or giving up my twenty-dollar bill, I asked him what the exchange rate was, just to make sure.

"About 600 Ps for dollar, but I give you beaucoup more," he said with another grin. Then he asked, "Have you MPC, too? I change MPC good, too."

"No, I'm not in the military," I reminded him. When I told him I didn't have any more U.S. currency, we exchanged what we had. I still didn't trust him and thought I may have just been ripped off for twenty dollars. But it wouldn't be a total rip-off, because I planned to pay him some of the Vietnamese money he traded me, for the cab fare when we got to the hotel.

The currency he handed me looked official enough. It had somebody's picture on it off to one side, but there was an empty spot on the face of the bill that looked like there should be another person's picture there. If this was real money, I figured they left that area blank, because the South

Vietnamese government changed so much, and they were never sure who should be represented on the bill.

We drove on for another twenty minutes or so, along wide, tree-lined boulevards, interrupted by shortcuts through smelly back alleys. The city was becoming very busy by that time, and I was getting very tired again after the tense night of travel. I was fascinated by Saigon, but the fatigue of the last couple of days was really getting to me.

As we got closer to what seemed like the heart of the city, the presence of both American and Vietnamese military was more noticeable and constant. Some buildings had concertina wire and sandbags around them. Vietnamese soldiers, in tight-fitting American-style uniforms and flak jackets, manned the perimeter fortifications of some of the buildings or sat in jeeps in driveways. It had been only a year and a half since the highly publicized "Tet Offensive" in 1968, when the Viet Cong attacked Saigon, so I assumed these troops were guarding against the recurrence of such an event.

As we turned onto the widest boulevard yet, several American servicemen, clad in jungle fatigues and nearly all unarmed, walked along the wide sidewalks near the shops. American MPs in specially marked helmets and flak vests walked along in pairs amid the pedestrians. Those were the first Americans I had seen since leaving the States, other than the few that were on the Pan Am flight and my hitched ride to Bangkok on the C-130. God, it was comforting to see them! What I was seeing was a very small sampling of the half million or so Americans in Vietnam that I heard so much about back home. I had a very strange feeling inside, knowing that most of these guys didn't want to be here at all, yet I was here by choice. The big difference was that I could leave when I wanted to, and wouldn't be ordered into a dangerous situation like many of them would, before their year-long tours of duty were over.

I also noticed that many of the signs and other advertising were in French and English, as well as in Vietnamese. Occupying armies over the last thirty years had made an enormous impact on this city's downtown area.

Off to the left, on the corner, was a large hotel, the "Caravelle." Sandbagged guard positions were set up near its front entrance, and barbed wire was strung around it at the ground-floor level. The cabbie saw me looking at it.

"Beaucoup reporters, press stay there," he informed me.

"Pull over, I want to go in there," I instructed him.

"That hotel, it number one. I thought you go to Long Hotel, it very close." The cabbie seemed a little confused, but pulled up in front of the Caravelle.

"You wait here, I'll be right back, I promise. I just want to see about something inside."

He believed that I'd be right back; after all, he did have my luggage in the car. I should have been more worried about *him* being there when I returned instead.

I hurried inside the main doors and directly to the cashier's desk. The clerk looked up at me and asked in English, albeit with a French accent, if he could help me.

I pulled out the Vietnamese currency that the cabbie had exchanged with me. "Is this official Vietnamese currency? I mean, could I spend it here in this hotel or in your restaurant?" I asked.

The clerk took some of the bills and studied them seriously, but a bit surprised. "Yes, this money is good; did you think maybe it was counterfeit?"

"No, no, it's not that," I said, feeling a little embarrassed. "Do you know what the official government exchange rate is for U.S. dollars?"

The clerk shrugged slightly and looked at a chart just to the side of his cashier's window. "Today the rate is 618 piastres to the U.S. dollar."

I immediately felt elated; the cabbie was for real! "Thank you very much!" I said to the clerk, then stepped over to the side of the lobby. I took another eighty American dollars from my wallet and put it in my shirt pocket. Then, I ran out the front door, where my cabbie was still waiting, but being hassled by the local military guards for parking in a restricted area.

I got back in the tiny cab and told the cabbie that I had gone into the hotel to cash a traveler's check, so I had more American money. I took the eighty dollars out of my pocket and showed him. He stared at the cash in wild excitement.

"I no can change that much. We go to someplace before hotel, okay?" he said, hoping I would agree.

Oh, what the hell, I didn't have any set agenda, and the Long Hotel had no idea who I was, or that I was coming. Even though I was tired, the thought of making some quick extra cash had revitalized me. Besides, this was something I thought Ron would be proud of me for doing.

We drove several blocks away from the Caravelle and away from Tu Do Street and the wide boulevards. The cab slowed and crawled through a maze of dirty back alleys that I realized weren't really the backs of buildings at all, but the fronts. They just looked like they should have been the back—disabled people, beggars, and desolate, despondent-looking children were everywhere. A small boy about eight years old was carrying a dead unplucked chicken by its legs, as he walked quickly through a small street formed by what appeared to be two gutters side by side. Two older boys ran up behind him, knocked him to the ground, and ran off with his chicken and around a row of tin shacks before anyone could react.

That incident brought the vivid reality of the poverty of Saigon home to me. What I had witnessed wasn't just a case of the block bully stealing the smaller boys' bag of marbles—it was more like the survival of the fittest. The big kids stole food from another family so that theirs wouldn't go hungry that night. Boys didn't "play" with chickens here like they did in Nuevo Laredo, they were nourished by them.

The cab stopped in front of a paint-deprived house with an old plywood facade. My driver asked if I would come inside with him to change the money. The place didn't exactly look like any financial institution I had ever seen. I declined his eager invitation.

"No problem, I take dollars inside and come out with beaucoup money for you," the cabbie announced. He noticed my hesitation at the thought of him leaving with my eighty dollars. "But you have my taxi, so I must return," he said, providing a purely business rationalization.

It was true, I did have his taxi for collateral, even though I questioned whether the little three-wheeled contraption was worth eighty bucks. So I agreed for him to go inside the half-open door, as I waited in the hot cab with its leftover exhaust fumes stinging my tired eyes.

I whiled away the three or four minutes he was in the building by watching the cancer of society muddling along the narrow street. I also began to realize just how exhausted I was from the heat and travel, and how great a bed would feel when we got to the hotel.

My driver came back out of the building, bearing a grin that would keep any dentist in business for life. I could see a wad of cash in his hand. He got back into the taxi, and, with a quick look around, he guardedly handed me the Vietnamese currency. I had about one hundred forty thousand piastres in my hand. He was jubilant, but my excitement was tempered by fatigue. Even though I knew he had probably made some commission on the exchange, I handed him ten thousand Ps as a tip and told him to get me to the Long Hotel.

Chapter 9

Experiencing Saigon

The Long Hotel was located a block from Tu Do Street, which was one of the busier thoroughfares in Saigon and served as a magnet of sin and good times for GIs on pass, AWOL, or worse. I knew from Ron's personal effects that the Tu Do Street area was where he went while in Saigon, and the Long Hotel was where he stayed.

The hotel announced its existence to the rest of the world with a simple white sign with painted red block letters jutting out over the sidewalk above the entrance. At least it announced that existence to the English-speaking world, since the sign said "LONG HOTEL" in English only. No French, no Vietnamese—which I thought a bit strange. The ten-foot-wide front of the hotel was open except for a steel accordion security gate pulled partly out about two feet from one side.

As the taxi sputtered to a stop in front of the hotel, a young Vietnamese boy, who looked to be about fourteen years old, dashed out and started pulling at my suitcase, which was on the roof of the cab. At the same time, he smiled and told me in staccato English that his hotel was "Number One! Number One!" My cabdriver, assuming he had a VIP fare to protect, tried pulling the boy's hand off my luggage, while simultaneously arguing with him in rapid-fire Vietnamese.

I leaned forward and grabbed each of their arms before they tore my suitcase in half. I looked at the boy and asked if he had a room for me for a few nights. He smiled again, calmed down, and said, "Yes, yes, GI Number One, Long Hotel Number One!"

With that settled, the boy and driver carried my suitcase and rucksack into the hotel and placed them at the foot of the counter. I paid the driver, and he departed, reminding me he would "be around" if I needed to change any more money.

There really wasn't a lobby, only a worn old countertop on one side, with well-used stairs next to it. This certainly wasn't the Dusit Thani in Bangkok. As I turned back to the counter, the boy was standing near my luggage, as if taking full responsibility for it. I noticed for the first time an old Vietnamese man seated behind the counter with only his head and face visible. When our eyes met, he became noticeably self-conscious. He smiled just wide enough for me to make out a line of black and rotting teeth, before he reached behind him for a room key.

In those few seconds of quiet, a sudden realization of peace surged through me. As I stood there, in the tiny lobby of that fleabag hotel ten thousand miles from home, I realized I was once again in Ron's world. After all the bullshit and turmoil I had experienced during the past few days, *here I was at last!* From his notes, I knew Ron had stayed here more than once. And now I was standing in the same spot and my senses were taking in the same sights, smells, and sounds that his had in the months before he died. This was a place that he, for whatever reason, had chosen to stay during his free time—a place he probably never told anyone else about. At that moment in time, I felt very close to my brother. But I also felt that I was invading his privacy somewhat. This hotel was *his* refuge. If for some reason I couldn't continue my quest beyond this very point, it would have all been worth it, just to stand there and experience that rush of warm feelings.

I'm sure the old man behind the counter and the boy must have thought I was crazy or some stoned deserter, but they allowed me those few seconds of silence and just stared at me, waiting for me to break the spell.

I looked at the boy, and in a new self-assured manner, asked him what his name was.

"You call me Johnny," he said with a big prerotten-toothed grin. "That is my grandfather—you pay him for room, forty thousand Ps, one night."

Now that I was here, I decided to get right down to business. I reached into my rucksack where I had packed everything pertinent to my investigation of Ron's death. After fumbling through some papers and assorted notebooks, I pulled out his civilian passport. The photo of his face on the inside was very clear and only a couple of years old. I showed the picture of Ron to the boy, covering the name. At first, he thought I was showing him *my* passport and was a bit confused. When he realized it wasn't me, he studied it more closely. Then all of a sudden his smile came back, and he surprised the hell out of me by shouting, "Sergeant Reilly, Sergeant Reilly!"

He showed the picture to his grandfather, who smiled and nodded his recognition as well.

I asked Johnny if he knew Sergeant Reilly well. He said he didn't, but that Ron had stayed at the hotel a few times and that he was "Number One GI."

Coming from a Vietnamese in Saigon, I didn't take Ron's being a "Number One GI" as a particularly heartfelt compliment. I figured to Johnny there were always about a half million "Number One GIs" in his country.

Nonetheless, Johnny did remember Ron's name without being coached. This I took as more of a tribute to Ron than the boy's compliment of questionable sincerity.

I explained to Johnny that Sergeant Reilly was my brother. I took out my passport and showed him the last names and the states of birth were the same. I was pretty sure he understood, because then he seemed to explain it to his grandfather in Vietnamese. Through difficult sign language and simple English, I explained that the Sergeant Reilly they remembered was now dead.

Their reaction to that news was sort of mixed. They almost seemed indifferent to Ron's death, probably because their whole country had been involved with so much dying for so many decades. Yet, they seemed a little sad that they were in the presence of someone who obviously cared for this particular casualty of *their* war.

Somewhere in Johnny's short past, he had been hardened by death just as I had. He decided to pull us out of the morass of emotions by abruptly announcing that my room would be half price, only twenty thousand Ps instead of forty. I guess that was his way of expressing his condolences for my loss. He briefly conferred with his grandfather and gave me a very plain-looking room key. I counted out twenty thousand Ps and laid them on the counter for the old man to verify.

Johnny picked up my bags and told me to follow him up the stairs. He said I would be staying in the same room that Sergeant Reilly always did. I didn't know if I could believe him or not, but how could I refute it? I decided to accept Johnny's statement at face value. I would be staying in Ron's usual room.

As we ascended the stairs, Johnny in the lead, it occurred to me that there was only one room per floor. We walked up a flight of stairs to a door, then another flight of stairs and another room. There were no numbers on the doors, so I made a mental note to count how many flights of stairs we climbed to get to the room. There were also no windows. The stairs and small landings outside each door were illuminated by small wall-mounted lamps midway between each flight. The stairwell had once been painted with a fresh coat of light green paint, but that must have been at least fifty years ago. Now it was decorated with chipped paint, cracked plaster, and dust, all accented with an overall coat of deterioration. It housed the same musty mildew odor that I was beginning to notice permeated the whole of Saigon.

We made it to what I figured must have been the top floor, or top room, since the stairs ended. I made a second mental note that I wouldn't have to count the stairs when I left the room after all. Figures Ron would stay in the "penthouse suite."

Johnny fidgeted with the key, got the door open, led me into the room, and dropped my luggage on the dilapidated full-size bed.

Penthouse, indeed! Aside from the sagging bed with no headboard, and a plain, but cigarette-burned bedspread, the only other thing in the drab room was a partially rusted folding chair. A well-used Casablanca-style fan hung from the ceiling in the center of the room. Johnny reached up and pulled the on-off chain that dangled from the fan, and it slowly started to revolve. I could hear a faint scraping noise about halfway through each revolution. The only light in the room came from a dirty seashell-decorated lamp, located on the wall above the bed's flat pillows.

Johnny seemed rather impressed with the accommodations, as he walked around the foot of the bed to the far corner of the room. He pulled open an opaque door to reveal a tiled cubbyhole. He acted as if I would *really* be impressed with this feature. I followed him over and peeked inside what appeared to be a shower and toilet, all in one fixture. A gigantic shower-head was mounted on one of the tiled walls, almost directly over a strange-looking commode. It was made of round porcelain and just kind of came up out of the floor, with a metal lift-off cover. A chain, which I presumed was the flusher, hung from the ceiling. The walls of the shower stall were stained and missing a few tiles, and the floor had actually grown about a quarter inch higher in some spots from mold and mildew buildup. *Ron really knew how to live,* I thought. But then I stopped and reminded myself that I was in a completely different culture, and that this was not meant to be a five-, four-, or even one-star hotel by American standards. Ron had come here just to get away from the war for a few days at a time—as if Saigon had become safe following the Tet Offensive. He also no doubt came here to get laid. The room had a bed, a toilet, and a shower—what else did he need?

Johnny started to unlatch my suitcase to help me unpack. I told him that I would do that myself later, because right then all I wanted to do was sleep. I tipped him, and he left.

I had lost all track of time over the past couple of days. I wasn't even sure what time zone I was in. It was as if time had no meaning in this part of the world, at least it was not as significant as it was back home. I knew, of course, that this was not true; any war, even one as confusing as the one in Vietnam, had to be run on time and with precision—didn't it?

Anyway, I didn't really care just then. I just wanted to sleep in a bed. My watch indicated it was early afternoon, for what it was worth. I made sure the door was locked, then pulled my luggage off the bed and sprawled out on top of the covers. I closed my eyes, thought about Ron's presence in the room, and let the scraping noise of the ceiling fan lull me to sleep.

After what seemed like only a few minutes, I was aware of banging on my door. When my eyes opened, I saw the same identical scene I had seen just before I closed them—the revolving ceiling fan and the dingy little room. Except now there was a small, elongated dark spot on the ceiling above my face. The knocking persisted. I couldn't believe someone would be waking me up after only five minutes of sleep. I pulled my arm over my face to check my watch, and had a hard time believing it was almost ten o'clock—I presumed that it was ten o'clock that night rather than the next morning. I had slept for about nine hours and couldn't understand why I didn't feel more refreshed. Must have been the heat and humidity.

As I brought my arm up to check the time, I noticed that the dark object on the ceiling was moving rapidly. I looked closer and determined that it was a small lizard, or gecko, that was scurrying over to a crack in the corner of the ceiling. Growing up in Wisconsin, I was unaccustomed to these little creatures. But once again, this was not the safe and practical Midwest. I just hoped he wasn't poisonous or hungry.

Tom Reilly at age seven, soon after his parents' death. Tom was sent to live with his sister and brother-in-law on their farm, but older brother Ron became his role model. *Brandon, Wisc., School District*

Tom, age ten, on the farm with the new Schwinn "Cutting Horse" that he would later use to run away from home.

Tom's older brother and hero, Ron.

Ron Reilly while stationed with the 25th Infantry Division at Cu Chi, South Vietnam, 1968.

Ron in a jeep at Cu Chi, 1968.

Ron (center) at his last duty station, Long Binh, South Vietnam, June 1970. He is hanging a pinup-girl calendar behind his desk.

The honor guard and firing squad at Ron's funeral in Brandon, Wisconsin, July 1970. *Brandon* (Wisc.) *Times*

Tom, clad partially in an Army uniform, outside the Long Hotel in Saigon, August 1970. He stayed at this hotel on seedy Tu Do Street because it had been one of his brother's old haunts.

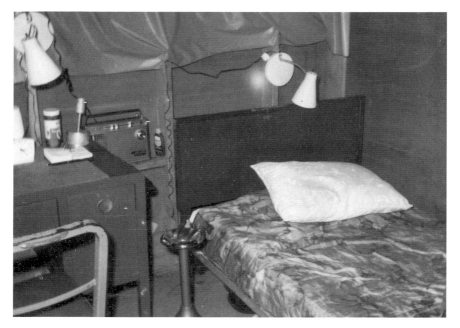

Ron's "hootch" at Long Binh where Tom slept during his visit.

The chapel at Long Binh where the memorial service was held for Ron.

"Next of kin" reaching for Ronald H. Reilly's name on the Vietnam Veterans Memorial in Washington, D.C.

The knocking continued. Now I could hear Johnny's voice call out, "Sergeant Reilly, Sergeant Reilly."

I went over and opened the door, still somewhat groggy. Johnny was standing there smiling. I told him that I wasn't *Sergeant* Reilly, but rather *Tom* Reilly. He looked a little confused, having probably never before heard the word *Tom* as a prefix to a name. After all, *Tom* was not a military rank like Sergeant, Specialist, or Lieutenant. I told him to just call me Tom. Since Johnny was obviously a streetwise kid, he could adapt easily to whatever anyone wanted to be called.

"You want girl? You want Number One boom-boom?" he asked excitedly.

His eagerness made me sense that there was a commission or finder's fee in it for him. At first I told him no, but my curiosity and nineteen-year-old libido told me I should at least check out what he had to offer. I followed him down the five flights of stairs. By the time we were halfway to the ground level, I began to hear the sounds of Saigon's street life outside. Pedicabs, mopeds, and unmuffllered Renaults, sounding more like chain saws, could be heard first, since they were the loudest. Farther down, on the last flight, a mixture of voices and faint rock music blended in, to round off the nocturnal overture. As we emerged from the tiny lobby, I felt the night air—the thickness and heat was just as uncomfortable there as up in the room.

Johnny's grandfather was still seated behind the check-in counter, maintaining the same stoic pose he had nearly ten hours earlier. Johnny told me to wait by the heavy steel security gate at the Long's entrance. He stepped out on the street, whistled, and waved his arm in a beckoning motion.

An old gray moped pulled up and stopped with a backfire and blue cloud of exhaust fumes on the sidewalk in front of the hotel's entrance. The driver was a small, weathered Vietnamese man who looked to be about forty years old. Seated behind him, riding sidesaddle, one in each direction, were two young girls, both dressed in slender, silk Oriental-style dresses, slit up the side to expose a generous view of thigh. The girl facing my side of the moped looked to be about my age. The second girl, who was looking over her shoulder at me, appeared to be much younger. Judging by their heavily made-up faces, it was apparent they were trying to look much older than they were. The older girl was more cute than sexy, but was trying her best to give me a sensuous smile anyway. I thought the little girl behind her, probably her younger sister, looked pretty pathetic, attempting to be sexy and desirous of male attention at her young age.

Johnny and the moped driver, probably the girls' father, watched me, as

I reluctantly looked at the moped's cargo of flesh, trying to avoid looking at the younger girl.

"Which girl you like for boom-boom?" Johnny asked, with a fourteen-year-old-going-on-thirty pimp's impatience.

My Midwestern morals caused me embarrassment at the matter-of-fact nature of the situation. I knew immediately that the younger girl was definitely out of the question. No girl her age in Wisconsin ever put on her mother's makeup, false eyelashes, high heels, and wore tight dresses slit up the side. No, the young one was out of the question. Her older sister, however, *was* cute! After all, since we were about the same age—well, she was a possibility.

"Which one you like? Or, you have both?" Johnny sounded more impatient, as if he had to show these "wares" somewhere else if I couldn't decide.

When I didn't answer him immediately, he decided to try to appeal to what all Vietnamese thought all Americans understood: money. "You have Lin for forty thousand Ps all night, she very good boom-boom. Or, you have her little sister for thirty thousand Ps, same-same. Or you want both, fifty thousand."

I got the feeling that Johnny had done this before, and so had the girls, but I didn't want to think about that if I was going to partake.

"Did Sergeant Reilly ever have these girls?" I asked Johnny. I wanted to be close to Ron, but I didn't want to be with the same girl or girls he'd been with. I couldn't see my brother with either one of these two, anyway. They just weren't his type, and I knew he wasn't into having sex with such young girls.

Johnny was a little taken aback by my question and didn't have time to think up a lie. "No, no, Sergeant Reilly he bring back girls from go-go bars up Tu Do Street."

I was relieved. So I decided to choose the older girl, and possibly come back in about ten years for her younger sister.

Paying for the use of another person's body was awkward for me to accept and to do. But as I had in Nuevo Laredo, I was learning that this was common practice in cultures outside of the sterile, provincial United States. But I would be damned if I would haggle over the price and value of this cute girl. Johnny, and others like him I'm sure, counted on such an attitude by the more puritanical, yet hypocritical, Americans.

So I took Johnny aside, paid him forty thousand Ps and told him I would like the older girl only. He said something to the older girl, then to the driver and the younger girl. The older girl, Lin, got off the moped, smiled at me, and stood next to me. The younger girl repositioned herself on the seat behind the driver, making sure to show off as much of a baby fat thigh as possible, and the moped took off down the street, backfiring again as the engine accelerated.

Johnny wasn't finished with his salesmanship yet. He said, "You want me to bring you whiskey, maybe champagne?"

Knowing I couldn't afford his mark-up, I flatly told him no. Johnny said "okay" defensively and turned and blended into the Saigon street nightlife.

Lin silently followed me up the five flights of stairs, as I wondered why in hell I had just "rented" her for the night.

A little over half an hour later, I was still asking myself the same question. It turned out that Lin's English was limited to "GI Number One, boom-boom, sucky-fucky, and me no like soul brother." Once we got to my room, she was undressed and lying naked in the middle of the bed with her legs spread apart—practically before I could get the door locked. Her sexy smile was gone, since I had already paid, and now it was apparently time to "get it over with," from her perspective. When I saw her there, I knew it wasn't going to be a very romantic interlude.

I obliged her by getting undressed and crawling on top of her, attempting to enjoy a little foreplay, but she wasn't interested in romance or foreplay. A few minutes later the act of sex—sans foreplay, romance, affection, or even a live pulse from my partner—was over. I decided I didn't want this "torrid love affair" to last all night after all, so I handed Lin her clothes, gave her a sizable tip, and showed her to the door. As she left, she turned back, smiled, and said, "GI Number One." It struck me that if all Vietnamese performed everything they did with such vigor and conviction as she had, we would be fighting their war for them forever.

Well, now that I had "had my tires rotated," as the guys back home would say, I felt like I wanted to go out on Tu Do Street to see what Saigon was really like at night. I planned to find a way to get up to Long Binh Post—Ron's last duty assignment—the next day and make contact with his unit. But tonight I needed to stretch my legs a little more and get some fresh-stale air.

I walked back down the stairs to the lobby. Johnny was nowhere around, and his grandfather was dozing in his permanent position behind the counter. I walked out onto the street and was relieved to see no mopeds with young girls on them waiting out front, although several did buzz by with all types of people on them. I decided to walk down to the corner, which was the intersection with Tu Do Street. It seemed the lights were brighter and that it was a bigger thoroughfare. There were more people along that street as well.

I noticed two American military policemen standing on the corner, decked out in jungle fatigues and wearing helmet liners emblazoned with their unit decal along with red-and-white stripes and a large *MP* on the front in white. Both had holstered .45 pistols and carried M-16 rifles. As I approached, they turned to look at me and became interested in my presence so close to Tu Do Street.

"Let's see your ID card, soldier," one of them said. The other one immediately asked what my unit was and to see my "pass slip."

I wasn't prepared to answer three things at once, let alone things that had nothing to do with me at all, since I was civilian. Even though I knew the MPs had jurisdiction over me because this was a combat zone, I was a little surprised at their cold attitudes. After what I had been through, I was just glad to see and speak to other Americans, but these guys made me feel defensive.

"I'm a civilian," I explained, pulling my passport out and opening it to the identification page. "I have a visa stamp in there allowing me to be here as a freelance photographer," I added quickly.

This seemed to pique their interest. The higher ranking of the two, a Spec-4, who looked only a year or two older than me, stepped a little closer and stared at me then at my passport photo.

"What are you taking pictures of over here?" he asked.

Since these guys didn't seem to be buying my story, I decided to try a new tack: the truth. "Actually, my older brother was stationed at Long Binh and died last month. I'm here to find out the details of his death," I said.

It worked. The Spec-4's expression suddenly changed from by-the-book, to one of compassion combined with a little unofficial disbelief. "You're kiddin'! You're not even in the military, but you come all the way over here from the World, just to see where your brother died?"

"I know it sounds strange, but I was real close to my brother, ya know, and I just wanted —"

"Okay, okay, I guess we believe you," the Spec-4 interrupted. "But what the fuck are you doing down here on Tu Do Street? And how long have you been in country?"

Not wanting to explain everything, I decided to answer his questions very specifically. "I just got to Saigon this morning," I answered.

"Well this ain't a good place to be out fuckin' around, especially for a civilian," his partner chimed in.

"My brother used to hang around here when he was on pass, and I just wanted to see what it was like."

"Your brother and fifty thousand other GIs on any given night. Hey, was your brother a lifer or draftee?"

"He was a lifer. He was a sergeant E-7 on his second tour over here," I said somewhat defensively, but feeling bad that I had to be. I figured these MPs were probably draftees that didn't want to be here at all.

"Well sorry 'bout your brother, I know that's a real bummer, man. But if you plan on walking down Tu Do Street, or anywhere else in this shithole city, you're gonna get hassled on every block by MPs like us," the Spec-4 lectured me for my own good.

"Yeah, and the El Cids in plainclothes are gonna really hassle you, since you're wearing civvies," his partner added.

They went on to explain that there were thousands of AWOLs, deserters, and soldiers with fake passes roaming around Saigon. To curtail this, the uniformed MPs and plainclothes CID (Criminal Investigation Division) agents routinely stopped most Americans to check them out. They also told me that my passport "didn't mean shit" in Saigon if I were stopped, because phony ones were easy to get on the black market.

Telling them that I would heed their advice, I asked if they knew how I could get to Long Binh Post. They told me Long Binh was only a few miles from Saigon and that an Army bus going there stopped in front of the Caravelle Hotel about every hour.

I thanked them for the information, and wandered off down Tu Do Street to take in the night scene. It was a street busy with activity. The street itself was cluttered with small foreign cars, pedicabs, taxis, bicycles, and the ever-present mopeds darting in and around the other vehicles. American GIs in twos, threes, and fours, shuffled along the sidewalks with the local Vietnamese pedestrians. The GIs were in fatigues and soft Army baseball caps, no helmets or other evidence of combat gear. They stood out because they were taller than the locals, and because they just casually strolled along, usually laughing or joking among themselves. The Vietnamese civilians, on the other hand, seemed to scurry along the street, much more serious in their demeanor. Unlike the GIs on pass, the locals had business in Saigon and were going about the routine of their daily lives. I wondered what the Vietnamese *really* thought of the big, easygoing, wisecracking Americans being in their capital city.

The main attraction for the American military along Tu Do Street was the red light bars. Sure, there were sidewalk and storefront vendors selling everything from ivory souvenirs to Sony stereos, but the main attraction were the bars and their "boom-boom" girls. Despite all the stories and warnings about crushed glass being put in bottles of beer and even up hookers' vaginas, despite the warnings of catching forms of VD not yet even diagnosed back in the World, and despite the threat of getting rolled or murdered, the American servicemen continued to flock to the temporary good time that Tu Do Street had to offer.

The names of the seedy little bars along Tu Do Street were not much different than the ones I'd seen in the red light districts of Bangkok and Nuevo Laredo. "The Orleans," "The Manhattan Club," "Windy City," "Whiskey-A-Go-Go," etc., etc., etc. It was almost as if there was a global corporation of flesh peddlers and every country had purchased franchises.

Even the most naive young soldier or Marine form Hickstown, USA, knew the Saigon bar scene was phony as hell and a rip-off. But they didn't care. I figured that just seeing the American names of the clubs in neon and hearing American rock music blaring from inside gave them a little taste of their much-missed hometowns. And unlike in the small towns that many of them were from, they didn't have to go into the bars on a Saturday night (or any other night, for that matter) wondering if they could get laid. In the bars on Tu Do Street, there was no "luck" involved in "getting lucky"—just cash.

After the brief and unfulfilling romp in my room, I wasn't interested in going into any of the bars. Neither was I interested in the many come-on looks from the girls standing in the doorways, announcing they gave "Number One Blow Job," or "sucky-fucky all night." Not only was I not physically inclined to pick up another girl, but I wanted to take in the whole street scene from a more objective view. Also, I figured I shouldn't encroach on the fun and therapy of those who had really earned it—the servicemen who were stuck in Vietnam and in desperate need of what Tu Do Street had to offer.

Just as I approached the next corner, a U.S. Army jeep with a MILITARY POLICE placard across the front pulled up to the curb where I was walking. The jeep carried two MPs. The one closest to me, the passenger, was a freckle-faced PFC about my age, his colorful helmet liner covering most of his short red hair. "Let me see your ID," he said, motioning me over to the jeep.

Here we go again, I thought to myself. After I showed him and his partner my passport and explained that I was a civilian and why I was "in-country," they told me I should return to my hotel room and get off the street. Actually, I think they just didn't know how to handle such an unusual situation, and I couldn't blame them. Considering my short hair and my age, I certainly looked like I should be in the military. By suggesting that I get off the street, I figured they thought they were saving both their fellow MPs and me a lot of time and hassle.

I decided that Tu Do Street was no different than any other third-world red light district, and I returned to my hotel after walking another few blocks. There I would force myself to get a regular night's sleep in order to start out fresh in the morning for Ron's unit, north of Saigon.

When I got back to the hotel, Johnny was sitting in his grandfather's place behind the counter. The security gate was about three-quarters closed now. Johnny jumped over the counter to open it for me. As he was doing so, he asked, "You like my sister, Lin? She Number One fuck, eh? She like you beaucoup!"

Now I understood why he had been so eager for me to pick out one of the girls on the moped. I guess it's good to keep the business in the family.

"Ah, yeah, she was good, I liked her," I said a little awkwardly. I didn't want to tell him that she had the boudoir manner of a dead sturgeon. I figured one should be left with a good impression of one's older sister, even if she was a whore.

"Tom, you have Polaroid camera?" Johnny asked, abruptly changing the subject. The way he asked it, I knew he already knew I had one.

This little shithead is more than just streetwise, I thought. He must have gone through my luggage while I was out of the room. Now I was getting pissed, but at the same time felt I was learning a good lesson: Never trust a local, no matter how sincere he or she seemed to be.

"Yeah, I've got a Polaroid, a brand-new one," I said. "Why do you want to know?"

"You want to sell it? I always wanted a Polaroid," Johnny asked as innocently as he could act.

I figured if I didn't agree to sell it, the camera would mysteriously end up missing from my luggage before I checked out anyway. "What will you give me for it?" I asked, knowing that I had paid about thirty dollars for it before coming to Vietnam.

"I give you twenty greenbacks for it," Johnny said in a businesslike manner.

"I paid forty for it back in the States," I lied.

"You pay too much, I give you twenty-five," he shot back.

I couldn't believe this kid! Not only was he streetwise, a pimp, and a crook, now he was a businessman quoting the value of goods sold in the

States! I figured the camera would only be a burden to me in the field, and I did have a Kodak Instamatic with me as well. I decided to offer him a new deal.

"Johnny, I think I can trust you," I lied through my teeth. "I'm going to make you a better deal. I'm gonna be leaving for the field in the morning to find my brother's—Sergeant Reilly's—unit. I'd like to leave my big suitcase here at the hotel for a couple weeks. I'd like you to watch it for me and make sure it's here when I return. If you agree to do that for me, I'll *give* you the Polaroid and four packs of film I brought along for it. That's a Number One deal for you."

Johnny made it look as though he was seriously pondering this deal for about five seconds. Then, apparently, not able to up the ante, he agreed.

I figured there was only a one in a million chance of ever seeing my suitcase again after I left Saigon, but clothes can be replaced. I decided to pack any necessities in my rucksack before leaving. After all, I wouldn't need several changes of civilian clothes and shoes once I left Saigon.

Once we agreed on the terms, Johnny asked if he could have the camera right away. I saw no reason not to give it to him, so he followed me up to my room. I went into the room alone and opened my luggage. I could tell someone, most likely Johnny, had rummaged through it, but it looked like everything was still there. Johnny either wasn't an outright thief, or he was smart enough to know he would be the primary suspect if anything was missing.

I got the camera and film, handed it to him, and asked if he would make sure I was awake by seven the next morning. He said he would, and I locked myself in, turned off the light, and lay in bed for what seemed like hours, listening to the scraping fan and thinking about what I had been through so far, and what might come next. I felt like I was getting five years older by the day.

Chapter 10

Long Binh Post

I didn't sleep well that first night in Saigon at the Long Hotel. It was just a long, drawn-out period of strange noises, stifling heat, sweat, confusion, and a little despair, when I allowed it to creep in. The only thing that kept me going was the thought of my brother and the idea of my self-imposed mission to obtain the details of his death. God, it seemed like months since I had had a good sleep and it felt like it would be years before I ever got one again. At my age, I didn't think I should be feeling so exhausted; I figured that was a symptom of old age. I guess I was growing older fast.

I must have been thinking about all this when I was startled awake by Johnny pounding loudly on my door. I became fully awakened and realized that once again I was tired after having just rested.

"It's seven o'clock, Mr. Tom," Johnny yelled from outside the door.

"Okay, okay. I'm awake," I answered.

Not knowing what I might catch if I stepped barefoot on the dirty floor, I had placed my rubber shower clogs on the end of the bed before retiring the previous night. As I put them on and staggered to the commode, Johnny said he was going to do his other morning hotel duties. *Yeah, probably as prince of all trades,* I snickered to myself. While relieving myself, I paid particular attention to the "appendage" I held in my hand. Even though I had used a condom with Johnny's sister, Lin, the night before, I was still nervous and suspicious. So far, no pain or change in appearance. Hell, I was elated by the fact that it was still there! I made a mental note to continue this inspection for at least the next fourteen days—if not for the rest of my life.

I retrieved my bar of American soap from its plastic travel container in my shaving kit. I asked and received permission from the gecko lounging in one corner of the shower stall if I could take my turn. Apparently he was finished with the stall, because he darted out and scurried under the bed. By now I figured this was really the little lizard's room and he saw me as *his* temporary pet.

Thank God for shower clogs! The floor of the oversized stall had about two centuries' worth of scum and mold built up on it. There was no real drain, just a hole in one corner of the floor. The tiled walls looked equally unsanitary. I made a point not to look down and especially not to bump into the walls while I showered.

I was sweaty again, five minutes after showering, but I figured I had to chip away at the perspiration layers when I had the chance, or my body would end up with a buildup similar to the one in the shower.

This morning I was finally going to make contact with American soldiers in Vietnam. Not just the MPs of Tu Do Street, or the C-130 crew that flew me down to Bangkok. Today I would hopefully get to my brother's last unit and maybe even talk to some people who actually knew him.

Not knowing exactly what this day would bring, I decided I should be ready for anything. I dressed in a green Army jungle fatigue shirt (sans insignia, unit patches, or name), gray jeans, jungle boots, and a Marine-style "jarhead" baseball cap. When Ron sent the military gear to me, neither he nor I ever thought I would actually be wearing it in Vietnam.

I put some underwear and socks, my toiletries kit, a towel, and my Kodak Instamatic camera in my rucksack. Ron's little notepad and "contact" book, along with some photos, went into one of my shirt pockets. My passport went into the other. Money, in the form of piastres, greenbacks, and traveler's checks, was everywhere on my person, and some was even hidden under the bottom liner of my shaving kit. I put everything else into my big suitcase, which was to remain at the hotel for safekeeping.

When I dropped off the suitcase behind the hotel counter at street level, I decided not to lock it with the cheap little luggage padlock. I figured the lock would be easily picked, or the suitcase simply cut open if anyone really wanted to get in it. Besides, I really believed I'd never see it or any of the contents again, anyway. After all, not only was I leaving it in Johnny's charge, I was also going out into the field during a war. Even if my suitcase survived the next few weeks at the hotel, there was no guarantee that I would. I felt as if I were saying good-bye to a terminally ill friend when I released my grip on the handle. The confusing part was that I didn't know which of us might be the terminal one at that point.

After Johnny accepted my suitcase, he gave me directions to the Caravelle Hotel, where the Army bus to Long Binh normally stopped. I thought it was strange that a bus carrying U.S. personnel would have a scheduled stop in downtown Saigon after the Tet Offensive. I knew from news reports and rumor that we had not ever totally secured Saigon. I hoped the bus wouldn't be the target of sappers tossing explosives, realizing that was probably the fear all the GIs had whenever they traveled anywhere in Vietnam.

But that general fear was overshadowed by the more specific fear I had that I would be prevented from taking the bus or getting any further along in my mission. After all, I was acutely aware that I wasn't really supposed to be there. The MPs on Tu Do Street told me my American passport didn't mean all that much, because a good counterfeit one could be purchased on the black market. The MPs were right: Even an authentic passport didn't prove you weren't AWOL or a deserting GI; all it proved was that you were an American, just like the half-million others in Vietnam. Also, the visa I had "obtained" in Bangkok had never been used or tested, since I had entered Vietnam via unsanctioned means. For all I knew, the visa could be an obvious fake. My best chance was to stop worrying and make it to my brother's unit and contact his acquaintances. Until then, I decided to plan on the confusion or sympathy of any Americans I encountered along the way to Ron's unit.

A half-dozen American servicemen and two Vietnamese locals were hanging out at the corner near the Caravelle, where Johnny told me the bus stopped. I was pleased to see that only two of the Americans were engaged in light conversation. The others, as well as the Vietnamese, seemed lost in their own thoughts as they waited. I figured I would do the same. That way I wouldn't be expected to talk to anyone, thus maintaining a low profile. I didn't want to draw attention to the fact that I was an American there under "special" circumstances who just needed a bus ride.

Only one of the soldiers, an E-5 buck sergeant, seemed to notice that my pants were not the standard issue, baggy jungle fatigues. He noticed, but didn't say anything to me or anyone else, obviously deciding he had enough of his own problems to be concerned about—like staying alive for his duration—instead of worrying about what some American was wearing.

I took up a position behind the others and remained very quiet, hoping I wouldn't be hassled by the bus driver or the other passengers. As I waited—and sweated off another pound—it occurred to me that I had no idea when the next bus would be coming along. There was no schedule posted at the bus stop, but I figured, since eight people had gathered ahead of me, it should be coming along soon. Rather than asking and sounding like a novice, I decided to just keep quiet and wait, sweat a little more, and hope I wouldn't have any problems getting to Long Binh. Once there, I would concern myself with why I came to Vietnam.

Just as I was thinking about all this, the U.S. military bus came lumbering around the corner. It seemed like a big, dull, dark green monster, creeping up the street in the curb lane in the midst of all the miniature Vietnamese vehicles that were darting around it, in their amoeba-like flow through the capillaries and veins of the busy city.

As the bus got closer, I could see that it was being driven by a black GI. The side windows had steel mesh grates on them over the glass, giving the appearance of olive drab fishnet stockings stretched over the windows. The grates were so heavy-duty that I could barely see in, but I did notice there were a few passengers on board. As the driver pulled to a stop in front of our little group, the brakes squeaked.

The others started to form a casual line in front of the bus, as people in any city do—a kind of polite, silent jockeying for position. I decided it was best for me to position myself after the last American GI and just before the first Vietnamese civilian. I guessed the civilians had been hired by the military to work on some of the bases.

I noticed the two civilians were busy pulling out laminated pass cards of some sort, and I felt a sudden wave of fear, because I didn't have any such card. I quickly looked ahead at the Americans, all in fatigues. None of them were producing cards, so I relaxed a bit. I supposed that being an American in uniform in Vietnam was pass enough to ride on a U.S. government bus. Trouble was, I was only wearing part of a uniform, and the part I was wearing was devoid of military insignia. Maybe the driver, who looked bored anyway, wouldn't notice. I stayed close to the last GI as we climbed the three steps up into the bus. My positioning in line worked perfectly. By the time the driver noticed me, he apparently only saw the mass of my fatigue shirt and Marine cap and was already looking past me to the Vietnamese who were directly behind me. When I got by the driver, I nervously glanced back. He was carefully checking their pass cards, comparing the photos with their faces. I quickly went to the rear of the bus and took an empty bench seat. When the two civilians took their seats, the bus jerked back into what one could almost call a traffic pattern.

One more stop somewhere in Saigon added a few more servicemen and another Vietnamese civilian. The driver made no announcement at this stop. I guessed that everyone that needed to be on the bus knew where they would board and where they would disembark. I took the bus ride on blind faith, much like I had taken the rest of my trip. There was nothing that told me that this was actually the bus to Long Binh. I was going only by what the MPs and Johnny had told me. Obviously there would be no signs or placards on the bus announcing its route in a combat zone. But, at least I was going where some American service guys were going, and that, oddly enough, provided me with a—perhaps misguided—sense of security. Being alone, young, and in a country at war, you had to take what you could get.

I was also pleased that no one else sat in the same row as me. The passengers were spread out all over the bus and had the luxury of having their own bench seats, except the Vietnamese, who doubled up two to a seat. This brought to mind an old quote of Ron's: "spread out or one round will get ya all!" He had said it in jest several times when he was on leave with me, and I never thought much about its significance until now. I squinted through the steel mesh windows to see if I thought any of the hundreds of people on the streets and sidewalks looked like a Communist sapper ready to attack the bus. They all did!

The bus was obviously making progress getting to the outskirts of Saigon. Here the street was wider and less packed with people and traffic than it was downtown. I also began to notice other military vehicles. Mostly jeeps and "deuce-and-a-halfs," the standard issue two-and-a-half-ton Army trucks with canopied tops. Some of the jeeps had steel potted MPs in them. A few others had their South Vietnamese equivalents, with their helmets marked QC. I remembered Ron once told me the Vietnamese military police were sometimes called "white mice," because of their white helmets.

Nearly every major intersection had a sandbagged bunker set up on at least one corner of the sidewalk, manned by South Vietnamese soldiers in their tightly tailored and bloused fatigue uniforms. I surmised that the Vietnamese troops could handle the tight-fitting uniforms, because they were used to the heat of this god-awful climate. The American soldiers, on the other hand, preferred their fatigues loose and baggy, to allow for more airflow. The two different styles probably had something to do with appearance and image as well. The South Vietnamese soldiers had their countrymen and the female population to impress; the Americans weren't there to impress anyone, especially the Vietnamese women.

Just when it seemed we were making good time, the bus slowed to a crawl, then came to a complete stop. I noticed that the traffic out the rear window and on the side was bunching up around us. The passengers in the front half of the bus stood up to see what the problem was. All I could see from my angle was a confused mass of vehicles, with our bus, still being the largest, making its way down to what appeared to be the source of the congestion.

As we got closer, I saw both MP and Vietnamese QC helmets ahead, near an Army deuce-and-a-half that was at an odd angle in the congested traffic. When we approached the scene, I was relieved to see it was some sort of traffic accident and not a military action. Near the truck, a young soldier frantically directed traffic around the accident. He was wearing a sweat-soaked, olive drab T-shirt, and a floppy-brimmed campaign hat, and was pointing an M-16 rifle skyward. Both the American and South Vietnamese military police were calming a crowd of onlookers who were milling about.

When it was our turn to drive past the truck, I got a brief look at the results of the accident. The huge military truck was at an angle, facing away from our bus, and didn't appear to be damaged. However, the front end was tilted upward and the heavy front wheels were resting on top of a completely crushed taxi. It was one of those small taxis Saigon was famous for, about half the size of a standard Volkswagen Beetle, even before the accident. Now it looked like a crushed, metal steamer trunk. All that could be seen of the occupants was a blood-soaked arm that was sticking out where the driver's side window, or possibly a sunroof, used to be. The arm hung grotesque and motionless, and judging by the degree of damage and the fact that nobody seemed to be in a hurry, I figured the body attached to that arm probably no longer contained a beating heart. Just another form of death in a part of the world that saw so much dying.

Soon, we were once again making pretty good time. Within about five minutes, we had turned off the street and stopped just outside the bunkers, concertina wire, and high fences of what appeared to be an important military compound. Some of the passengers were standing up, when the driver stood, turned partway around, and announced in a bored voice that this was "Tan Son Nhut." Since this was a military bus and the defensive bunkers were quite formidable, I figured this must be the part of Tan Son Nhut that housed the American airbase.

Just when I began wondering if this bus actually did go to Long Binh, one of the GIs up front hollered out to the driver, who was just about to exit the bus, "Hey man, how long of a wait here, before going to Long Binh? I don't want to be AWOL."

"We'll leave in about ten minutes," the driver answered.

Long Binh! Realizing I was getting close to my destination, I fumbled through Ron's little notebooks that I had stuffed in my pockets. I turned the pages, until I came across the one I was searching for.

There it was. *"SFC Royce and Mr. Edwards—civilian—Long Binh Post, Inventory Control."* Maybe they were still there, especially the civilian, Mr. Edwards. If I could find them, maybe they could help me. Of course, I had no way of knowing what their connection had been to my brother, or even when he had known them. Ron had been on his second tour in Vietnam, and his notes were difficult to decipher chronologically. Also, I didn't know if Sergeant Royce or Mr. Edwards were still in Vietnam, or, for that matter, if they were even still alive. But it was worth a try.

Three more servicemen in fatigues came out the main gate and boarded the bus. A minute or so later, the driver got back on, after taking a short smoke break. He surveyed his human cargo, then sat down in his seat and started the engine. We pulled away from the main gate and drove a short distance before turning onto what looked like a highway.

We were now definitely out of Saigon and driving through open country. Except for the occasional stretch of concertina wire along the roadside, and a fortified bunker, I felt as though we could have been driving through the American countryside. The fields were lush and green, with sporadic patches or rows of short trees—darker silhouettes connecting the ground to the sky. I had a hard time relating what I saw to the Vietnam portrayed on the nightly news back home.

The corridor we were traveling on from Tan Son Nhut to Long Binh seemed to be a well-used piece of highway for the military. U.S. Army trucks and jeeps surrounded us in all directions. The few civilian vehicles there almost looked out of place.

Just when I was feeling relatively safe in this war-torn country, the bus drove by the rusted wreckage of two APCs (armored personnel carriers) in the ditch on the near side of the highway. They had both been there for a long time, perhaps even since Tet nearly two years earlier, and one was on its side. I supposed the military brass had decided to leave them there as a reminder, just in case any other service personnel got to feeling too safe along this allegedly controlled section of road. Without having firsthand knowledge, I got the distinct feeling that no place was actually under the total or constant control of the Americans—or their South Vietnamese military counterparts.

We traveled farther along the highway, and I noticed the ditch on the right side of the bus suddenly changed. It looked as though the sandy soil had been bulldozed up high and flat across the top. There was a huge hurricane fence, about ten feet high, with several parallel rows of concertina wire laid out like overgrown slinky toys, spaced several feet apart outside the fence. Every fifty yards or so there was a large heavily sandbagged bunker built up high inside the fence. The bunkers were all manned by American soldiers, wearing flak vests and steel helmets. The bunkers were defended by machine guns and M-16 rifles. I imagined what couldn't be seen was even more deadly to potential intruders: electronically controlled claymore mines set outside the fence.

This formidable-looking perimeter seemed to go on for about a mile, until the bus turned into what apparently was the main gate of Long Binh Post, where the size of the bunkers and number of sandbags increased. The main drive was lined on both sides with similar fortifications. Two manned armored vehicles were parked near the entrance, apparently to assist with security.

After driving through the outer gate, the bus pulled over to the side into a sally port area, before entering a huge, sprawling military base, where, I was to learn, most of the planning and logistics support for the war was conducted.

Two MPs, dressed in full combat garb, complete with flak vests, boarded the bus before anyone got off. Each was armed with an M-16 and a holstered .45-caliber semiautomatic handgun. One of them took up a position facing the passengers, just inside the front of the bus, next to the driver, M-16 pointed up in the ready position. The other walked through the bus checking the passengers' identification papers.

The American servicemen aboard produced green laminated military identification cards for him. The MP recognized one of the American passengers and said something to him with a short laugh. Then he continued on towards the rear, where I was seated. I was becoming more nervous by the second at the thoroughness of his identification check. He stopped at the remaining two Vietnamese civilians and took his time to completely check out their IDs and work permits. He spoke two or three words to them in Vietnamese, and they answered in a litany of sentences. It seemed obvious he didn't have a clue as to what they answered.

After he seemed satisfied that the two civilians belonged on the base, he walked back to where I was seated. I could tell my Marine baseball cap, with its pleated points on the crown, was only the beginning of what piqued his interest. From a few steps away, he could see my fatigue shirt was devoid of any patches or other insignia, not even the usual "U.S. Army" stitched in bold black letters over the left breast pocket. *Just wait 'til he gets a look at my light gray jeans,* I thought!

"Who are you?" he asked, with just a tinge of disgust in his voice.

I had already pulled out my passport and was handing it to him. "I'm an American civilian."

He cradled his M-16 in the crook of his arm, as he turned to the photo page of my passport.

"I also have a visa stamped on one of the next few pages. The visa gives me permission to be here in Vietnam." I was trying to provide him with just enough information to be cooperative, while not sounding overconfident or like a smart-ass.

"I don't care about your damned visa. What are you doing coming on this base?"

"I'm coming to see Mr. Edwards, another civilian who works in the Inventory Control Center," I said matter-of-factly. Again my heart was racing, and it was all I could do not to let it show outwardly. I was so close to making contact with an acquaintance of Ron's—if I could just get past this MP and gain access to the base.

I sensed the MP was trying to look as though he was doing his job, but like the MPs in Saigon, he probably didn't have a clue how to handle such an unorthodox situation. A teenaged civilian in half-military garb entering the base to allegedly visit another civilian was probably not SOP (Standard Operating Procedures).

I knew he wanted out of this situation as much as I did, so I decided to help us both out by lying a little more. I pulled together the last ounce of my limited street sense and went for broke. "Sergeant First Class Royce, who works with Mr. Edwards, arranged the whole thing—they're expecting me, you can check it out if you want." I was certain my pounding heart was rocking the bus by now.

"What unit do these guys work at?" the MP asked, but I could see he was weakening. After all, when was the last time an American threatened the security of Long Binh Post? I hoped my youthful collegiate looks counted for something.

"They work in the Inventory Control Center," I told him, trying to sound a little impatient, as if he were really delaying me. I hoped like hell there was an Inventory Control Center at Long Binh.

Of course, I also worried that if such a unit *did* exist, the MP would go back to his guard shack and telephone them. Even if those guys still worked there and remembered Ron, they sure as hell weren't expecting his kid brother to show up out of the blue. My whole story was a gamble, but I had to continue, I was so close.

"So—you know how to get there?"

It worked! I won!

"Yeah, I was there a couple of days ago, before I went to Saigon," I lied again. Now my heart was going wild, not in fear and anxiety, but in jubilation.

The MP apparently decided he had wasted enough time on me. He handed me back my passport, nodded without resuming eye contact, then turned and walked to the front of the bus and exited with his partner.

We drove through the inner gate, and I was "officially" on the base. The bus stopped just inside the second gate, and most of the passengers exited. A couple of the GIs remained seated. I figured I could either get off here or travel farther inside the sprawling base, since it appeared the bus was going to continue on some sort of route inside Long Binh's perimeter.

Since I was already on the base, I decided I should put some distance between me and the main gate MP, before he had second thoughts. I didn't want to ask anyone where the bus was headed, or if they knew where the Inventory Control Center was. The less attention I drew to myself, the better.

I couldn't believe how big Long Binh Post looked through the steel mesh windows of the bus. It appeared to be set up in the shape of a huge doughnut. Buildings and streets were all organized in a wide circle. The doughnut "hole" was a large expanse of open field, vegetated with short, dry grass and scrub brush. It looked to be at least a mile in diameter and had no roads crossing it. The buildings seemed to be on higher ground than the expansive empty center.

The bus followed a main street, and I assumed it would make scheduled stops around the base, which was confirmed when we pulled up to an enclosed bus stop.

Across the street on the left side was a huge, single-story building, surrounded by a tall hurricane fence with thick strands of razor wire across the top. The building was situated well inside the menacing-looking fence. I also noticed more fenced-off areas close to this building, and sandbagged guard towers located at all corners of the facility.

The bus stopped directly outside this formidable-looking compex. Two MPs wearing fiberglass helmet liners got on the bus as passengers. I wondered if this could be the main stockade for U.S. servicemen in Vietnam. Ron had mentioned to me in one of his letters that Long Binh housed such a prison. I decided this wasn't a good place to leave the bus. Ron never mentioned working very close to the stockade.

As we began to pull away, the driver looked into his rearview mirror and yelled to the remaining two GIs, and me "Are you guys going to headquarters?"

Both nodded their affirmation from their more forward seats, and, trying to blend in as much as possible, I nodded my intention of getting off there as well. I figured "headquarters" would be a good place to disembark and ask someone how to get to the Inventory Control Center.

The bus then turned off onto another street and headed up a slight hill. The buildings looked much newer in this part of the base. I was surprised to see the exterior of one was painted yellow, a color one doesn't normally associate with government structures—especially in a war zone. The bus stopped, and the two GIs and I got off. It felt good to get out of the bus. Even though Long Binh was only a few miles north of Saigon, the trip had been an emotional ordeal.

I was careful to exit quickly past the two MPs that had boarded at the stockade stop. I'm sure my paranoia was much more real to me than it was to them, but I was nonetheless relieved they didn't pay any attention to me, as I made my way past their seats.

Not really wanting to go into the very official-looking headquarters building to ask for directions, I caught up with the other two GIs who had gotten off the bus ahead of me. They were walking along in no particular hurry and engaged in a jovial conversation.

"Hey, do you guys know where I could find the Inventory Control Center?" I asked, catching them a little off guard.

They stopped and turned to look at me, then at each other. "Isn't that over by—"

"Yeah, I think it's over by the Medivac Hospital," the second GI interrupted.

They were really trying to be helpful. The one closest to me pointed to some buildings in the distance. "You see that water tower way over there? Not that one, but the one way over there? I remember there's some kind of inventory supply center over there," he said with a certain air of authority.

The other guy reiterated, "Yeah, there's like an office building next to a big warehouse over there. One of the base chapels is close to it, too, just down the hill a little from it."

I saw what they were pointing to, and it looked to be about a mile or a mile and a half around the "doughnut" from where we were. I turned and started walking down the long driveway leading away from the headquarters building.

One of the GIs yelled to me, "Hey man, you're not *walking* all the way over there are you? I mean another post bus will drive over that way pretty soon."

I yelled back that I could use the walk and thanked them for their help. Now that I was on the base and surrounded by probably twenty thousand Americans and a few thousand supposedly friendly South Vietnamese civilian workers, I figured I was in a fairly safe environment again. I also didn't want to be hassled anymore by MPs or bus drivers. I just wanted to get to *somebody* who had known my brother.

As I walked down the gradual hill from the base headquarters, I was still elevated enough to see a panoramic view of Long Binh. It was truly amazing. It looked to be about ten or twelve square miles of modern one- and two-story buildings, most constructed of corrugated steel or cinder block. Except for the stockade facility and occasional rows of two-story wooden barracks, the place looked more like a modern industrial complex than what I had thought a military base in a combat zone would look like. I could even discern a swimming pool and baseball diamond mixed in among the mass of structures.

One thing that did, however, catch my eye and remind me that the sprawling complex was run by the military, was the several red-and-white-checkered water towers that were dispersed around the base. It seemed like every base I'd ever seen in the States had them. My perception was that this base should be located Stateside instead of in a war zone, especially the war zone that was shown on the national news. I was beginning to realize that the whole topic of Vietnam, as depicted by the media, was flawed with misperceptions and confusion.

As I walked along alone, I became aware of the constant thumping, muffled rotor sound of Army helicopters circling overhead. Two Hueys constantly flew over the base's perimeter and swept over the deserted open field in the center. I assumed they were part of an elaborate security system, on the lookout for anything that wasn't supposed to be there. The side doors of the Hueys were open, and machine guns were very visible from the ground. This was one feature, I thought, would not be seen at a military base in the States.

As I got back to the main road circling the base, I realized that I still wasn't used to the stifling heat. Walking had always been relaxing and enjoyable to me, but in that heat and high humidity, it just wasn't the case. It felt like I was walking through a huge bowl of hot Jell-O. My clothes were soaked and sticking to my skin, even though my shirt was the loose-fitting standard issue jungle fatigue variety that the other Americans were wearing here in Vietnam. I'd have thought the Department of Defense could have designed some other type of clothing to wear in this horrendous climate.

The base seemed quiet, as I trudged along in the direction the two GIs had pointed me to. What appeared to be a base bus passed me without slowing down. I had made no gestures indicating that I wanted a ride, nor was I at one of the marked bus stops. A few other military vehicles also passed me as I walked.

I was getting thirstier and more uncomfortable the farther I walked, and I worried that I might not have enough fluids inside me to replace all the sweat that was spewing from my every pore. An Army canteen was packed in my big suitcase back at the Long Hotel. I wished I had had the foresight to put it in the rucksack. I was out of salt tablets as well.

I noticed both rooftop and window air-conditioning units on most of the buildings I passed and could hear the whispers of their motors. Imagine that! Air-conditioning for our troops in Vietnam. I knew if these buildings had air-conditioning, they certainly had cool drinking water as well. I tried resisting the temptation to walk into one of the buildings and ask for a drink of water, but water was all I could think about.

No, I told myself, *You can make it, you're over halfway there!* I was afraid if I went into a building, there would be too many questions to answer. I figured the people Ron wrote about in his notes would be more sympathetic and willing to help me than someone he hadn't known. *I can wait,* I told myself. *I can wait.*

Just as I was repeating that mantra, I began to hear strange voices. "Hey guy, you okay? Where you going? You sure you're okay?" someone kept asking me, but I wasn't fully comprehending why. "I think the heat's got to you. Where you going? What's your unit?" the voice kept asking. "You can't be walking around in the middle of the road like that. Can I help you get somewhere?"

Then I realized a guy in fatigues was holding me by my upper right arm and was steadying me against the side of a jeep. "You need some water and salt tablets fast. I'll help you," he said. The "he" didn't look much older than me and wore the insignia of a Spec-4.

I pulled together some strength between waves of light-headedness and stammered, "Inventory . . . Control . . . Center . . . Mr. Edwards."

Next I realized the young Spec-4 was awkwardly loading me into the passenger side of the jeep. Before I realized we had driven anywhere, the soldier and another guy dressed in fatigues helped me out of the jeep. I was in the middle, as they half-carried/half-dragged me towards the entrance of a building a few yards from the jeep. Through my blurred vision I could make out part of a very official-looking sign over the door casing. I thought I saw the word *Inventory* in black letters against a white background.

As the three of us pushed our way inside the entrance, I immediately heard some shouting. I felt my whole body begin to tremble, and alternating waves of heat and chills rushed through my head and neck. The temperature in the building must have been at least thirty degrees cooler than it was outside; it felt like I was stepping out of a sauna and into a deep freeze—a change too drastic for the body to regulate.

My helpers sat me down on a very institutional-looking green vinyl sofa. An American man who could have been in his fifties, and who was dressed in a white shirt instead of fatigues, put a paper cup of cool water up to my lips and told me to drink slowly. My first instinct was to gulp the fluid and ask for more, but the older man carefully controlled the flow. A different hand held two small white pills up to my mouth. The man with the cup of water told me to take the pills if I could—they were salt tablets.

For the first time since encountering the Spec-4 in the jeep, I began to recognize what was happening. The heat, coupled with the exertion of walking in the sun, had gotten to me. Even though Wisconsin is hot and humid in the summer, it is not like the Vietnamese climate. Also, in the Midwest, the cool spring and mild, early summer months gradually ease the body into the sticky, summer heat of July and August. There was nothing gradual about Vietnam, everything about it seemed harsh and immediate.

In a few minutes the Spec-4 jeep driver leaned over to me, put his hand on my upper back, and said with a half-smile, "You'll be okay, just rest a little while."

I looked up, and clearly saw his face for the first time. Actually, he looked younger than me. I could feel myself stabilizing and my head getting less foggy. "Thanks, but where am I?" I asked him.

"You're at the Inventory Control Center, where you told me you were going. You were about ready to keel over from the heat, so I figured I could either bring you here or take you to the hospital. This place was closer. Figured you knew the people here. Well, good luck, I gotta get going."

"Thanks again," I said, as he turned and walked out.

As I sat there getting stronger, the older gentleman came back out to see how I was doing. "Thought I'd better check on you again, how are you now?"

"Gettin' my senses back at least. Is this the Inventory Control Center?"

"Yeah, who were you coming to see?" he asked in a helpful tone.

"Well, I'm not sure. Is there a Mr. Edwards or an SFC Royce working here?"

"I'm Carl Edwards," the man responded, sounding a bit curious that a stranger would show up asking for him.

"Well, Mr. Edwards, I really appreciate your helping me with the water and all. I'm a little embarrassed about how I got here."

"You still haven't said why you were looking for me," Edwards pressed.

"Did you know a Sergeant Reilly, Ron Reilly?"

With that question, the older man's demeanor changed—from helpful and curious to sad. "Yes, I knew Sergeant Reilly," he said very slowly, looking away. "You're his younger brother, aren't you?" he asked, renewing eye contact with me.

"Yes."

"Your name is Tom, right?"

"Yes."

"Well, hell, I'm sure surprised to see you here. Your brother was a good man, well liked by everyone. He talked about you sometimes. Told us you were in college. What the hell are you doing here?"

"The Army didn't tell me how he died. He meant a lot to me, so I came here to find out, and to see where it happened," I explained. The water, salt tablets, and air-conditioning were starting to revive me. I was so relieved I had finally made contact with a colleague of Ron's. It had been a long and difficult journey in a relatively short period of time.

"I assume by the clothes you're wearing, that you're still a civilian," Edwards said in a half-questioning tone.

All of a sudden I felt a little self-conscious. After all, I was wearing a Marine cap, an Army fatigue shirt, a civilian pair of pants, and jungle boots. Not exactly military *or* civilian dress. "Yeah, I'm still a civilian, for now. I flew over on a Pan Am flight, but ended up in Bangkok for a few days, but that's a long story. Is this where Ron worked?" I asked, looking around inside the building.

"Yeah, that was his desk and work area over there," Edwards said, pointing to a corner desk. "We haven't replaced, ah, I mean nobody works there now," he said trying not to hurt my feelings.

It was obvious nobody worked there; the desktop was completely bare. The swivel chair behind it was neatly pushed up to the desk's edge. There was a two-month calendar on the wall near the desk, displaying July and August beneath a sexy Asian model. Ron had sent me a photo the guys had taken of him standing on his desk changing the calendar from March and April to May and June. Since this was late August, I assumed Ron had changed the calendar page again at the beginning of July, about two weeks before he died.

I went over to the work area and slowly ran my hand over the bottom half of the calendar. This was apparently quite touching to Mr. Edwards, because he cleared his throat a couple of times and said with a fatherly smile, "Ron was our official calendar changer. He hated it when the wrong month was turned up."

I went behind the desk, pulled out the chair, and sat in it, imagining Ron's presence as, one by one, I slowly pulled open the empty drawers. I felt a sense of saddened fascination by being at this exact spot in the world.

It was all Mr. Edwards could handle. "Ah, Tom, why don't I give you a little time to yourself. I'll go over to Ron's unit, his barracks, and let them know you're here. There's a guy or two that will probably want to talk to you, okay?"

"That would be fine, Mr. Edwards, thanks," I said, not looking up as he left the room. I was aware of other people working in other parts of the building behind various cabinets and partitions, but none were near me. I just sat there and enveloped myself in what I sensed was my brother's presence. For a few minutes I just wanted to be with Ron's things and stare at that calendar, especially at the date of July 16th, the day he died.

Being there at his workstation, I realized that so far the trip had been well worth the effort and expense.

Chapter 11

The Details

In what I guessed to be about twenty minutes, Mr. Edwards came back to the Inventory Control Office, followed by two servicemen in fatigues. One was older, probably in his mid-forties, short and with a well-worn face. The black metal rank insignia on his collar was made up of several chevrons and rockers. I recognized the rank as that of master sergeant. The other soldier was much younger, maybe about twenty-two, with a slight build and short, reddish hair. His collar rank indicated he was a specialist 4th class, or the equivalent of a two-stripe corporal. Both servicemen had quizzical looks on their faces when they saw me.

Mr. Edwards was the first to speak. "Tom, I'd like you to meet Master Sergeant Olack. He serves as the first sergeant of headquarters company that Ron was assigned to. This other gent is Specialist Osborne. Both of these guys said they wanted to meet you when I told them you were here." With that, Mr. Edwards stepped back, and the other two moved towards me—by then I was standing behind Ron's desk.

Sergeant Olack took the lead, extending his hand to me as he warmly smiled—an expression that he seemed to use sparingly. "Good to meet you, Tom. How the hell are ya?" he said, grasping my hand.

"I'm doing okay, Sergeant," I replied, wondering why Mr. Edwards was introducing me to *these* men.

Spec-4 Osborne likewise shook my hand and said "hello" in a quiet, more hesitant manner than Olack had.

"I've heard a little about you from your brother," Sergeant Olack continued. "By the way, you can just call me 'Top' like everyone else around here. I'm acting company first sergeant until they can pawn the damn job off on someone else," he laughed, half-winking at Osborne.

"So you guys knew my brother?" I asked.

"Yeah, we knew him. A damn good guy, too," Top said.

Osborne remained silent during this conversation, I thought maybe in deference to Top's more senior rank, but couldn't be sure. Maybe he was just shy.

"So, what brings you to this ass-wipe part of the world?" Top asked, in the vernacular of the grizzled lifer that he obviously was.

"I came to find out how my brother died, and where it happened."

"You mean *nobody* told you?" Top asked.

"No, just that he died of nonhostile causes, which could be anything," I answered.

"Well, I'll be a son of a bitch!" exclaimed Top. "I helped the captain write you a letter. You mean you *never* got it?" he asked incredulously.

"No, I checked with the Army almost every day and nobody could tell me anything, so I decided after a couple weeks to come here myself."

"Who all's with you?" asked Top.

"Nobody, just me."

"You mean no other relative or government people? You came here *alone?*"

"Well, yeah, I was the next of kin. The government and Army told me not to come, but I did anyway," I explained.

"You come here on a MACV flight?" Top asked, with some confusion. I knew MACV stood for Military Assistance Command—Vietnam, and its aircraft were the mode of transportation for nearly all the troops arriving to and departing from the war zone.

I was getting a little disappointed that Top was more concerned how I got there than telling me about how Ron had died. I figured he would eventually tell me, so I humored him with answers to his questions for the time being. Osborne and Mr. Edwards were also listening intently in the background.

"No, I came over on a civilian Pan Am flight."

"No shit! You just bought a goddamned ticket and came over to this here war zone like a fuckin' tourist?" Top seemed to be fascinated with the whole concept.

"Well, not exactly. I wasn't allowed into Vietnam at first, and had to go to Bangkok to get a visa," I continued explaining.

"A *visa*? So they let you in country with a damn visa now?"

"Well, I didn't actually need it, because I ended up coming in from somewhere in Cambodia by truck." I knew this would surely fire up Top even more.

"Wait, wait, wait just a goddamned minute! Somehow you got your young ass into Cambodia, then you just rode by truck to Saigon, and then out here? That means you would have crossed the fuckin' Ho Chi Minh Trail, that's *Charlie* country, boy! Worse yet, that whole fuckin' area is controlled by the *NVA!*"

"Yeah, that's about it, but there wasn't any trouble, I got here okay," I said, hoping to end the discussion.

Top then looked hard at both Osborne and Mr. Edwards, who also displayed looks of disbelief on their faces. Then he turned back to me and grinned from ear to ear. "Boy, you got a fuckin' set of balls on you the size of Texas! Glad you're here! Your brother would be proud of you, or maybe he'd belt you in the head with a fuckin' two-by-four for bein' stupid. Either way, welcome to Vietnam, where the beer is warm and the women ain't!" Top proclaimed, by way of bringing the subject to a close. "So where ya staying, while in this lovely vacation spot?" he asked good-naturedly.

"I left some things at the Long Hotel on Tu Do Street in Saigon, but I'd really prefer to be out here with you guys."

"Hell's bells, boy! You sure know how to pick the fuckin' *garden* spots don't you! Tu Do Street is no place for you to be, but then again you *are* Reilly's brother, aren't you?"

I just smiled my confirmation.

"Osborne here and I will take you over to the company area and get you billeted," he said, putting his burly arm around my shoulder and directing me towards the door, with Osborne trailing behind. "Don't waste your time with Edwards over there, he's just a *highly* paid government civilian. Around here, the Army runs the war, ain't that right, Carl?"

"Whatever you say, Top, whatever you say. You just take care of that boy. He's pretty important to all of us," Mr. Edwards said.

"We'll get you settled in here, then we'll talk later, if that's okay with you?" Top said as we left the air-conditioned building and stepped back outside into the blast furnace. I was hoping the salt pills and water I had taken would help me survive the oppressive heat. I wouldn't want to pass out again in front of Ron's Army friends.

It was about a hundred-yard walk down to the barracks area, which was closer to the inside of the "doughnut" than to the office building. There were several two-story barracks, all with sandbagged fortifications around them. Other low sandbagged walls lined paths leading from each barracks to what looked like a shower and lavatory building. Farther down another fortified path was a one-story building with a "Mess Hall" sign over the door. Unlike the main perimeter fortifications, there were no weapons or men present behind any of the sandbags.

Just before entering one of the barracks, Top turned back to the trailing Osborne and said, "Do me and Tom here a favor; go find Sergeant Reynolds and tell him I'd like to inconvenience him for a few days. Explain about our guest and tell him to find a new place to sleep the next few nights, or until I tell him otherwise."

"Roger that, Top, he won't mind," Osborne said with a sly smile, as he turned and headed in a different direction.

"Damn straight he won't mind! I'll kick his ass, if he does. Damn buck sergeant doesn't deserve his own room yet, anyway. That was Sergeant Reilly's room, and now we'll just kinda keep it in the family, so to speak!" Top laughed.

I could tell I had made contact with the right guy. Top Olack, as with many first sergeants, really ran the show around his company. Sure the officers, especially the company commander, were *officially* in charge, but the first sergeants, also known as "Top" or "Topkick," were the ones that got things done. Moreover, since all were staunch lifers, they got things done the *Army way,* give or take a few bent regulations when necessary, like letting unauthorized civilians stay in a war zone barracks.

"You timed your little visit here right on the money. The company CO, Captain Gilliam, just left on leave. He'll be gone a couple weeks, so that leaves me and a couple green-assed lieutenants in charge around here. But don't worry about them. They're up on Army regs and all, but they're more worried about gettin' their heads blown off in a rocket attack, or some shit like that. Put 'em all together, and they ain't got enough common sense to spit at!" Top enjoyed proclaiming, with an adequate amount of frustration. "Let's go up to my hootch, you look like you could use a beer, I know I could—least until Osborne gets your area squared away."

Right then I couldn't have turned down that invitation, even if I had wanted to. Top was, indeed, fully in charge, and, after all I'd been through on my own the last few days, it was okay by me. In fact, it was a great and comforting feeling.

We went up one of the open-framed wooden stairs to the second floor of his barracks, which was the one closest to the mess hall. He unlocked a padlock on a plywood door that simply had the word *TOP* written on it with a heavy black marking pen.

The room, only about six by eight feet, had walls and flooring of unfinished two-by-fours and plywood. A cot with a footlocker at the end took up one wall, and on another wall was a two-door metal wall locker. The inside of the walls were lined with sandbags halfway up to the ceiling. A small window was higher up on one wall, with a single sandbag perched on the sill. Leaning against the wall, near the cot, was an M-16 rifle with a loaded magazine. A steel helmet and flak vest hung on a hook beside the M-16.

Pretty Spartan living quarters, I thought. Spartan, that is, except for a mini-refrigerator that was in the middle of the remaining interior wall. The fridge had a single row of sandbags up both sides and on top of it, revealing only the door. An Army-green extension cord ran up the wall behind it and plugged into an outlet near the ceiling light fixture.

Upon seeing this, I chuckled to myself. What more could a lifer NCO ask for in a combat zone? He had his cot, his weapon, and a place to store cold beer, not necessarily in that order of importance.

Top went down the hall and returned in a minute with a black molded plastic chair, indicating that it was for me to sit on. He then opened another padlock on the door of his refrigerator, reached inside and pulled out two cans of Budweiser—very cold! Handing one to me, he popped the other open, as he sat down on his cot. I wasn't much of a beer drinker, but anything cold would have tasted great right about then. Besides, I could tell Top was already beginning to accept me, either because I was Ron's brother, or because of the journey I'd taken from Cambodia through Charlie country, or both. I didn't want to disappoint him, so I guzzled about half the can, following his lead.

"Aaahh, now that's what life's about, ain't it?"

I disagreed with him, but didn't dare say so. "Sure is!"

"So, I figure now you want to know about your brother, uh?" Top asked.

"Yes, I do."

"Well, first off, let me tell you he was a good guy. Because of his time in, I considered him my most experienced NCO, even though I had a couple other E-6s in the company. In fact, Reilly, er Ron, went up for the E-7 promotions board a few weeks before he died. I knew he'd get it. He felt confident he aced the board, but they never got the results to him before he died. I went over and checked the day after, and sure as hell, he made the promotion to E-7, sergeant first class. I thought to myself, that's really the shits. A man works hard to get the promotion he wants, then dies the day before the results come out."

"Top, you still haven't told me *how* he died," I said, hearing a hint of impatience in my voice.

"Well, one day a few days before it happened, he told me and another NCO he was having chest pains. Said he could barely get out of his bunk in the mornings. You know, he was a heavy smoker, hell, we all are around here. Because of this, Ron thought he might have lung cancer or tuberculosis, or some such shit. So I told him to take some time off and get his ass over to the base hospital for a checkup. He went over there one day and had some chest X rays taken, came back, and said the pain was getting worse. I told him not to go to work—you know, stay in his bunk and take it easy for a few days, least 'til he got the X ray results back. Me and the other guys would check up on him a couple times a day, but he was usually asleep."

"Did the base hospital tell him anything they thought might be wrong?" I asked.

"Don't know about that. I saw him a couple nights later in the mess hall. Christ, he looked terrible. Said he didn't have much appetite the last few days, but knew he needed to eat something. I told him I would take him back over to the hospital the next morning to get some more tests done, maybe even have him admitted for a few days. Didn't say if he wanted to do that or not, just wanted to get the chest X ray results back and hoped that would say what was wrong. I really felt bad because I knew he was hurting so. That was the last time I saw him alive."

"What happened after that, Top? The telegram said he died about 0825. Was that the next morning after you saw him in the mess hall?" I asked, pressing him for more information.

"Well, apparently he got up, still feeling like shit, but got dressed and went down to the ammo room and sat and talked to Sergeant Hammond, our armory NCO. The ammo room is on the first floor of his barracks, Ron's room was in the back of the second floor. He sat there in an old stuffed chair, just making small talk with Hammond for about twenty minutes, then left, saying he was going back up to his room because he was still feeling pretty bad.

"Apparently he never made it up the outside stairs. All of a sudden Hammond, still down in the ammo room, and Osborne, who was walking on the other side of the barracks, hear a Vietnamese cleaning gal, who we hired a couple of months before, screaming outside the front stairs. When they get there, they see her standing over Ron, who is sitting on the steps about halfway up, slumped against the wall.

"When they got to him, they could see his eyes were open, but not focused, and when Osborne checked, he found Ron wasn't breathing and didn't have a pulse. They pulled him off the steps and quickly laid him on the ground. Osborne began CPR, while Hammond ran and flagged down a lieutenant from another unit driving by in a jeep. Osborne still wasn't getting any response, so they loaded Ron into the backseat, and the lieutenant drove to the base hospital like a crazy man. All the while, Osborne kept up the CPR in the back of the jeep.

"The emergency room staff worked on Ron for another half hour or so, but he was gone. What a goddamned shame," Top said, now with tears in his eyes, matching the ones that were streaming down my own face.

"So that explains why Osborne was so quiet around me today," I said slowly, after taking a minute to recover a little.

"I guess so. The lad felt real bad that he wasn't able to revive Reilly. I tried to tell him that it wasn't his fault. Christ, Ron could have been unconscious on those steps for ten minutes or more before the charwoman found him in that condition. But Osborne still feels shitty anyway, especially when he saw you here today."

"Hell, Top, all I want to do right now is thank the guy for trying. Sounds like he really did his best to save him. It's not his fault," I said through some of the strongest emotions I hoped to never again feel in my life.

"It would probably help if he heard that, coming from you," Top advised.

"I'll make sure he does," I said. "Can you show me *exactly* where Ron was when they found him? It's really important to me."

"Sure, finish your beer, and I'll take you there, it's just one building over from here."

"Thanks, Top, I really appreciate all this, although I wish I never had to come here to hear it. Did the doctors tell you what the cause was?" I kept probing, as if I hadn't heard enough painful details for one day.

"Massive heart attack, they called it something else, though, —athero . . . something or other. You can talk to the folks at the hospital, too, maybe tomorrow."

With that, we crumpled our Budweiser cans, adding them to several already in a wastebasket, and exited Top's barracks.

We walked up one of the sandbagged paths to the next barracks. As soon as my eyes focused on the front stairs, I felt as if something was squeezing *my* chest. My legs turned to cement, and a strong wave of emotion permeated my senses.

Just before we got to Ron's barracks, Osborne came around from the far side of the building. He appeared a little surprised to run into Top and me. I had the distinct feeling he wanted to turn away, unnoticed by us, but it was too late.

"Hey Osborne, I just explained to Tom here what happened to Sergeant Reilly. Maybe you could show him how you and Hammond found him on the stairs," Top suggested carefully.

Osborne looked down for a moment, heaved a huge sigh, then climbed to about the fourth step from the bottom, sat down, and slowly leaned against the building next to the stairs. He sat there for a few seconds, motionless and staring at the ground, and I saw tears welling up in his eyes. The same was happening to me, again.

It was a very somber moment for me to see another GI, dressed in fatigues, sitting in the position my brother had been in when he died.

All I could do was to go and sit next to Osborne on the same step. "Top tells me you really tried to save him," I said slowly, in a voice fractured by tears and emotion.

"But I couldn't," Osborne replied, through his equally strong emotions and tears. "I just couldn't save him, and it's been hard for me, especially seeing you here today."

"It's okay, doesn't sound like anybody could have saved him. But you tried hard, and I just want to thank you for that," I said placing my hand on his knee.

Sensing it was time to end this moment of agony for the both of us, Top softly asked Osborne if he got Sergeant Reynolds to sleep somewhere else so that I could have his room.

"Yeah, Top, Reynolds already moved his stuff out, so Tom can move in anytime. Reynolds's gonna bunk in the open bay, so Tom can use the room as long as he needs it," Osborne said, getting up to leave.

"Just one more thing, Specialist," I said before he left. "Where did you lay Ron on the ground, you know, after you removed him from the steps and started CPR?"

Osborne looked a little surprised again, but slowly walked a few feet from the bottom of the stairs and pointed to the dusty ground just off the sandbagged path. "We laid him here; his head there, his feet there," he said, sweeping his hand over an area as long as a man is tall.

"Thank you very much for all you've done," I told Osborne, as he looked at Top and walked away.

My eyes focused on some dark gray stones, about one to two inches in diameter, which were laying where Osborne indicated Ron's head had been placed a little over a month before. I knelt down and picked up those specific stones and put them in the lower pocket of my fatigue shirt. I told Top Olack I was sure the Army wouldn't mind me taking the stones, and he readily agreed.

"Want to go see your new sleeping quarters, the place where your brother bunked?" Top asked.

"Sure," I said, as we walked up the stairs, through the open bay area of the empty barracks.

In the back corner were two small private rooms normally used as quarters for the NCOs. The lower-ranking men had their bunks situated in two rows in the open bay in the middle of the barracks. Top opened the unpainted plywood door of the end room, and I stepped in. Even though my mind knew that another serviceman had been living there recently, my heart felt Ron's presence in the small enclosure.

The room was similar in size and roughness to Top's in the other barracks building. It had the standard bunk, footlocker, wall locker, and a small desk with a lamp on it next to the bunk. A reading lamp was mounted on the wall over the headboard. Nearly every square inch of the wall opposite the bunk was decorated with *Playboy* and *Penthouse* foldouts. A large piece of rose-colored oilcloth was tacked up as a makeshift curtain over the room's one window.

I asked Top if he remembered if this was how the room looked when Ron occupied it.

"Well, I haven't been here for a month since your brother lived here, but that wall sure as hell wasn't covered with all this naked shit. The only things I remember Ron having on the walls was a calendar over there next to the wall locker, I think, and a picture of you and some woman, here above the bunk. But all the furniture in the room, I mean, the bunk, this desk, and the lockers, were all your brother's."

As he described it, I knew exactly what picture Top was referring to that Ron had on the wall. I had found it in his personal effects that the Army had sent me after his death. It was a picture taken several years earlier of me standing next to our sister, Jean, on the farm in Beaver Dam. It had been taken just before I ran away to Ripon. Jean and I were both smiling widely in the photo; we were very close to one another. When I mailed it to Ron in Okinawa, he told me in a return letter that it was his favorite family picture. I had remembered that comment as I tearfully went through the items the Army sent me—all in one cardboard box, containing all that was left of his entire life.

It seemed right that Ron would have that particular picture on the wall of his last living space.

"How 'bout I give you some time alone here? I'll send someone over with the rucksack you left in my hootch. I'll come get you about 1730, ah, that's 5:30 in civilian time, for chow in the mess hall. If you need to use the can, or wash up or anything, the latrine is the next building over with all the screens on it. Okay?"

"Okay, Top." Despite the persona of the rough, tough, mean lifer master sergeant that he wanted to portray to his men, I knew he had a good heart and soul under that olive drab veneer.

He turned to leave, then poked his head back into the room and said, "By the way, Tom, if anyone in the company area asks who you are or what you're doing here, you have my permission to tell them it's none of their fuckin' business, or better yet, just tell them to see me, all right?"

"Okay, Top, I appreciate it," I answered with a smile. His Army veneer was still intact as he turned to leave.

I closed the door and stared at each piece of furniture in the tiny room, trying to ignore the naked women on the wall staring back at me.

I stepped over and opened the dark green wooden footlocker at the end of the bed. The top shelf was empty. I imagined Ron having his shaving gear and rolled up socks and towels in the divided compartments of this removable shelf, much as he had when I stayed with him for a few days in Fort Hood, Texas. The bottom of the footlocker was also empty. Apparently Sergeant Reynolds had moved all of his personal items out, to make room for mine.

I laid down on the camouflaged blanket that covered the bunk and placed my head on the pillow, closing my eyes and feeling the presence of my brother all around me. I thought about this room being his last home. Because he was a solitary person, I knew this was the place he could be at peace with his thoughts, closing out the world, with its people and the war that surrounded him. Here, he would read my letters, and, at the small desk, he would sit and write back to me. Here was where he had laid in such pain the last few days of his life, wondering and worrying what was wrong, why he was having chest pains.

His last letter to me had made no mention of the pains, which meant they either hadn't started yet, or he didn't want to alarm me with the details. I would never know for sure.

Surely, at only thirty-two, he would not have expected heart problems. He always seemed healthy, always passed his Army physicals. He did mention one time to me several years earlier that he almost hadn't passed a physical exam to go to Vietnam on his first tour, because of high blood pressure. But he told me he had "taken care of the problem." At the time, I didn't know if that meant he had treated the high blood pressure or simply got the guy to pass him for combat duty. The way he told me the story, I now strongly suspected the latter.

I also remembered bits and pieces of conversation among other family members that Ron had had rheumatic fever as an infant, and that the disease had damaged his heart in some way. But if that were true, how could he have passed all those Army physicals for ten years, and seem and look so healthy? Surely, I thought, if there was a medical problem serious enough to kill someone his age, it would have been diagnosed earlier. He couldn't have bribed or talked his way out of every physical exam, could he?

Yes, I needed to talk to the doctor at Long Binh Hospital. I had too many questions. Now that I knew how and where Ron died, I needed more answers concerning the *why*. I had come too far not to be more thorough.

I reached up and flicked on the reading lamp over the bunk pillow. Running my hand over the wall above the bunk where Top said the family picture had hung, I found a small nail hole. It was the only nail hole in the plywood wall, so I figured it was where the photograph of Jean and me had been. It would have been positioned so that when the lamp was on, the photo would have been illuminated and visible from the pillow. I wondered how many times, especially in his last days of suffering he had looked at that picture. Sad, very sad. I felt so bad that the brother I loved so much had felt such pain and died without me being there to help him. In a way, I understood how Osborne felt by not being able to save him with CPR. But apparently it just wasn't meant to be.

Even though the words I came to hear had been said, sad as they were, I felt some solace in the fact that Ron had not been murdered. There was no person or thing for me to direct any revenge upon. Now I could focus my attention on the sorrow I felt at his loss and getting through the rest of my stay in Vietnam safely, so I could return to someday finish college like Ron wanted.

All of a sudden, there was a knock on the door. I was actually glad for the interruption—it shocked me out of my excruciatingly sad thoughts.

I got up to answer the door. Standing on the other side, was a soldier who looked even younger than me. He was holding my rucksack and an unopened can of Budweiser.

"Sir, I was told to bring this over to you," he said, in a distinctive Southern accent. The cold beer was a dead giveaway who had sent this guy.

I took my rucksack and the beer and thanked the young soldier.

"That's okay, sir. I didn't know Sergeant Reilly, because I just got here a couple of weeks ago, you know, after he . . ."

"Yeah, okay. Thanks again, and by the way, you don't have to call me 'sir.' I'm a civilian. Just call me Tom," I told him.

"Okay, Tom, but welcome to the unit anyway," he said, turning to leave, having accomplished his mission.

Ron had told me in a letter he sent just after he arrived in Vietnam on this tour that a lot of the soldiers weren't much older than me, and they seemed to be getting younger all the time. That letter went on to state he was sure glad I was in college so that I wouldn't have to come to Vietnam. How ironic, since, here I was, not only *in* Vietnam, but standing in his very room.

I stored my few personal things in the footlocker, then went to the latrine building to wash up. Returning to my room, I met Top, who was just coming to get me for dinner.

"You hungry yet?" he asked.

"I haven't had much of an appetite lately, but I could eat something," I answered.

"You probably haven't had much good old American food lately either, eh?"

"No, not any really. I don't really know most of what I've been eating for the last few days," I told him, thinking how much I appreciated being back with Americans.

"Well, I'm not so sure you'll be able to recognize what's served in the mess hall either, but it usually stays with you longer than that fuckin' gook shit!" he said, snickering.

We entered the mess hall. Apparently we were early, since there were only about a dozen servicemen and a couple of American civilians seated at some of the tables.

I noticed Mr. Edwards right away. He was sitting at the end of a long table across from Specialist Osborne. Mr. Edwards smiled broadly at me, and Osborne turned to look at me over his shoulder, and I was relieved to see him smile as well. I hoped that our talk was helping him to get over his self-imposed guilt over not being able to revive Ron.

"Here, Tom, take a tray and get ready for some fine government cooking—Army-style," Top said, handing me a tan fiberglass tray that was divided into separate compartments.

"Actually, Top, I've eaten Army food before. I spent some time with Ron when he was stationed at Fort Hood last year, before he came here. I don't mind it at all," I informed him.

"Well, to tell you the goddamned truth, I think the chow we get here is better than what we got Stateside," Top said, almost bragging.

Glad there are some benefits to being in Vietnam, I thought.

"Of course, the guys out in the boonies eatin' C-rations might disagree," he laughed.

I followed Top through the chow line, manned by servers on the other side of the counter, who were dressed in white. Each one methodically dumped a scoop of a different food into the compartments on our trays. Upon reaching the end of the serving line, Top helped himself to a cup of black coffee, and I filled a glass with milk from a dispenser. I didn't see much difference between this mess hall and the one at Fort Hood, except for the sandbags outside.

I trailed along behind Top, as we walked over and sat down with Mr. Edwards and Osborne.

During the ensuing small talk, I commented that this mess hall made it seem like we were back in the States, and wasn't what I had expected to find in Vietnam. As soon as I said it, I wondered if I had spoken too soon. After all, I had only been at Long Binh less than a day.

But to my surprise, nobody at the table seemed to take offense at my comment. "Long Binh Post isn't the Nam you see on the television news back in the World," Top said, munching on a fried chicken drumstick. "Oh sure, we've had our share of shit here, with rockets and mortar attacks, but now any action is just the little inside shit from the locals. I mean, you've seen a lot of Vietnamese civilians on the base. Not all of them are friendly—all the time. Some are here just gathering information and biding their time. A few months ago a couple were nailed out in no-man's-land, setting up time-delayed mortars set to go off when empty cans fill up with rainwater, detonating them. Could be days or even weeks after the little bastards rig 'em up. How many gooks did the cowboys kill out there Osborne, four or five?"

"Yeah, Top, it was something like that," confirmed Osborne.

"Shit, the EOD demolition guys were out there for a week with metal detectors, trying to figure out where all the mortars were hid," Top added.

"Where is 'no-man's-land?' " I asked.

"It's that big damn field you see right in the middle of Long Binh," Mr. Edwards said. "Don't ever go out there, means nothin' but trouble."

"I wasn't here at the time, but this base was really lit up during the Tet Offensive back in early '68," Top continued. "This place, Saigon, Tan Son Nhut, and Bien Hoa were all big targets of the gooks in this sector. Guess the little fuckers wanted to work in air-conditioned buildings too, for a change," he laughed.

"Ron was just finishing his first tour over here at that time. I remember him telling me about it. He had to stay a week longer, because he couldn't get down to Saigon from Tay Ninh," I said proudly.

"They probably kept his ass here for more reasons than that. They needed every swingin' dick that could fire a rifle or thump-gun (M-79 grenade launcher) at that time," Top said.

"I first came in country during Tet," Mr. Edwards interjected. "What a nice welcome for a civilian job under a new job contract. Then in February of '69, the base came under siege again. That got pretty hairy, with gunships dropping flares all night long so our guys could see the gooks. But after a while, things simmered down around here, and it's not been so bad."

"That reminds me, Tom. Your brother's last tour was with the 25th Infantry up at Cu Chi in Tay Ninh Province. We all worked with a guy named Jim Royce, another NCO who served with Ron when they were both at the 25th a couple years ago. Royce and your brother were pretty tight. He 1049'd, I mean transferred, back up there to his old unit after Ron died. I'll bet he'd like to see you while you're in country. That is, of course, if you'd like to see him," Top said, with a slight bit of hesitation in his voice.

"Sure, I would like to meet him. Ron told me in one of his first letters when he got over here this time that he was working with an old buddy of his from the 25th," I said excitedly.

"Yeah, those two were good friends, drank a lot of beer together at the NCO Club," Osborne added.

"Okay, Tom, give me a day or two to put it together, and I'll see if I can't get you up to Cu Chi. It's not quite like here at Long Binh, though, is that okay with you?" Top asked.

"If you can arrange it, I'd like to go there to see Ron's old combat unit," I answered.

I knew what Top meant when he said Cu Chi wasn't like Long Binh. That area of South Vietnam, Tay Ninh Province, was known for a lot of heavy action all throughout the war. Ron had served a year and a half there, beginning in 1967, with a combat outfit, the 4th Battalion, 9th Infantry of the 25th Infantry Division, or "Tropic Lightning," as it was called. He proudly wore the division's patch on his right uniform sleeve. He sent me several pictures in and around the 25th Division's base camp at Cu Chi—those pictures looked more like the television news stories back home and less like Long Binh Post. He also received the Bronze Star Medal while serving with the 25th. Yes, I knew that Cu Chi was *not* the same as Long Binh.

After chow, Top, Osborne, and I walked back to Top's hootch to have a couple more cold beers for dessert. Seemed to me that drinking beer was the national pastime in the company area, at least at Long Binh. During the small talk in the mess hall, Top had mentioned he had been in the Army for nineteen years. I wondered how many beers he had consumed during that time period. Not that anybody was counting!

While working on my third beer in Top's hootch, I felt myself getting very drunk and very tired. However, the normally quiet Osborne was becoming more talkative. "Goddamned shame, that's what it is," he suddenly blurted out, startling me a bit.

"What's the fuckin' goddamned shame, Osborne?" Top asked.

"Here's this guy, Sergeant Reilly, on his second or third fuckin' tour here in Nam, and he died here in the company area. That just really sucks in my book! I mean, he goes through all the heavy shit up in Tay Ninh and lives through it just fine. Then he comes over here on a gravy assignment at this damn base—and buys the farm! Just doesn't make fuckin' sense, does it, Top?"

"Osborne," Top said with the voice of experience, "dead is dead. You think Tom here cares *how* his brother died over here? Shit no, he doesn't, all he knows is his brother came to Vietnam and came home in a fuckin' box.

"Let me tell you what does count though, and Tom, you listen up to what I'm gonna say. The only fuckin' thing that counts was how he lived. And I'm here to say to both of you, Sergeant Reilly was a stand-up guy. Everybody liked him, and I liked having him in this unit.

"We had a memorial service for him over at the chapel. Hell, it was fuckin' standing room only. That'll show you how well liked he was. Hell, probably nobody would show up for me if I bought the farm—'specially Osborne here. Ron was just good fuckin' people, end of story!" Having said that, Top raised his Budweiser in a toast and said, "Here's to Sergeant First Class Ron Reilly, good guy, and good fuckin' soldier!"

"Fuckin'-A, I'll drink to that!" proclaimed Osborne as he raised a new can of beer in answer to Top's toast.

"Thanks, Top, I'll drink to that, too," I said, feeling emotional from the effects of his brief eulogy and the beer.

"By the way, Top, does Tom know about Mai yet?" Osborne asked the first sergeant.

"We haven't talked about her, have we, Tom?" Top asked, turning directly to me.

"Who's Mai?" I asked, surprised at the mention of a new name.

"Well, Mai was a Viet civilian gal that used to work in the office here with Ron and Edwards. Cute little thing, maybe twenty-five years old. She was here before Ron got here in April, and well, you know, she took a liking to Ron, and the two of them started seeing each other for maybe a month or so before he died." Top explained.

"Yeah, that makes sense," I offered. "Ron mentioned in a letter that he was dating some civilian girl over here that lived in Saigon. Never told me her name, but that must be her."

In fact, this made a lot of sense to me. *Everywhere* Ron went, he had a girlfriend. He never married, saying he felt the military was no place for wives or kids, but it seemed he was never without female companionship wherever he was stationed. I think more than he realized, he used the military as an excuse not to settle down with one woman. I knew he had been deeply in love one time when he was younger. She was a blond from the Chicago suburbs. I always got the feeling she had broken his heart and he decided never again to get that emotionally involved with just one woman. So he played the field, usually dating just one girl near his duty station for several months or for the entire tour. But never anything lasting.

"Where is this Mai now?" I inquired.

"She doesn't work on base anymore," Osborne said. "Seems like she was pretty hooked on your brother, as they spent a lot time together in Saigon on their days off. Anyway, his dying was just too much for her. We thought she was gonna go off the deep end when we told her he was gone. She wouldn't believe it, so Top and Edwards took her over to Graves Registration the next day where they had Sergeant Reilly's body. She had to see for herself. Anyway, she took it pretty hard and quit the same day. Haven't heard from her since."

"Wow," was all I could say. "That's really sad."

All of a sudden I realized there was another person out there in this world, suffering the same dreadful grief that I was over losing Ron. Sure, I knew all these other guys liked Ron, he was a very likable guy; but here was someone special. And, according to Osborne, she loved him very much, even though she had only known him for a short time.

"Does anyone know how to contact her? There must be some paperwork on her if she worked here," I said.

"Oh, I know where she lives. I took Sergeant Reilly to her house and dropped him off there one time when I drove into Saigon by jeep," Osborne said matter-of-factly.

"You want to go see her or something?" Top asked, in a surprised tone.

"Yeah, maybe," I answered. "I mean, here's someone who really cared about him in his final days. Did she know he was having chest pains for a few days before he died?"

"Not really. Sergeant Reilly told me to have Edwards tell her he just had a touch of the flu and didn't want her to catch it from him. He didn't want her to know he was hurting at all," Osborne explained.

That sounded like Ron, I thought to myself. He didn't say anything to me either. "I was hoping maybe tomorrow morning I could go see the doctor that tried to save Ron over at the base hospital. But I'd sure like to try and find Mai, too, maybe tomorrow afternoon, if possible," I said in a way that sort of solicited help from my drinking companions.

"You think you could find Mai's place again in Saigon?" Top asked Osborne.

"I think I can, it's on the north side, at least." Osborne replied.

"We could probably do without you around here for a day. Take Tommy boy here over to the hospital tomorrow after breakfast, then take him to find Mai's house. Tell the motor pool you need a jeep to run down to Tan Son Nhut, or some bullshit like that," Top instructed Osborne.

"Roger that, Top," Osborne answered.

We all had one more beer, and it was sack time, especially for me. It had been quite a day.

Chapter 12

In Search of Mai

As with most people, beer always made me sleepy, so I was glad I'd had several Budweisers in Top's hootch. Without those brews, it would have been impossible for me to get any sleep that first night at Long Binh, being in Ron's former bunk. As it was, I kept waking up about every ninety minutes, fully aware of where I was attempting to sleep.

At one point, I even reached up and clicked on the reading lamp over the bunk. In my mind's eye, I could see Ron seated at the small desk next to the bunk, writing a letter, and, finishing it, putting it in a red-and-blue–edged airmail envelope.

In the distorted shadows of the dim lamp, I looked at the plain wall adjacent to the bunk. I could see the small nail hole where the picture of my sister and I used to hang. I wondered how many times Ron couldn't sleep in this bunk and turned on the lamp to get some comfort from his smiling siblings. I wondered how, in obvious pain and discomfort, he spent the last few nights of his life in that same room, trying to find some relief during his sleepless hours.

Like the proverbial moth to the flame, I was glad and relieved that I was here in this one particular speck on the globe, but oh, how much it hurt. But, just like seeing the steps where he died and retrieving the stones his head had lain on, being in his former bunk was worth all the hardships and frustrations I had encountered on my journey. This was what I had come for. And I knew at that precise moment I would never regret this journey for the rest of my life, no matter what the cost in current emotional pain. Being here brought me closer to Ron and helped me put closure to his unexpected death.

The reading lamp was still on when, through a fog, I heard knocking on the door and voices outside in the open bunk area. Opening the hootch door in shorts and T-shirt, I saw the face of the obviously hungover Osborne. Beyond him I could see some of the forty or so other GIs who slept in the open barracks bay, in various stages of getting dressed and ready for the day.

"It's 0600, Tom," Osborne said slowly, his voice half-muffled. "Top thought you might want to sleep in an extra half hour. You can meet us in the mess hall after you shit, shave, and shower," he added, the last four words spoken more as one.

"Ah, yeah, I'll meet you guys there in a little while," I answered, my mouth feeling like it was filled with dry peanut shucks.

I grabbed my shaving kit and left the hootch for the latrine. Most of the other guys didn't pay any attention to me, but a few of them, who were milling around their bunks, noticed me come out of Ron's old room. A couple made eye contact, with looks I interpreted to be genuine compassion; two or three nodded a greeting to me, which I returned. Apparently the rest of the guys in the company had been told the identity of this civilian who was staying in their barracks. Remembering what Top had said about Ron having been well liked, I felt as though I was being accepted because I was his brother. It was a nice feeling.

After completing the three Ss in the latrine that Osborne referred to, I went to meet Top and him for breakfast. Top was sitting at a table having a cup of coffee and a cigarette. Osborne was sitting at the same table, leaning his head on his arm, with only a glass of water in front of him.

I fell in line with some of the other guys from the unit. We shuffled along, holding our trays up for the servers to spoon out various breakfast foods. One of the servers I encountered asked if I wanted grits. I'd heard of grits before, but not knowing exactly what they were, I answered, "I'll try one."

The server, a short black guy, gave me a look like I just arrived from Pluto. "Smart-ass!" he muttered, putting a spoonful of what I thought looked like runny oatmeal on my tray. I knew, of course, that grits were part of Southern cuisine, I had just never come face-to-plate with this particular delicacy.

When I sat next to Top, he was alert and friendly as ever. Osborne, on the other hand, was still very hungover. I wasn't feeling so great myself, but thought a good breakfast, with or without grits, would help.

"Goddamned Osborne drinks *one six-pack* of beer, and he's shot for the whole next day," Top roared, slapping Osborne on the back. "How you doing today, Tom?" he asked me.

"I'm okay. I didn't drink as much as he did last night," I said gesturing towards the motionless Osborne.

I figured Top had been consuming a six-pack or more of beer nearly every night since before I was born and had probably built up a tolerance to any ill effects the next morning.

"Just as soon as Mr. Osborne, here, gets his wits back, he'll drive you over to the base hospital. The guy you want to meet with is Major Sanders—he's the doctor who was there when your brother was brought in. I'll call him and let him know to expect you later," Top said.

Osborne slowly got up to leave, saying I should meet him in front of my barracks in thirty minutes and he'd drive me over to the hospital.

"We got to get you out of those jeans and into some Army pants, you stand out too much. I'll get you an Army fatigue cap, too, so you can shit-can that *jarhead* one you've been wearing," Top said, referring to my rather unconventional wardrobe.

I gulped down the rest of my breakfast—except for the grits. To me they tasted like sawdust, and their consistency reminded me of a runny papier-mâché glue mixture. Maybe that's just how Army grits were; I vowed to myself to someday try *real* grits back in the World.

Top walked me over to a supply building, and after a good-natured love/hate conversation with the supply sergeant, an E-6, he got a pair of jungle fatigue pants and an Army baseball-style cap for me.

After changing into the new baggy pants and cap that matched the fatigue shirt I was already wearing, I had to admit I did blend in more. Unless someone had reason to look closely, they would not notice that my "uniform" was completely plain—no name, no unit, and no rank markings of any kind. It didn't even have the "U.S. Army" patch on it anywhere. Of course, it helped that all the servicemen in Vietnam who did wear such markings had them done in combat black and green, rather than in full color like back in the States. This was done because the colorful patches would stand out like a beacon in the jungle to the enemy.

When Osborne met me in front of the barracks, he agreed that from a distance, he couldn't tell me apart from the other soldiers. I thought it was a good idea to blend in more, but couldn't help thinking that I would also be considered a regular soldier by the enemy in the event of an attack. However, I figured the VC or NVA didn't really care if a target was GI or civilian, as long as he or she was an American. And, there was no mistaking an American, or at least a Westerner, from the locals in Southeast Asia.

Osborne said he was getting over his hangover, as he drove me over to the base hospital, which wasn't all that far from the company area. I asked him to take me the exact route he and the lieutenant took the day they drove there trying to revive Ron. Osborne said he wasn't sure because he was involved with CPR the whole way, but took me the shortest route, which he assumed the officer took.

I was amazed that we arrived at the hospital in only about three minutes, driving normal speed. Osborne probably thought it took them a half hour as he worked on Ron in the jeep's backseat. I didn't express this to him, though, because I knew it was still a sensitive subject. I was glad he and I had formed a kind of bond during the short time we had known each other. I think it helped him relinquish some of the unnecessary guilt he felt over the incident. I knew it helped my grief process, knowing that I was in the presence of the guy who tried so hard to save my brother, even if his efforts had been in vain. I also knew I could never thank him enough for trying to save Ron.

When we entered the hospital, he took me down a hall and introduced me to Major Sanders, who was doing paperwork in his small office. Osborne then said he would wait for me in the main lobby.

Major Sanders was a clean-cut man I guessed to be in his late thirties. It surprised me a bit that he was wearing a light khaki summer dress uniform. Every other American I had encountered in Vietnam wore olive drab jungle fatigues, with the exception of the civilian, Mr. Edwards.

When I entered his office, he stood up, and with a warm smile, extended his hand across the desk to shake mine. "Sergeant Olack called me about a half hour ago and told me you were coming over to see me. I must admit, Tom, this is a first for me. We don't get too many relatives dropping in here. Matter of fact, I'm sure you're the first, but I'm glad you came," he said cordially.

"Well, sir, I appreciate you taking the time to meet with me," I answered.

"Nice clothes, by the way," Major Sanders said, smiling. "Not exactly Army regulation, are they?"

"Well, sir, I'm not exactly Army, either. I thought I would blend in a little better over here if I looked more like other guys."

"Don't worry about it, Tom, I'm a doctor, not a line officer, nor would I want to be," said Sanders. "But you didn't come here to get a critique on your choice of clothes, did you?" he asked, growing more serious.

"No sir, I was hoping you could tell me more about my brother's death. That's why I came to Vietnam. I've already seen where he died, but I guess I'd like to hear what his medical condition was," I said, getting more serious myself.

"As you might expect, Tom, we get a lot of combat-type cases in here every week, not as many here as, say out in the other base camps, but we see our share when they get overloaded, or if the case is more unique. But, of course, your brother's situation was different. We just don't see thirty-two-year-old soldiers in seemingly good physical condition die of heart attacks. In fact, your brother was the first I'd seen in fourteen years of practicing medicine. It was really baffling to my colleagues and me.

"First, I want to reassure you that there was no way we could have revived him. And believe me, I'm not just saying that, either. The Spec-4 and lieutenant that brought him over here did a great job, because they were still administering CPR when our emergency staff took him from the jeep and placed him on a gurney. We had to pull the Spec-4 away just to check Sergeant Reilly's vital signs, the kid just wouldn't give up."

"I know, Specialist Osborne is taking it pretty bad," I said quietly.

"He was performing it correctly, too, from what I saw. But I knew your brother was DOA when I first saw him. The staff had the crash cart out and were shocking him, you know, with the paddles, to start his heart again. I know this sounds like a cliché, Tom, but we did everything we could, and kept trying for nearly another thirty minutes, but he was gone."

Cliché? It's a cliché when you hear that phrase on television, maybe, but it's no longer so when you hear "we did everything we could" *when it's about your own loved one,* I thought to myself.

"But I still don't understand why it happened. I'm satisfied with everybody's efforts to revive him, but why did it happen, do you have any ideas?" I asked, almost pleading for answers.

"Has anyone told you we performed an autopsy on your brother?" the major asked.

"I heard something about that from the escort sergeant," I replied.

"Well, we generally don't do autopsies over here. Unfortunately, it's all too obvious why the person is deceased. But in suspicious or unusual cases, the Army reserves the right to perform an autopsy, even without notifying the next of kin, which I presume is you, in this case." Major Sanders seemed to throw in that last part, just in case I objected to them doing an autopsy on Ron. I didn't.

"I'm glad you did it," I reassured the major. "Did it show why he died?"

"Yes, I think very clearly. I did the autopsy myself, along with a cardiologist, because we expected a problem with Sergeant Reilly's heart. He showed all the signs of a classic heart attack when we received him.

"The autopsy did, in fact, reveal some preexisting contributing factors. First, your brother suffered from severe atherosclerosis, a buildup of plaque in the coronary blood vessels around the heart. This condition is usually caused by poor diet, smoking, or family history. By the way, Tom, has anyone else in your family had any problems with heart disease or strokes that you know of?" Major Sanders asked.

There was that word *stroke* again. I hadn't heard it since my parents died a dozen years earlier! "Our mother and father died of strokes about a week apart several years ago," I answered.

"A week apart? How old were they when they died?" he asked, becoming even more interested.

"Our mother was forty-two, and our father was forty-nine."

"Christ, I'm sorry. But what we saw in your brother, and what you're telling me, lends credence to the hereditary theory," he said. "We also saw that your brother had high blood pressure and didn't seek any treatment for it, according to his medical records. I know that his appearance didn't fit the classic high blood pressure scenario, but it's not all that uncommon to *not* fit the physical profile."

Now, Ron's casual mention of high blood pressure and "getting it taken care of" on one of his Army physicals hit a nerve deep within me. Since his medical file didn't indicate any treatment, it meant he had "taken care of it" by either bribing or talking some orderly out of listing something on his fitness for combat exam. I wished he had taken his condition more seriously. Even more, I wished whoever discovered the situation wouldn't have given in to Ron's pressure.

"There's one more thing the autopsy revealed. This surprised both the cardiologist and me. Ron's heart did not resemble the heart of a guy in his early thirties. Rather, it looked to us more like it came from a seventy-year-old man. It had obviously been damaged at an early age and was forced to work much harder than would be indicated by his chronological age at the time of his death. Did he ever have, to your knowledge, any severe childhood diseases, like rheumatic fever, diphtheria, or such?"

"I was told he had rheumatic fever as a small boy and almost died from it," I quietly answered, not even sure what rheumatic fever was.

"Well, unfortunately, all that you're telling me fits. I don't know how the hell Sergeant Reilly ever got over here, but he never should have been in Vietnam, especially in combat. You see, take all of the internal conditions he had, and mix it with this type of harsh climate, and everything becomes aggravated, eventually resulting in tragedy. Your brother was a ticking time bomb, especially over here. Incidentally, because of your family history, Tom, I strongly suggest you get checked out with a thorough physical before you get much older," Major Sanders recommended.

My head was reeling with all the information he just told me, so I didn't want to inform him that I had just passed *my* Army entrance physical a couple weeks before—without bribes or other persuasion. "His unit told me Ron had come in for some chest X rays a few days before he died. Do you know anything about that?" I asked him.

"Yes, I heard about that later. There was some confusion about where his medical records were the day he died. Turns out the radiology department had the records and were going to contact his unit that same morning with the results. They said he wanted them to see if there was something wrong with his lungs, like tuberculosis. The pictures didn't reveal any form of TB, and sadly, the type of X rays used wouldn't have shown the atherosclerosis either. What Sergeant Reilly really needed was a whole battery of tests performed, but as you know, we obviously never got the chance," explained the major.

"Is there anything else you think I should know about why he died, doctor?" I asked.

"I think that pretty well sums it up. I submitted an autopsy report to his commanding officer. I'm surprised you, as next of kin, didn't get a letter from him explaining the cause of death. That would have saved you a long trip."

"For some reason, I never received anything but a telegram and a lot of Army people telling me they didn't have any details beyond him not dying from hostile action. I really appreciate your help. And besides, doc, I needed to come here to find out for myself, anyway," I told him.

"I understand," Major Sanders said, as he got up again to shake my hand and wish me good luck on my return trip.

I walked out of his office on my way to meet Osborne back in the hospital lobby where he said he would be waiting.

"Did you get the info you needed?" he asked.

"Yeah, thanks for bringing me over here," I said. "And, thanks again for trying to save Ron," I added, remembering what the doctor told me about Osborne's unrelenting CPR efforts.

Osborne became quiet for a second, then said we could go into Saigon right from the hospital if I still wanted to try to find Mai.

"That would be good, but first I have a favor to ask. Last night Top mentioned a chapel where a memorial service was held for Ron. Could we drive by there first? I'd like to see it."

"Sure, it's not out of the way," Osborne replied.

It turned out the chapel was just down from the hospital. How convenient, I thought.

The nondenominational chapel was a one-story wooden building with a peaked corrugated steel roof. The exterior walls were painted white, with dark brown trim. A small brown-and-white steeple sat on the roof's crown near the front. There was a small footbridge over a drainage ditch at the front entrance, leading up to a sidewalk lined by a short picket fence.

Knowing that Ron had not been a churchgoer, even though he believed in God, I imagined he probably never entered this building when he was alive. But it was very touching to me that the guys in his unit and the few civilians he worked with had held a special memorial service for him at this chapel.

Osborne parked in front of the chapel and told me that so many people attended the late afternoon service that several had to stand outside to listen.

"Just outside the front door there, next to the sidewalk, is where we stuck his M-16 upside down in the ground by the bayonet and put his helmet on the butt, while taps were played," Osborne said, pointing to a spot in the sandy dirt covered by sparse grass.

I thanked him again, and we did a U-turn in front of the chapel and began driving around the "doughnut" of Long Binh Post on the main streets.

I felt totally incognito, since I was wearing a complete fatigue outfit, albeit without insignia. I was also riding in a jeep from the unit's motor pool, driven by a guy from the unit who was authorized to use it. For the first time in a week, I felt almost "official," not like I was sneaking around. If it wasn't for the oppressive heat and the reason I was there, I might have been feeling pretty good.

On our way to the main gate, we passed that same dismal-looking place with the concertina wire and guard towers I thought might be the stockade. "Exactly what is that place, Osborne?" I asked, now sounding more like a tourist. "Is that the stockade?"

"That? That's a place nobody wants to visit. That's LBJ—Long Binh Jail, the main stockade in South Vietnam for MACV," Osborne said with an ominous tone.

"What kind of prisoners—U.S. or enemy?" I asked.

"Mostly U.S., but there are probably a few special gooks there, too. The MPs and *El Cid,* the Criminal Investigation Division, run that place. I guess it's mostly a holding place for the serious cases, you know like fraggers and guys who rape civilians—before they get sent back to Leavenworth. They also have a lot of deserters in there, too," Osborne explained.

"Fraggers—aren't those the guys that try to kill their own officers?" I asked.

"Yeah, they don't only try, sometimes they do. And sometimes the targets aren't just officers, but noncoms, too," Osborne continued. "Some guys say it's an overexaggeration about fragging, but my personal opinion is, there's a lot more of that shit happening out in the bush than gets reported. You gotta figure, about three-quarters of the guys don't want to be here in country anyway, and a lot don't want to be told to charge something of no value and maybe get themselves killed for nothing. I don't know what I'd do if I were out in the field, but I don't think I could frag one of our own guys, no matter how hairy the shit got," Osborne stated.

I didn't know how I would respond, either, if I were ever put in those circumstances; but like Osborne, I was sure I could never consider killing one of my own leaders. I knew Ron had seen action on his previous tours with the 25th Infantry Division, but he never talked about it. I knew he never would have reacted by doing anything that would put him in the stockade, fragging or otherwise.

By that time, we were clearing the sally port at Long Binh's main gate, and soon we were back on the main road to Saigon, which was only a few miles away. I was amazed at all the people and various types of vehicles on the road, both military and civilian. Some of the locals drove old cars or trucks of all sizes. Others were on assorted bicycles, mopeds, and other strange-looking three-wheeled vehicles. The people passed in both directions at varying speeds depending on their mode of transport. And surprisingly, none of the vehicles—large or small—seemed to interfere with the others, except for the occasional honking of horns.

It appeared that most of the Vietnamese civilians wore black or white clothing, or a combination of those colors. Occasionally a loud pink or yellow shirt stood out in the sea of black and white garments. I thought it odd that the machines being used for transportation were colored in dusty reds or blues, which contrasted to the austere black and white clothing of the drivers.

Back in the States the news always made mention that the VC wore black pajama-type clothing. From what I saw, nearly the entire population dressed like this, especially in the countryside outside Saigon. I wondered again how many of the people Osborne and I passed on that road, going about their daily activities, were actually the enemy. Everything seemed so peaceful, during the day.

We were soon entering the more built-up areas of Saigon. Three- and four-story apartment buildings along the tree-lined avenues were interspersed with blocks of stores and shops. Osborne, trying to remember the way to Mai's house, slowed down at nearly every intersection, trying to recall specific landmarks to guide him. As we drove deeper into the city, I saw far fewer U.S. military vehicles or American personnel on the streets. With just Osborne and me alone in the jeep, I felt much more conspicuous.

"I'm looking for a corner that has a big faded 'Canada Dry' sign on it, you know, the ginger ale drink. It'll be on the end of a building," Osborne said soliciting my help. "That's where we have to make a right turn off this street."

We drove through a couple more intersections, then he saw the sign before I did. "There's the Canada Dry sign! Okay, we make a right and go about four blocks back into these houses," Osborne said, somewhat relieved he was on course to Mai's house.

After we turned off the larger boulevard, the neighborhood got poorer very quickly. Replacing the taller apartment buildings were rows of mostly one- or two-story stucco houses, some in pastel colors, and all in varying degrees of decay. The farther we drove, the worse the small houses seemed to get.

Everything was dusty, even the naked or half-naked children playing in front of the shacks, or at the edge of the street. Old people and young mothers alike squatted in the open doorways of some of the residences, idly watching their children or grandchildren play.

Now I was really feeling conspicuous! Two Americans in an American Army jeep looked very much out of place in this neighborhood. It didn't seem to bother Osborne as much, because he had been here before to drop off Ron.

"You sure you have the right street?" I asked Osborne loud enough so only he could hear me over the jeep's motor.

"Pretty sure this is the right one. I know we turned at the Canada Dry sign when I brought Ron here. Should be a house with a yellowish front door just about . . . here!" Osborne exclaimed with an air of satisfaction.

I looked at the house. It was different from the rest of the houses on the same block, not only just because it had a pale yellow door. It was much nicer and in less need of repair than the neighboring houses. In fact, my thought was that it was kind of cute, relatively speaking.

Osborne parked the jeep in the street in front of the house, as there was no other traffic on the street. He stayed with the jeep, as I walked up to the front door, not really knowing what to expect, or even what I would say to Mai if she were home. I knew she at least spoke English, which was a requirement for her to work in an American office at Long Binh. She was obviously more educated than the barracks' cleaning women, who spoke only a few words of English.

I knocked on the door a few times and waited. No response. I knocked again, not wanting to make too much noise and be noticed by the neighbors—as if we weren't already. Still no answer. I got a little bolder, cupped my hands around my eyes, and looked through part of a window next to the door. The window had a valance at the top and a curtain covering the bottom half. There was a small, two-inch gap between the two that I could see through.

The house was empty inside, except for a few scraps of paper on the floor. It was obvious that nobody lived there anymore. Just then, over my shoulder, I heard voices. Turning around to leave, I saw an elderly Vietnamese woman speaking animatedly with Osborne in her native language. But, with her hand and arm gestures, I could see she was trying to tell him that the occupants had vacated the house. Osborne seemed to be getting the same message from the old woman's singsong voice and semaphored hand signals.

"Are you *sure* this is the right house?" I asked Osborne.

"Yeah, I'm sure, I definitely remember that yellow door and those curtains in the front window. It's also the best-looking house on the street, and I remember that, too," Osborne confirmed.

I went up to the old woman and asked, "Mai, Mai?" not even sure if I was pronouncing it correctly.

To my surprise, she smiled and answered me.

"Mai." She made more arm gestures, indicating going away, while repeating Mai's name along with other Vietnamese words. Unfortunately, Osborne only understood a few Vietnamese words in order to communicate with the cleaning women at Long Binh. This was far beyond his knowledge of the language, and I didn't understand anything except Mai's name. But it was obvious, from the neighbor lady's attempts to communicate and the empty house, that Ron's last girlfriend had, in fact, moved away. She could be *anywhere* in the country by this time. Perhaps she had gotten a job at another U.S. installation, or even in Saigon. The possibilities were endless.

I thanked the old woman as best as I could, and suggested to Osborne we head back to Long Binh, resigned to the fact I would not be able to find or talk to this mysterious girl named Mai.

"Well, I was glad to see she lived in one of the nicer houses on that street," I told Osborne, as we drove out of the neighborhood.

"That's because she was working for our government. That time I drove him over here, Sergeant Reilly told me she lived with her mother. Any of the locals who work for us have a pretty good standard of living, especially if it was just the two of them living there," Osborne explained.

I was somewhat disappointed to realize I would not get to meet Mai, but I also was relieved I wouldn't have to see her grief, coupled with mine. I did, however, feel satisfied that we had given it a try.

Osborne and I had an uneventful drive back to Long Binh. Because of my full fatigue uniform, we breezed right passed the MPs at the heavily guarded main gate. Osborne didn't even give my unauthorized presence a second thought; maybe he considered me a part of his unit.

When we got back to the company area, I located Top and told him about the day's events. He was interested in the conversation I had had with Major Sanders at the base hospital. He was also glad I got to see the chapel where Ron's memorial service had been held. He told me he was planning to take me there himself if Osborne hadn't done it. Top also expressed little surprise that Ron's girlfriend apparently had moved. The way he put it, she was "pretty shook up" over Ron's death.

Top also explained that while I was gone, he had had a chance to get in touch with Sergeant Royce, Ron's friend at the 25th Infantry Division. He told me Royce was very surprised to hear that I was in country and wanted to see me, if possible. Top told me Royce felt like he already knew me, because Ron had talked about me a lot while they served together at the 25th on their previous tours. Top mentioned that Royce said it would be difficult for him to leave his unit, as he had just gotten back from R&R in Thailand. But, if I was willing to come to Cu Chi, he would make time to "tip a few beers" with me. Top also told me that he and Royce had worked out a good plan to get me up to Tay Ninh Province the next morning. All I had to do was be ready to leave right after breakfast.

It was so much easier working with these guys than trying to do it on my own—especially these more senior NCOs who had been "around the block" a few times and knew how to skirt the Army regulations.

Chapter 13

Cu Chi—
The Reality
of War

I awoke the next morning again to the sounds of the other soldiers outside my private hootch. They were reluctantly getting ready for another day of work in Vietnam—another day they could check off on their countdown calendars until they could return to the World. This whole scenario of early morning rising rituals gave the place more of a college dorm atmosphere than that of an Army barracks in a war zone. Knowing that I would be en route to Cu Chi base camp after breakfast made me wonder if that place could also be likened to a college campus—something told me it wouldn't.

I met Osborne for breakfast in the mess hall. He explained that Top was putting the final touches on my transportation to the 25th Infantry at Cu Chi.

After breakfast, Top quickly walked over to meet us, a sneaky grin on his rugged face. "Well, Tommy boy, you still want to get up to Cu Chi and see what this war's all about?" he asked jovially.

"Yeah, I'd like to see if I can meet with Sergeant Royce, that is, if you've been able to arrange for me to get there," I answered.

"We don't have a lot of time, so I'll explain the plan as we go. Let's get up to your hootch, so you can get your shit packed and ready to go," Top said. Then he turned to Osborne and said, "Osborne go check out a jeep from the motor pool and meet us back here in ten minutes; hustle your ass now!

"Shit, Tom, wish I was goin' with ya," Top said, in a mood that was probably expressed by the majority of the older lifers, who felt they weren't doing their job unless they were in circumstances where they stood a good chance of getting their guts blown away. "All I have to do is get you down to Tan Son Nhut this morning, then you can catch a supply truck up to the 25th near Cu Chi. You can take the base bus down to Tan Son Nhut and be there in plenty of time for the supply transport."

"Sounds good, Top, I really appreciate it," I said trying to sound matter-of-fact. "How am I gonna get on the supply truck?"

"Easy. There's gonna be three or four deuce-and-a-halfs—you know, the big canopied trucks. Anyway, when they leave Tan Son Nhut there will be a divisional MP jeep in the lead, the three or four trucks, and a unit jeep following in the rear. I know the first sergeant over at your brother's old unit. He said he'd have the last truck and the rear guard jeep stop near the bus stop just outside of Tan Son Nhut's main gate long enough for you to jump in the back of the last truck. The guys from the 25th in the ass-end jeep will know about you, too. Hell, the only reason they're there is to prevent any gooks from jumping into the truck. Then it's about a forty-five-minute ride up Highway 1 to the 25th base camp near Cu Chi. Nothin' to it!"

Since Top Olack seemed to have it all worked out, there was nothing for me to do but agree with the plan. "Sure . . . sounds okay with me, if those guys are willing to give me a ride," I answered Top, who was still gloating for putting together such a clandestine plan.

"Good! I guaranfuckinteeya you'll be with your brother's old friend tonight; not that I'm trying to get rid of you, ya know."

"Nah, I know that, Top. I just really want to thank you for all your help," I said to reassure him that his conniving had not been in vain.

"Well, you'll thank me by gettin' your bag and your ass in Osborne's jeep outside and let him drive you to the main gate. Now, when you get to Tan Son Nhut, wait out by the bus stop for an MP jeep followed by three or four deuce-and-a-half trucks. The MP jeep will have '25-25' and some other numbers on the front bumper. The trucks will have '25-4BN9' stenciled on their front and rear bumpers. Just be sure you *only* get into one of the trucks with that unit designation. The '25' is for the 25th Infantry Division, and the other numbers are Royce's unit, 4th Battalion, 9th Infantry. You get in the wrong truck, and no tellin' where the fuck you'll end up in this goddamned shittin' country!"

"Thanks for all your help, Top," I said again while he was ushering me out of the barracks to where Osborne was waiting in the jeep just outside.

"You just remember to keep your ass and head down out there if the shit starts flying, or *you'll* be going home in a box, too," Top said, as he turned me over to Osborne and walked away, apparently not being one to stick around for long good-byes.

Osborne asked if I was ready, then ground the jeep into gear, and off we went to the main gate. Along the way, he went over the same information that Top had just given me regarding the unit markings of the vehicles I was supposed to watch for. It was a real comfort to know that both of these men had gone out of their way to help me, and that they were genuinely concerned for my safety. After all, they had only known me for two days. I saw firsthand how being in a combat zone can bring people closer together, which I thought was ironic, because the same war was dividing the entire population back home. But then, the people back home weren't here, where all that mattered to any American was ending a year's tour of duty with a beating heart and all of one's body parts.

Osborne drove in an obvious hurry, as we proceeded through the expansiveness of Long Binh Post. Soon we were passing Headquarters Hill and the abundantly fenced prisoner stockade. I saw why Osborne was in a hurry when we arrived at the main gate just as a dusty green Army bus pulled up to the bus stop. Osborne brought the jeep to an abrupt stop in a swirl of dust, jumped out, and ran over to the nearest MP. He quickly returned to the jeep and motioned for me to grab my bag. "That's your bus to Tan Son Nhut, better get on right now, because the next one won't be here for another hour."

I grabbed my rucksack, which was filled with my meager belongings, and hurriedly followed Osborne to the bus. When we got to the open passenger door, he stuck his head inside, and with a tone of real authority told the driver, "This is General Allbright's nephew. Make sure he gets off at the main gate to Tan Son Nhut, got it?"

The young driver—who had been half-slumped over the steering wheel, waiting for more passengers to arrive—suddenly righted himself in the seat, as if whoever General Allbright was might be entering the bus himself. "No problem, I'll make sure I see to it personally," the Spec-4 answered.

Osborne turned back to me, winked, and shook my hand, as I climbed up the bus steps past him. "I'm glad I got to meet you, even if it was only for a couple days. Good luck out there." Then he added with seriousness, "You be real careful out in the field. I've never been in the real shit, so I can't tell you what to expect or how to act. But if anything starts happening, just get down to the ground. It's not gonna help anything if you get zapped, too."

"Thanks, I really appreciate what you've done for me here. I wish you luck, too," I answered him, as the driver closed the door.

"Just take a seat anywhere, sir. I'll let you know where to get off," the driver said, with a professional politeness in his Tennessee drawl. I was, however, a bit uncomfortable with someone who was probably a year or two older than me referring to me as "sir." I was also amused by Osborne's little added twist stating that I was a general's nephew. What the hell, whatever worked!

The drive back to Saigon was uneventful and certainly not as exciting as when I first traveled to Long Binh from the city a few days earlier. Part of this had to do with traveling over familiar ground, but mostly with the fact that I was feeling a little more comfortable with the progress of my adventure. Anyway, a major part of my trip—the logistics of getting around— was now being ironed out, and that gave me a lot less to be concerned about.

After the bus made its routine stops in Saigon, we finally arrived at Tan Son Nhut Airbase. I recognized the main gate even before the bus driver informed me we were there. "This is the bus stop you need to be at, sir," he said, as I was exiting the vehicle.

"Thanks a lot, I'll be sure to tell my uncle, the general, how helpful you've been to me," I said in a snobby but friendly tone, continuing Osborne's charade.

"Gee, thanks a lot, sir!"

There were several American Army and Air Force servicemen, as well as a few Vietnamese civilians, waiting at the main entrance bus stop. I took up a casual position near the back of the group. The only officer I noticed was a young Air Force lieutenant who looked to be in his mid-twenties, and he didn't pay any more attention to me than the rest of the people there. They all were wearing their universal "bus stop expressions" anyway.

As I bided my time waiting for my "ride," I realized just how busy a place the big airbase was. There was a disjointed procession of both military and civilian vehicles entering and exiting all the while I waited. I wondered if the trucks in the small convoy from the 25th were actually inside, and if they were, how long it would be before they were loaded and came out, so I could hitch my prearranged ride.

After waiting in the heat for almost an hour, my eyes were getting tired from the strain of reading every vehicle bumper that exited the base, searching for one with the 25th's decals. My optimism remained high, because I had no reason to lose faith in Top Olack's well-laid plans. But, as Ron's favorite saying went: "There's the right way, the wrong way, and the Army way." According to that philosophy, I could be waiting at that bus stop for days!

Another hour passed. Everyone who was at the bus stop when I arrived had cycled through to their destinations, by getting on other buses, being picked up by jeeps, or being picked up by civilians, driving the indigenous two-, three-, or four-wheeled vehicles. New faces and ranks kept coming to the bus stop to replace those who left. But there always seemed to be about the same number of people waiting. After another hour went by, I considered myself the veteran of the bus stop. I found one of the only bits of shade just under the overhang of the roof, and whether it was psychological or not, I could have sworn it was a few degrees cooler in that spot—probably down to a balmy 105 degrees, or so.

Then, just as I started wondering if I had any salt tablets left to prevent dehydration, an MP jeep left the main gate, followed closely by a lumbering deuce-and-a-half grinding its gears. The white decal on the front bumper of the jeep was "25-25MP"; the decal on the truck was "25-4BN9"! These were the vehicles I was waiting for! At last! The next truck out of the gate also had the same unit marking on its front passenger side bumper. Then a third similar truck came through the gate, and I could see another jeep behind it, bringing up the rear, just as Top Olack had described. At least something in this seemingly screwed up war was going according to plan, albeit a little late.

The sight of those jeeps and trucks slowly coming out of the gate and making a right turn to pass in front of the bus stop was enough to stir me out of my boring and hot wait and into a renewed state of excitement. The front two vehicles slowed down almost to a stop just beyond my position, to allow the back three to catch up.

I grabbed my rucksack and casually started to walk towards the end of the convoy, hoping to make it look to anyone watching like I was going to cross the street between the last truck and the rear guard jeep when they stopped to regroup. As I reached the back of the third truck, I was able to make eye contact with the two GIs in the last jeep. The driver was busy leaning out looking to the front of the convoy. The other soldier stood up, looked over the windshield, and asked if I was "Reilly." I nodded my answer, too afraid to say anything or look in any direction but at him. He responded with a hand signal indicating that I should jump into the back of the truck just in front of his jeep. The truck was all but stopped at this point, so I immediately stepped close to the tailgate, threw my rucksack over it, and heard it land somewhere inside the canopied cargo bed. Then I realized that getting myself into the truck would not be so easy. The bottom of the tailgate was about even with my chest. I knew the driver had been instructed to slow down or stop to allow me to get in, but I knew he could not stop for long. I also knew he could not see me or judge my progress. Knowing all this, and not wanting to draw any unnecessary attention, I drew up all my heat-depleted strength, found a handhold, and pulled myself up and over the closed metal tailgate. The truck was about two-thirds full of cased supplies and a few vehicle parts, but the rear portion was free and clear for me to land in. With the little remaining strength I had, I pulled myself up and signaled the men in the rear jeep with the universal thumbs-up sign of success. Both the driver and passenger smiled, then looked at one another as if relieved that I made it. The passenger nodded back to me and motioned for me to keep down. The driver gave two quick honks of the horn, and my truck lunged forward into the street. By the whine of the heavy engine, I sensed that he was trying to make up lost distance between the lead vehicles and us.

As I settled into my newfound mode of transportation, I felt both relieved and physically exhausted from the exertion of climbing up into the truck. I laughed to myself about getting used to traveling clandestinely in the backs of trucks—this was the third one in the last week. First, there was the vegetable truck that got me from the Dusit Thani Hotel in Bangkok to the remote airstrip outside of town. Then there was the anxiety-filled ride under the tarp of the truck that got me across the Ho Chi Minh Trail and back into Saigon. And now this! I had to admit I felt a lot safer in the company of Americans, especially with 30-caliber machine guns mounted on both escort jeeps and the M-16s for the drivers and passengers. I also felt fairly safe being in the fourth vehicle from the front, just in case there were any mines along the way.

I knew we were driving on Highway 1, the main route between Saigon and the Province of Tay Ninh, of which the city of Cu Chi was the main population area. The highway was paved, making the ride fairly smooth. It would have been almost enjoyable except for the heat and diesel fumes flowing back over the top from the exhaust stack near the cab. I sat on a case of some unknown supplies that I repositioned on the floor. From this vantage point I could see out a short distance. Although there wasn't really a lot to see. The terrain was still flat in all directions that I could see. Small clumps of short trees and shrubs sprang from out of nowhere, many of them forming boundary lines for a field or rice paddy. Once we were in the open country, the traffic, once again, thinned out considerably. Occasionally we would pass pedestrians walking slowly along the shoulder of the highway, some carrying farm tools. I wondered if any of the people I was observing put their tools down at night and picked up rifles or rocket launchers to use against the same Americans that casually drove by them during the day.

Every once in a while the convoy would slow down to a near crawl to maneuver around some local traffic creeping along the highway. At one point we came to a complete stop for about five minutes. I peeked out over the tailgate in an attempt to determine the cause of the delay. I couldn't see any particular reason for stopping, but I did notice the two soldiers in the jeep behind me looked nervous as hell. The passenger soldier had moved out of his seat and into the back of the jeep, where he manned the mounted machine gun. The driver kept one hand on the steering wheel, clutching the front stock of his M-16 rifle with the other. They were both concentrating on something to the front and left of the column of vehicles and didn't notice me looking out the back of the truck.

Suddenly both servicemen relaxed; the driver put his rifle down between the two seats of the jeep, and the passenger returned to his seat. In a few seconds, the convoy started moving again, amid the sounds of grinding gears and accelerating engines. I hoped that I would be able to see what had been the cause of the delay, and increased my vigilance when we got farther up the road.

I kept peering out the back of the truck, and in about thirty seconds I saw what all the commotion was about. Off to the left side of the road, an old rusted Citroen car was tipped over on its side in a ditch. The windshield was riddled with bullet holes. One of the tires was smoldering, releasing a feather of black smoke skyward. A small group of Vietnamese civilians and two ARVN QCs were standing around near the back of the car in an uneven semicircle. By now we were picking up speed, but I caught a quick glimpse of a body sprawled on the grass beside the road. In the fleeting moment I had to take in the sight, all I could see was that the person, gender unknown, was dressed in the common black pajama-bottom pants and what appeared to be a white tunic. The reason I couldn't determine the victim's gender was because the upper torso and head was covered in blood, which glistened grotesquely in the sunlight.

I knew I had just witnessed the aftermath of violence caused by the war, and it made my knees weak. My senses told my brain I had just seen a dead casualty in vivid blood tones not more than twenty feet away. I tried to tell myself the poor soul could have been the victim of a car accident. Hell, even people in pastoral Wisconsin got killed in car accidents along the highway. But, something kept telling me that this was not caused by any kind of automobile accident. I remembered the bullet holes in the windshield. I assumed that our convoy had stopped just long enough for our MPs in the lead jeep to see if they could be of any assistance to their South Vietnamese counterparts.

We continued down the highway for about half an hour, and I couldn't get my mind off of what I had just witnessed. All of a sudden the appearance of tranquillity portrayed by Long Binh Post was gone. The sight of the bloodied corpse and the manning of weapons by the soldiers in the rear jeep made Long Binh seem farther away than the twenty or so actual miles it really was. I sensed I was getting closer by the minute to the war scenes shown on the nightly news back in the World. Even though that corpse was not an American, he or she had been a member of the human race.

Soon our convoy slowed down again, and I looked back at the rear guard jeep just in time to see the soldier riding shotgun signal me to get down out of sight. Since I didn't sense any alarm in his demeanor, I surmised this caution was more for my concealment than for my safety. I was correct. The convoy came to a stop before entering the main gate of the big base camp that housed the 25th Infantry Division. I felt relieved that we had made the trip from Tan Son Nhut with only the one incident, which had not directly involved us. My only concern was to make it onto the base without being detected and without my accomplices getting into trouble.

No problem. After the brief stop for the gate guards, our mini-convoy drove right in. I still kept down and out of sight, however, not forgetting my unauthorized presence. My curiosity compelled me to see what the base camp looked like, so when I guessed that we were well inside the compound, I raised up again to get a look.

I could only see where we had been, of course, because of my position in the back of the truck. I did see in the distance a rather formidable-looking perimeter, consisting of an earthen berm with copious quantities of concertina wire and sandbagged gun emplacements. The magnitude of the base was awesome. As far as I could see, row upon row of single-story large garrison tents, corrugated steel Quonset huts, and several wooden one-story buildings filled the landscape. All of the structures, even the tents, had three-foot or higher sandbag walls built just outside them. Many of the footpaths connecting the buildings were also lined with sandbags—at least waist high. My immediate thought was: How did they get all these sandbags in place? I remembered Ron saying that the 25th Division had come to South Vietnam in early 1966, so I figured the ten thousand or so men would have had time over the last few years to fill and place all the sandbags.

As we proceeded farther into the base camp, we passed a professionally lettered wooden sign which read "ALOHA—25th U.S. INF. DIV.—HAWAII'S OWN—Elevation 12 Meters." On both sides of the lettering was the unit's patch, a red taro leaf bordered in yellow, with a yellow lightning bolt in the middle. Ron had said he was proud to serve with the 25th, nicknamed "Tropic Lightning." He informed me the outfit had picked up numerous battle streamers in both World War II and Korea before being deployed to South Vietnam. I had also read in the papers, only a few months before, that several units of the division had been used in the push into Cambodia, which had ignited antiwar demonstrations on college campuses back in the States. This included the killings at Kent State as well as the riots that I had witnessed during my last semester at the University of Wisconsin–Madison. I found it eerily ironic that I had smelled the tear gas of those campus riots only a few months earlier, and now I was halfway around the world, in the middle of one of the main military units that had taken part in the operation that had incited the riots.

After negotiating a few turns down several different "streets," our convoy came to another stop. I looked out the back and watched the two soldiers get out of the jeep behind me. The passenger grabbed his M-16, stretched, and then walked up to the tailgate. The driver walked away, also carrying his weapon.

"Enjoy the ride?" the passenger asked, grinning at me.

"Yeah, it was okay," I smiled back. "I guess we're here, eh?"

"Yup, we're here. Home of the fightin' MANCHUS," the soldier said. "My partner went to find Sergeant Royce. He's the one who told us to get you here in one piece."

"Well, you did, and I really appreciate it, thanks! By the way, what was going on with that car on the side of the road?" I asked.

"Just some local official got himself blown away by Charlie this morning. Must have happened after we drove down to Tan Son Nhut earlier, 'cause it wasn't there when we came by the first time," he answered casually.

The GI seemed so nonchalant about the roadside episode that I decided I would only look greener if I pursued the topic any further. Seems like this sort of thing happened with enough regularity in Tay Ninh Province so as not to warrant much reaction on the part of the Americans serving there.

Just then, I noticed the jeep driver near the entrance to one of the barracks, standing near a tall, thin, older man in jungle fatigues and no service cap, and pointing towards me. The older guy seemed to dismiss the younger soldier and then began walking directly towards me, revealing a distinct limp that he tried to minimize with his authoritative gait. As he got closer, I could see that he was probably about thirty-five years old, with the leathery skin of someone who had spent much of his life in a tropical climate. His hair was salt and pepper and cut close to his scalp. He stopped about five feet in front of me and just stood for a moment, with his hands on his hips, staring at me.

"You Reilly?" he asked in a voice so gruff at first I thought he must have been kidding. But when I looked into his narrowed eyes, I realized he wasn't. He appeared to be a man who hadn't kidded anyone about anything since Eisenhower was in the White House. At least he wasn't an MP, and I could see the sergeant first class rank insignia on his uniform collars.

"Yes, I'm Tom Reilly, Sergeant Reilly's brother," I answered.

"Well, I'll be goddamned!" the sergeant said, a wide smile breaking across his iguana-hide face, as he reached for my hand. I shook his hand in return, and it occurred to me that all of Ron's friends had handshakes so firm it was like shaking a piece of machinery.

"I'm Royce. Welcome to the 25th Infantry Division, or, ah, at least a part of it anyway!" he boomed. "I see these guys gotcha here in one piece. I'll make sure you stay that way," he winked. "Jump down out of that truck."

"I'm glad to be here. Hope I'm not gonna get you in any trouble by sneaking on base," I said, voicing some concern.

"*Fuck no!* I doubt if anyone around here minds an American coming on base. It's the goddamned VC we don't like sneaking in. Of course, they normally announce themselves at the perimeter wire, if we're lucky," Royce said smiling. "Let me look at you, Tom," Ron's old friend said, stepping back a few feet. "I feel like I already know you through your brother. You know we spent our last tour together here at the 4/9th?

"I want you to know how bad I feel about him dying. He was good people, and I miss him. We did a lot of boozin' together, even took some R&R together down in Penang. He was a good guy. Hope you know, he thought the world of you, back in college and all," Royce continued.

"I know, he was a good guy, a great brother to have. Taught me a lot about the world. I guess that's why I came here. I wanted to know about the details of his death, see the place and all; but I really wanted to see more about his life over here, too."

"Well, I think he'd take it as a real tribute that you're here. Of course, he'd probably kick your ass if he knew beforehand you were planning on coming over here," the sergeant said.

We turned and started walking towards a barracks building, and I noticed the base camp had much more in the way of fortifications than Long Binh had. The sandbags lining nearby walkways and around the entrances to each building were much higher here. Also, there were many more sandbagged bunkers and trenches dug between the buildings. There was no vegetation visible at all—the entire area that could be seen within the huge base camp was flat and sandy. One thing similar to Long Binh Post was the droning *thud-thud-thudding* of Huey helicopters constantly flying nearby, although here it seemed like they were flying around the perimeter of the camp rather than over it like they did at Long Binh. I was sure the men stationed here were so used to the chopper rotors they didn't even hear them anymore.

I also noticed that the buildings themselves, whether barracks or service sheds, looked different than those at Long Binh. Here, they were sort of a brown and worn-out Army green, with a good covering of dust from the sandy soil on which they were built. One of the buildings, appearing to be some kind of utility structure, had one corner covered by a fairly new dark green tarpaulin. Around the edges of the tarp was evidence that some of the boards and metal roof had been burned. This damaged building was only about fifty feet from the barracks that Royce was leading me to.

"What happened over there, Sarge?" I asked.

"Oh, that? That's just a little greeting card we got from Charlie 'bout a week ago. Nobody got hurt though," Royce answered with perverted humor. "Now Tom, I want you to know that the accommodations here aren't gonna be like you had down at that 'country club' called Long Binh. And there's a better chance of things *goin' bump in the night* around here compared to Long Binh. But we'll talk about that later," Royce said as he led me into a one-story barracks that was heavily sandbagged outside. "Since I made platoon sergeant, I got my own private hootch up here in the front part. You'll be bunkin' in here with me, if that's okay," he said as we entered the building.

"That'll be fine, Sergeant, I wasn't expecting a room at the Holiday Inn," I assured him.

"Really? This used to be a Holiday Inn," Royce laughed, making me acutely aware that I had been wrong about him having shown no sense of humor since Eisenhower . . .

He opened an unfinished plywood door to his room, which, unlike Top Olack's at Long Binh, wasn't padlocked. Upon entering, I noticed that the room was smaller and even more Spartan than Olack's. There was no window, and sandbags were piled waist high inside two walls, which made up the corner of the building. The standard footlocker and wall locker were against another wall. In the corner nearest the door was an M-16 rifle, with a loaded magazine, a steel helmet, and two metal ammo boxes of "233 cal. ammunition," which was stenciled on the outside. Hanging on a large nail above the rifle and helmet was a green flak vest. I had not seen any of these in the barracks or hootches at Long Binh.

"Not much, but I call it home, and so will you while you're here," mused Royce.

As I surveyed the inside of the room, I saw only one place to sleep. "If you have a sleeping bag, I'll just curl up on the floor," I said trying to sound accommodating.

"Hell no, you won't! Top, First Sergeant Miller, that is, said he'd send over a cot for me later; you'll be sleeping in my bunk. Don't worry, it's no problem. And you can stay as long as you like.

"By the way, it's cool that you're here. Top Miller's a good guy. When I told him about your little visit here, he was pretty impressed. But he and I just don't want the officers to know about you being here. The CO would get his ass bent out of shape if he knew you were here. Our CO's a good officer, and we don't want to piss him off. But don't worry, he never comes around the barracks. The only brass to come around here sometimes is the platoon lieutenant; his name is Jacobs. You can't miss him—he's got curly red hair and looks like he's about twelve fuckin' years old! Don't worry about him, either; on the remote possibility he finds out you're here, me and Top will smooth it over. See, he's a draftee who got into OCS. He doesn't want to be over here anyway, he thought he was going to Germany, but got the shit surprised out of him. Top and I told him we'd protect him until his DEROS (date of estimated rotation from overseas) back to the States in a couple months."

"That's all pretty good to know," I said. Just like Ron always said, the NCOs really run things in the Army at the local unit level.

"Top told me at chow this morning he'd send over a steel pot and flak jacket for you in case we get any incoming while you're here," Royce said nonchalantly.

"Do you get much *incoming* here?" I asked, with both excitement and fear.

"Not a lot. Charlie kinda goes in streaks. Sometimes we go a couple months with nothing; then we'll get a few mortars and rockets a couple nights apart. You can't figure out Victor Charlie. What we get around this part of the base is mostly harassment fire. That's because we're fairly close to the perimeter, I guess. The VC sneak up to the edge of no-man's-land outside the wire and see us through their binoculars during the day. But sometimes, the middle of the base gets hit, too. Like I said, hard to try to guess what Charlie's thinking," Royce explained.

Sergeant Royce then went out for a few minutes and returned with two cans of Budweiser, apparently the drink of choice for NCOs in South Vietnam, or perhaps the only beer available by contract to the government.

For the next couple of hours we talked about a topic we had in common—my brother. Seemed like Ron and Sergeant Royce not only were good friends, but also respected each other. Royce, like Ron, seemed to be a man who didn't need a lot of friends around him; one or two drinking buddies were sufficient.

He explained how he had met Ron when he first arrived at the 25th Division in 1967. They were assigned to the same company a few weeks apart, and as new guys with similar personalities, gravitated towards each other. They had spent nearly that whole year's tour of duty and their voluntary six-month extensions together, and then kept in touch after rotating to new assignments in the States. Ron went to Fort Hood, Texas, and Royce was assigned to Fort Ord, California. Both disliked Stateside duty and wanted to return to Vietnam as soon as possible. As with Ron, Royce's motivation to get back to the war was not patriotic. He wanted back for the benefits. Ron had explained to me once, and Royce confirmed it, that each time an NCO went back to Vietnam, he would usually be in good standing for another stripe promotion. Also, the pay was tax-free, and each serviceman got an extra amount of pay each month for "hazardous duty" while in Vietnam. However, I also knew, the more I listened to Royce, that he, again like Ron, felt that a war zone was where a career soldier belonged.

Ron had even told Sergeant Royce about me writing to Senator Proxmire of Wisconsin on his behalf, hoping to speed up the orders that would get him back to duty in Vietnam. Royce couldn't believe this scheme had gotten results and said he was in the middle of trying to find someone in his home state of California to write a letter to his senator, when he got his orders to return to the war zone as well.

Royce continued his reminiscing about his time with Ron, talking about an R&R they once spent together—with plenty of local female company—in Penang, Malaysia. He even showed me a black-and-white photo of Ron kneeling in a Buddhist Temple, being blessed by a priest. I told him the same photo had been sent to me along with Ron's personal effects. I'd wondered who had taken the picture. Royce said that had been a great week—two NCOs running around in civilian clothes, just like tourists. Royce said they rode in rickshas, fed wild monkeys, and screwed their heads off with the local women the entire week before returning to Vietnam.

I told Royce that Ron had called me collect at my apartment in Ripon from Penang on my birthday that year. I added I didn't even know where Penang was until Ron explained he was on R&R in Malaysia with a buddy of his. I assured Royce that Ron sounded like he was having a great time, too. I remembered that call because it had made my whole week for me!

As we were ending our discussion about Penang, we heard someone knock loudly on the closed hootch door. Royce got off the end of his bunk where he had been sitting, opened the door a few inches, and looked out. I could only see the muzzle of an Army .45-caliber pistol pressed through the cracked door to Royce's forehead.

"You sonofabitch!" Royce exclaimed, opening the door all the way.

Outside stood a huge man who looked like he was in his late forties. He was dressed in fatigues, which bore the unmistakable rank insignia of chevrons, rockers, and a diamond, indicating that he was a company first sergeant. His face and arms were dark tan, and his head was nearly shaved. The man lowered his pistol and held out a steel helmet and flak vest in his other burly hand. "You must be young Reilly," he bellowed as he stepped inside the now very crowded hootch.

"Yes, First Sergeant, I am," I said.

"Well, I'm Miller, and I brought you some welcoming presents, here," he said tossing the helmet and body armor on the bunk. "I told that pansy-assed Top Olack over at the 'country club' we'd take care of you, and god-damn it, we will!" he proclaimed. "And if Royce and I can't, maybe this shit will."

"Thanks, sir," I said, immediately realizing my mistake in calling him "sir" rather than "sergeant."

"Don't call me *sir!*" he growled, good-naturedly.

"I know, I know. You're a sergeant, and sergeants work for a living," I said, backpeddling, recalling the NCO's mantra I had heard several times from Ron.

"So, how long you plan on staying in our little piece of heaven?" Top Miller asked, now holding the .45 pistol down at his side, muzzle pointing towards the floor.

"Not long, just a day or two."

"Well, you stay as long as Royce and I can keep you away from the brass. You're welcome in my unit. I didn't know your brother, but Royce here says he was okay. That's good enough for me. I'll be sending a cot over here later. Make sure Royce sleeps on it—you take the bunk, okay?" the first sergeant said, turning to leave.

"Ah, Top?" Royce said while pointing to the pistol.

"Oh yeah, almost forgot," Top said, removing the magazine from the gun, checking the chamber by pulling back the slide, and handing the weapon to Royce.

"See ya later, Top, and thanks for the help," Royce said, calling after the gruff, older first sergeant. "Have you ever fired one of these?" he asked me, holding up the pistol.

"Not a .45, but I have a semiautomatic .22-caliber pistol at home. I load it with a magazine like that one," I replied.

"Top and I thought it would be good for you to sleep with it at night. Also, keep the steel pot and flak vest handy. Remember where they are when you go to sleep. Just precautionary, that's all. In case we get an unscheduled wake-up call from fuckin' Charlie. You hungry?" Royce asked, abruptly changing the subject.

"I could eat something."

"Let's hit the mess hall for some early evening chow before it gets too busy."

With that, Royce and I left his hootch and walked to the nearby mess hall via a sandbag-lined path. Another similar path led in a different direction, to a building Sergeant Royce said was the latrine.

The outside of the mess hall was heavily sandbagged, even more so than the barracks. I guessed the VC knew this structure could have more than a hundred Americans in it at certain times of the day. Because of this, the main entrance was also sandbagged nearly to the roof on both sides of the door. Two large, dug-out bunkers were located one each a few yards outside the front and the rear of the building. All of these fortifications created a nice illusion of dining in safety—that is, if you could call eating in any mess hall *dining*.

Inside, the place was empty except for two bored-looking GIs who were drinking coffee and smoking at a corner table. The servers behind the chow line looked equally bored, as they set out large stainless steel troughs of food for the evening meal. Here, the servers wore regular fatigues, and few had on white chef's hats. At Long Binh, they all wore white uniforms and chef's hats.

The interior of this mess hall was also different from the one at Long Binh. This one seemed much more rustic and devoid of any of the little extra trappings that were visible in Long Binh. The only thing interrupting the drab interior decor was a large, red-and-yellow 25th Infantry insignia on the main wall, accompanied by an equally sized battalion crest for the 4th Battalion/9th Infantry. I reckoned it was good for a soldier to know what unit mess hall he was eating in!

As Royce and I made our sideways shuffle along the food line, one of the servers, a black Spec-5, started grumbling to Royce that we were too early.

"Just quit your godammned bitchin', Luther," Royce snarled back good-naturedly. "And where's the fuckin' rainbow Jell-O you said you'd get me?"

"Someday, someday. We'll make a 55-gallon drum of it just for your lily-white ass!" Luther said indignantly, trying not to smile.

"Sure, sure, someday. Don't forget what I do for a living. Someday I may get this lily-white ass blown off out in the boonies, then you'll miss me!" Royce responded in a way that indicated he'd been carrying on like this with Luther his entire tour.

Sergeant Royce just didn't look to me like a rainbow Jell-O type of guy.

During our meal, which I must admit was pretty good, I asked Sergeant Royce where everyone in the company was. I said I hadn't seen anyone in the company area, except for him, Top Miller, and a few other guys.

"Most of our company is out in the boonies with Bravo and Delta companies for the next five days or so, depending on what they run into. The 'black boxes'—sensors we set up last month—indicated some gook activity the brass apparently hadn't planned on so soon after we went into Cambodia. So about half the battalion is out beatin' the bush and playing hide-and-seek with Charlie."

"How come you and Top Miller didn't go out with them?" I asked Royce carefully, so as not to insult him.

"Hell, some of us have to stay behind to man the store," he said smiling. "Fact is, the guys left real early this morning, and I knew yesterday you were coming, so Top gave me a little slack time. Besides, since I 1049'd in here a few months ago from Long Binh, we have two E-7s in the platoon. Nobody at battalion admin noticed till after I was here. So me and Sergeant Malaskey, the other E-7, sort of switch off with each other for poundin' the bush. Besides, I'm shorter than he is, so I said I needed to stay in this time. He'll still be in country another four months or so after I've DEROS'd my ass back to the World."

Seemed like a good explanation to me. After chow, we walked back over to Royce's barracks. When we got there, we found a folded canvas and wood-framed cot leaning up against his hootch door.

"Top always comes through," Royce grinned.

Royce walked me through the barracks, which was situated as an open bay of bunks with their associated lockers nearby. One other private room was at the far end of the open bay, similar to the barracks at Long Binh. However, the group living area seemed to be less organized and had a lot more personal photos and foldouts near most of the bunks compared to Long Binh.

Towards the far end, three soldiers lounged on their bunks conversing, while Santana played on a nearby radio. Only one was wearing a full fatigue uniform, but without his cap. The other two wore various pieces of Army clothing—one just green Army-issue boxer shorts and a matching T-shirt. The third guy wore a black Led Zeppelin T-shirt under his open fatigue shirt and an orange bandana tied around his forehead as a headband.

As we approached them, they showed little interest in Royce or me, except Mr. Headband, who called out to Royce. "What you got there, Sarge, another FNG for us? Better tell him he missed his chopper ride to the boonies this morning."

"Shut up, Wilson. This isn't any FNG, he's the brother of a friend of mine from a past life. He's not even in the fuckin' Army, so I guess that means he outranks a pothead like you!"

This comment got a stare from the three, but little else. They weren't very interested, and Royce apparently deemed them not worthy of a long explanation.

As Royce and I walked back towards his hootch, he explained the three guys were all "short-timers," all having less than thirty days left on their tours in Vietnam. Each unit would leave behind a skeleton crew to guard the barracks area when the company deployed to the field. If at all possible, they would pick some of the short-timers for that purpose.

"Sarge, what's an FNG?" I asked, as he ended his explanation of the three soldiers.

"Fuckin' New Guy," laughed Royce.

We went back to Royce's hootch, set up the cot, and with a small amount of effort, rearranged the hootch to accommodate both of us for the night.

Later on, we hung around outside the barracks reminiscing about Ron. When the sun disappeared below the horizon, the sky looked like a Maxfield Parrish painting, with pastel oranges and blues blending together. In the midst of the colors, tiny black specks began appearing just above the horizon, in the early evening sky. First, there were just a couple of dots, then more; and then I heard the unmistakable sound of Hueys.

"That'll be the aviation battalion bringing in some 'ground-pounders' from the bush," Royce said casually, with what sounded like a hint of pride.

"Is that your unit returning already?" I asked, hoping to see several companies land right in front of me.

"No, judging by where the Hueys are taking them, that's probably part of the 23rd Infantry, the 'Tomahawks,'" Royce said, as we watched the Hueys emerge out of the sunset then drop down just out of view inside the base camp's perimeter. It looked like they landed about a half mile from our position.

Only a few seconds after the last chopper was down and out of sight, there was a tremendous, uneven roar of gunfire that seemed to come from the perimeter in the area where the Hueys had just landed. Phosphorus flares could be seen relighting the darkening horizon. I couldn't believe what I was hearing! I jumped and shot a surprised look at Sergeant Royce, who seemed unconcerned.

When he saw my confused reaction to what was happening, he just smiled and indicated there was nothing to worry about. "That's just the perimeter boys doing their version of a 'mad minute.' The guys in the perimeter bunkers lay down about a solid minute of rifle and machine gun fire at the woods and fields just outside their kill zones. If Charlie was planning a surprise for the guys coming home after a mission, it makes him think twice about it. Also, it lets our guys on the perimeter have a little fun and let off some steam. Sure as hell wastes a lot of taxpayer's money, but we don't worry about that over here," Royce explained.

By the time he finished talking about it, the gunfire had stopped. There was no mistaking that I was in a *real* combat zone, even though none of that gunfire had been directed at actual enemy targets.

Royce and I went back into his hootch, where he said he had some more pictures of Ron to show me from their R&R in Malaysia. He removed a small Sanyo radio box from his footlocker. When he opened it, I could see it obviously contained personal items such as letters and photos. Ron had also had a similar-size box among his personal effects that contained the same type of things. I couldn't help but be amused about the fact that these senior NCOs could fit their entire life's private belongings into a container not much larger than a cigar box. At least the tangible things could be stored in such a container; the memories and experiences these guys had were enough to fill several lifetimes.

He showed me pictures of him and Ron in hired rickshas, another picture with a group of local children, and yet one more of Ron in civilian clothes hand-feeding a monkey in the middle of a small road. I knew Ron had a soft spot for children, but I didn't think he liked animals all that much!

BOOM! BOOM!

Thundering sounds came from just outside the barracks, shattering the peace of the moment. Royce's hootch shook with each explosion. An empty beer can jostled and fell from a sandbag where it had been sitting.

BOOM! BOOM! BOOM!

"*Shit! That's not ours!*" Royce screamed at me, already grabbing for his helmet and flak vest. He frantically reached across the small room and literally threw the other steel pot and vest to me. "Put that on and let's get the fuck outta here!" he yelled as he picked up the .45-caliber pistol Top had brought to his hootch. "Here, just in case," he hollered at me, shoving the magazine into the handle of the weapon. "Don't forget to chamber the first round!"

Grabbing his M-16 rifle and a metal box of ammo, he screamed for me to follow him.

BOOM!

I heard another as we ran out the barracks door. Out of the corner of my eye, I glimpsed the visual effects of the last explosion. It was nearby, although, just how close was hard to estimate, because the whitish, yellow flash made the surrounding area look pitch black. Huge sparks cascaded up and out in dozens of arches, which all happened in less than a second.

Aside from seeing the last explosion, all I could comprehend was that I was running behind Sergeant Royce, my pulse slamming inside my eardrums.

"*DOWN!*" screamed Royce from in front of me. His scream coincided with a distinctive hissing sound that came from behind and above us.

I hit the dusty ground hard, my flak vest, which was only slung over my right shoulder, came down hard and heavy between my shoulder blades. The front lip of my helmet caught the ground and started rolling off my head. Like a madman, I grabbed forward to retrieve the steel pot and pulled it back on to protect my head.

B-O-O-M!

The next explosion was even louder than the others. This time I felt the sandy ground shake from the concussion of the exploding shell. White light momentarily invaded the inside of my dark helmet sanctuary, that was now half-cocked over my head.

"You okay?" I recognized Royce's voice yelling back at me.

"Yeah!" I answered him.

"Come on!" he ordered.

I could feel him yanking on the shoulder of my flak vest, pulling me forward. His strong grasp kept me from getting up to run. Half-crawling on my knees, and half-pulled by Sergeant Royce, I sort of rolled into a sandbagged bunker. I had no idea where the bunker was located. I just knew I was down inside it, a couple of feet below ground level. I maneuvered my body into position against the interior of the bunker. My face was as close to the earthen wall as the lip of my helmet would allow. I could smell the sand mixed with the unmistakable aroma of cordite wafting into the bunker from the nearby explosion.

More hissing sounds, each followed by a loud boom, although not as close as the one I had heard out in the open before I got inside the bunker.

Then, just as suddenly as the attack had begun, it was quiet again. Quiet, that is, except for the wild pounding of my heart and the sound of sweat beads dropping from my forehead and crashing onto my cheekbones. The fear I felt was incredible and overpowering! It heightened my senses of the immediate area, at the same time, blurring everything just outside the bunker.

"You okay, Tom?" Royce asked from a few feet away, as I was now comprehending my location inside the bunker.

"I . . . ah . . . I'm fine, Sarge," I tried reassuring him, even though I wasn't sure if my words were even coherent.

"Good, let's just sit here for a minute to see if Charlie is up to anything else tonight," he said peering through one of the bunker's gun ports. "You still toting that .45?"

"Yeah."

"Well, chamber a round and make sure the safety is on. Let's just wait," Royce said, pulling back the bolt on his M-16.

Jesus Christ, I thought, as another sharp blade of fear sliced through me. *Did he mean a* ground attack *might be next? I mean, mortars or rockets I knew could be deadly, but* real *enemy soldiers attacking?* That was something else—almost too real for me to imagine! Hopefully this was just Sergeant Royce's experienced caution at work. "You really think they'll attack?" I asked Royce, remembering there weren't many guys around our particular barracks area due to the field assignment.

"You never know with Charlie. Usually they just shoot off a few mortars to let us know they don't enjoy us being here. Sometimes they back it up with a ground attack, if they think they can breach the perimeter."

Just as he was saying that, we heard the staccato sounds of automatic rifle fire coming from the closest part of the base perimeter, perhaps a hundred yards and a few buildings away from us. All of a sudden a roar of other automatic gunfire erupted from the same area.

I pulled myself up to look out one of the other gun ports of our bunker and saw several white phosphorus flares in the sky just outside where I imagined the main fence line fortifications were. The heavy thudding of Huey helicopters flying over us vibrated the dust from between the sandbags inside the bunker. I watched as the choppers flew in a loose zigzag pattern over the area lit up by the flares. First one, then another, dropped their noses down and fired several rockets into an area well outside the base camp perimeter.

"Perimeter boys must have seen something out there, or at least *thought* they saw something," Royce said with a wary grin.

After firing several rockets each, the Hueys banked to the right and looked like they were making a large arc back to inside the base. The small-arms fire ceased at the fence. Less than a minute later, I heard a clickety-clackety sound accompanied by a whooshing noise, coming from high in the sky to our left. Enormous explosions could be heard in the distance outside the perimeter.

"That'll be our arty giving some insurance rounds to the area where they thought the mortars came from," Royce said, referring to the artillery fire. He still looked out the gun port in front of him, but seemed more relaxed now, which helped me to calm down a little bit, too.

"You think they'll still attack?" I asked, with a nervous concern, greatly contrasting the deadly fear I had felt a few minutes earlier.

"Nah, they just wanted to harass us. Maybe they just felt like making Uncle Sam spend a quarter-million bucks on them tonight," he grinned again. "Let's go see if any damage was done," Royce said, motioning for me to follow him out of the bunker, wobbly legs and all.

Upon exiting, I noticed the bunker entrance was only about fifteen feet outside the front door of the barracks. We had "hit the dirt" about halfway from the barracks to the bunker, or at about eight feet. I could have sworn I was running behind Sergeant Royce for the length of a football field. Strange how sheer panic affects one's senses and perceptions.

Royce and I slowly walked around to the rear of the barracks, where there were two more bunkers similar to the one he and I had taken cover in. My legs were still shaking as we rounded the building.

"Wilson? Alphabet? Where are you guys?" Royce began softly calling with concern, as we neared the fortifications.

"We're here, Sarge, we're okay."

Three silhouettes emerged from one end of a bunker closest to us. I knew "Alphabet" was the nickname given to any young soldier who had a name too complicated for the older NCOs to pronounce.

"Fuck, Sarge! I don't *need* this fuckin' shit! I'm down to twenty-two days and a wake-up! I just don't need this shit!" Wilson grumbled, looking around to see how close he had come to going home dead or wounded.

"Relax, Wilson, Charlie doesn't want your sorry ass!" proclaimed Sergeant Royce.

Alphabet and the other GI just stood looking around with their hands on their hips. Alphabet was wearing one flak vest and holding another. Apparently one couldn't be *too* safe when one was a short-timer. I'm sure both these guys were thinking the same thing Wilson was openly grumbling about.

Everything was quiet again, except for several soldiers, who came into our barracks area from other places deeper within the base camp, obviously also curious about any damage or casualties.

Sergeant Royce began walking away in the open area around the barracks, as if looking for something. "Hey, Tom, come over here," he yelled to me from several yards away.

When I walked over to him, he pointed to the ground. In the semidarkness, I could see a shallow crater, still smoking a bit. The crater itself was maybe four feet across, with ragged edges. Around the outside were piles of sand and bits of metal that were shining in the minimal light—up to about twenty feet away in most directions.

"This is the one that landed closest to us, you know, the one that hit before we made it to the bunker," Royce said.

"Yeah, I'll never forget that one," I answered, unnerved by the closeness.

Then Royce backed up to the edge of the crater and started pacing out a straight line towards the bunker we had been in. "About forty-two meters," he declared, as he ended his pacing at the spot we had hit the ground.

"Well out of its effective kill range, but close enough to hug the ground over," the experienced NCO said, slapping me on the back. "Let's get a beer, the excitement's over for the night!"

My heart rate was returning to normal, and I followed him back inside the barracks. Once in his hootch, I took off the helmet and flak vest, stowing them neatly at the end of the bunk where I knew I could find them again, if needed. I also made sure the safety was on and placed the .45 on the floor under the bunk, where my head would be later on that night.

There was no question in my mind about what precise part of the world I would be sleeping in that night!

Chapter 14

An Unauthorized Patient

I slept like a baby that night—and not because Royce's bunk was all that comfortable. Experiencing the fear of the mortar attack made me feel like I weighed three hundred pounds—at least fifty pounds of it being my eyelids. Maybe the physical drain was just the body's way of helping the mind block out the whole episode. Whatever it was, I had gone to sleep as soon as my head hit the thin pillow, and I wasn't cognizant of anything until I heard Sergeant Royce stirring in the hootch early the next morning.

He was coming back from the latrine, with a green towel draped over one shoulder and his shaving kit under his arm. When the door opened, I could tell it was already light outside. The daylight was reassurance that the fearsome activities of the previous night were indeed in the past. His shaving kit signified a comforting return to normality.

"Good morning," Royce said, when he saw I was beginning to return to the world of consciousness.

"Morning," I groggily returned his greeting.

"Just saw Top over at the latrine. Said he'd be over with some coffee for you in a little while. I already told him you're okay, but he wants to make sure for himself, after our little episode of fireworks last night."

Not really wanting to be too far away from Royce, I hurriedly shaved and showered and returned to the barracks. Top Miller had just joined Royce in his hootch with a thermos of coffee and a couple of extra cups. Soon the small living quarters was filled with the smells of black coffee and cigarette smoke. Top chain-smoked unfiltered Camels, of course.

"Well, Tommy, how'd you like the welcome Charlie decided to give you last night?" Top asked jovially.

"Well, it certainly was different," I answered.

"The good thing was nobody got hurt, and they didn't hit a fuckin' thing in the company area. Saved me a lot of goddamned paperwork!"

"Did you get a report yet from our guys in the field?" Royce asked.

"Yeah, not much happened yesterday. Based on intel they were ready for a hot LZ (landing zone), but it wasn't. Second platoon thought they saw something and opened up, but couldn't find any blood trails or weapons. Shit, Alvarez is insisting he was grazed by a bullet and wants a Purple Heart, but he's not gettin' one. Bastard probably got scratched by a branch when he dove for cover. In my book, that's not worth a PH. So, end of the first day, no body count—them or us."

"So, Tom, I hear you're a college boy, eh?" Top asked, turning to me and changing the subject.

"I was, up until a few months ago."

"Were you one of those long-haired, hippie-pinko bastards back there demonstrating against us baby killers over here?" Top asked me, grinning.

"No, I wasn't."

"Didn't think so, or you wouldn't be here now," Top said approvingly.

"Actually, I'm not going back to college right away. I already enlisted in the Army before coming over here. I'll report for basic training in October." I decided to tell Top and Royce my plans, probably to gain a little more respect from them while I was in *their* world.

"*Jesus H. Christ!*" Top bellowed. "If that doesn't beat all! You got shit for brains, son?"

Sergeant Royce stopped pouring a warm-up cup of coffee and just stared at me. "You know your brother was proud of you going to college, Tom," he said, sounding a bit disappointed.

"I know, I know—but college is different all of a sudden, and Ron's death . . . well, I just couldn't go back right away. I'll finish someday, I know I will. I'll get my degree for Ron someday."

"So you went in on the Delayed Entry Program they got now?" Top asked.

"Yeah, I have ninety days to report."

"Did you get to sign up for an MOS—a job?" Top asked.

"Yeah, I'm guaranteed to be a military policeman."

"An MP?" Top thought for a moment. "That's a hell of a lot better than being '11 Bravo.' You don't want to be no ground-pounder like us."

"You know, with your brother dying over here, you don't have to come to Nam. Make sure you go to Germany or stay Stateside. Okinawa or Subic Bay isn't bad, either. Just don't volunteer to come over here," Royce advised.

"Your brother would probably come back and kick you in the ass if you volunteered to come back over here," Top Miller chimed in.

"Don't worry. I'm leaning more towards going to Germany for a couple of years. The MPs do more city-type police work there than the combat MPs here. That would train me more for a civilian law enforcement job if I didn't stay in the Army," I said.

"Do your time in the service, learn a good job, maybe even get a few more college credits, but then get the hell out," Royce said, almost pleadingly.

"It's okay, guys," I said more adamantly, hoping to change the subject. "I'll go in, get out, and finish college just like Ron wanted me to do."

"Good! That's settled!" Top said. "I'm gonna drag my ass back over to HQ and do some paperwork. You guys have fun today—no matter what the fuck you're planning to do. And don't forget Royce, you still owe me for the ghost time this week."

"Yeah, yeah, yeah, Top, you know I'll cover it before I DEROS," Royce answered. "Tom, what do you say we hike over to the motor pool. I'll check out a jeep and show you around the base camp."

"Sounds good, let's do it." Royce must have been reading my mind, because I had been hoping to see more of the 25th than just the company area.

The sun was already baking the dusty orange-colored ground, as we walked from the company barracks area to the battalion motor pool. It was only about a third of a mile, but as I walked along with Royce exchanging small talk, I began to feel like something was wrong with me.

My legs seemed heavy, and I was having difficulty focusing on what he was saying. Even though it was only mid-morning, it was hot outside— damn hot. I was feeling the heat, but thought that after being here for a while, I should have been getting more acclimated to it. But, now, as we walked, I started to feel *cold*. My mind told me that it was inappropriate to feel cold in this climate, but my body said the opposite.

When we got to the motor pool, Royce asked me to wait outside and he'd return with a jeep for our tour of the camp. I remembered hearing his words, but I didn't know if I answered him, not that a response from me would have been necessary, anyway. Soon I was standing outside the motor pool's operations building, all alone and getting colder with each passing second. Soon, the coldness turned to the chills; the chills made me shiver; the shivering forced me to lean against the outside wall of the building.

I couldn't understand what was happening to me, but felt very alone in my suffering. By this time my teeth were chattering with the chills, as if I were back home in Wisconsin ice fishing in January without a coat. But this was Vietnam; I *knew* it was hot. The shivering was getting worse. I struggled to go inside the operations office to look for Royce, but my feet seemed nailed to the sandy ground. All I could do was lean up against the building, then I slowly started sliding down, eventually into a sitting position.

Come on Sergeant Royce, where are you? Something is wrong, I don't know what, and I need you to help me! Due to the field maneuvers, there was almost no activity at the motor pool, nobody coming or going. Come on Royce, where are you?

All of a sudden I was aware I had leaned over onto my left side from a sitting position. Then I was pulling myself into a fetal position, in an effort to stay warm. I could smell the hard-packed sand of the earth, but I couldn't sit or stand up.

"*Tom!* What the hell . . . ?" I heard Royce's concerned voice. He sounded so far away, but he was right there, gently shaking and pulling me some, so that I could sit up.

I felt Royce and someone else—who was attached to arms and a fatigue shirt—pick me up and move me.

"I . . . I . . . I'm freezing, Sarge," was all I could say. Now I was conscious of them putting me into the back of a jeep.

No, no, I thought—*not* the back of a jeep! *That's what happened to Ron!* No, not the backseat of a jeep! *I'm not going to die here,* was the only thought going through my mind.

"You're okay, Tom, you're okay," Royce said in a soothing way, all the while holding me down in the back of the jeep. By then we were moving. Someone else had to be driving, because Royce was in the back with me. Or maybe, there were five or six people in the jeep? My senses were not serving me well at the moment.

"Take care, buddy, we'll get you to the base hospital," I heard a strange voice say from afar.

No, no, *not* the jeep! *Not* the base hospital! This is what happened to Ron! Was he cold and shivering just before he died, too?

Any attempt I made to escape the vehicle was met by strong arms restraining my movements.

"Go get somebody out here!" I vaguely heard Royce yell.

I was conscious of *what* was happening in sort of a detached way, but couldn't understand *why* it was happening. Why would I be shaking from chills in such a hot climate? Maybe it was something I ate? Maybe it was a delayed reaction to the fear I felt from last night's mortar attack?

"Let's get him transferred to the gurney," I heard a woman's voice say, as several sets of hands picked me up. I was trying to sit up on my own, feeling a little strange that all these people had to help me out of an open jeep. Then I was laid out on the thin mattress of a hospital gurney and wheeled into a building.

A woman with short red hair and dressed in jungle fatigues was near the front of the gurney. She seemed to be in charge, barking short, crisp instructions to the others. I strained through half-focused eyes, trying to identify a hazy silhouette that was standing at the back of the gurney—it was Sergeant Royce, looking at me with a very concerned expression.

I was aware that my shirt sleeve was being pushed up, and a blood pressure cuff was being wrapped tightly around my upper arm. My shirt was hastily unbuttoned, and I felt the metal of a stethoscope on my chest. Strange, I thought, that metal piece is usually cold when pressed to your chest; today it felt *warm*. My body was beginning to ache from the violent shivering.

The female was lifting my eyelids and peering into my eyes. Despite my shaking, I could see an attractive face only inches from mine. As she pulled back from examining my eyes, I saw the two parallel black fabric bars on her fatigue shirt collar. She was a captain.

"Where's this man's dog tags?" she hurriedly asked of anyone in the room. I felt the tightening of a blood pressure cuff on one arm, the stinging prick of needles in the other. Another female in fatigues was poking around the arm that had been given the injection, apparently trying to find a vein for an IV.

"Where's this guy from?" the captain asked impatiently, after not getting an answer to her first question about the dog tags.

"He doesn't have any dog tags," I heard Royce's voice in the distance, but out of my sight. I was glad he was still in the same room. "He's a civilian, ma'am," Royce said, barely audible over the scurrying around in the emergency room.

"A civilian? In an Army uniform? You have some explaining to do later, Sergeant!" the captain said sternly.

"Yes, ma'am. But what's wrong with him? He's a friend of mine just visiting the base, and all of a sudden he starts to shiverin' like that. He seemed fine earlier," I heard Royce saying to her.

"Well, Sergeant, we're going to stabilize him right now, but my first guess is he's got an attack of malaria. We'll do a blood test to verify."

"Is he gonna be okay with the medicine you're giving him?" asked Royce, concerned.

"If we confirm malaria, your young buddy here is in for a couple of bad days, even with the medicine," the officer said, backing off considerably from her initial brusqueness. Now she, at least, seemed a little more sympathetic.

I felt groggier by the minute, but my shivering seemed to be decreasing considerably. My muscles—from my neck to my ankles—ached like I had been dragged around behind a horse.

That was the last complete, coherent thought I remembered having for a while. Then, for what to me was an undetermined amount of time, I could vividly distinguish my body temperature going from teeth-chattering cold to extremely uncomfortable heat. The heat caused me to sweat from every pore, soaking the sheets as if they had been drenched by a sudden cloudburst.

I could remember brief bouts of consciousness that seemed to run together as if they were only minutes apart. I felt vaguely aware of a few faces, different faces, hovering over me at different times. First, there was a blond female, then a brunette. Then, was it Royce? Maybe even Top Miller? They all kind of ran together in a whirling haze, constantly changing their positions around me. The female faces seemed concerned about other things near me; Royce and Top seemed concerned about me.

Strange that all of these people were around me for such a brief period.

The heat and sweating continued. Why was someone pricking my arms with needles every couple of seconds? Why was another person wiping my forehead and lips with a really cold cloth, and yet another was telling me to sip ice cold water? Why was all this activity happening during the course of only five minutes?

Then suddenly the heat was gone. So was the sweating, except the bedsheets still felt damp. I opened my eyes and the haziness was also gone. I looked around and saw that I was in a hospital room with at least twenty other beds in it, occupied by patients. I was in a bed at the end of the room. The patient next to me was sleeping, and the top of his head and side of his face nearest to me were wrapped in white bandages. The guy in the bed directly across from me had his right leg in a cast and elevated about eight inches above the sheets. He was sitting up in bed, but his face was mostly hidden behind a thick paperback book he was reading.

I realized the room I was in was actually a large Quonset hut. I could discern some muted noise and activity outside, but the inside quiet was only disturbed by the muffled purring of what I assumed to be an air conditioner. I was surprised to hear the sounds and feel the cooling effects of air-conditioning. This was only the second temperature-controlled room I had been in while in Vietnam. The first had been the Inventory Control Center at Long Binh.

Just as I was getting more acclimated to my surroundings, a nurse entered the large ward and began fussing with a patient here and there, stopping to read the chart of another. She was working her way closer to my bed. She stopped and checked the bandage on the guy's face in the next bed, though he never moved.

When she turned to look at me, I recognized her as the blond I had seen while dreaming a few minutes earlier. When she made eye contact with me, a curious smile came over her face. Her expression was new to me. In my dreams she looked very serious, and I thought for a moment this was really someone different. "So, how's Mr. Civilian doing?" she asked, placing a thermometer under my tongue. Why do nurses and dentists always ask you questions just after putting something in your mouth so you can't possibly answer them?

I smiled and nodded, indicating that I felt much better. Actually, I felt very fatigued, and every muscle ached, but I no longer felt the alternating shivering cold and burning heat. Since she was taking my temperature, I assumed those were the symptoms she was referring to.

"You had us a bit worried, *Mister* Reilly," she said, lifting my wrist to check my pulse. Thirty seconds later she removed the thermometer and made some notes on a chart at the end of my bed.

Now was my chance to ask her some questions, since I had nothing in my mouth and she wasn't occupied by taking my pulse. "Where am I, Lieutenant?" I asked, noting the single gold bar on her collar.

"You're at the 12th Evac Hospital at Cu Chi, Republic of Vietnam, in sunny Southeast Asia," she replied in a distinctive cadence. "And, you just went through an attack of malaria."

"How long have I been here, I mean, here in the hospital?" I asked her with genuine curiosity.

"How long do you *think* you've been here? Just a game I like to play with malaria patients," she said with a hint of mischief.

"I don't know, really. Maybe about an hour, maybe two hours, max?" I answered, trying to sort through my dreamy haze.

"Well, the number two is right," she said. Then leaning closer, she grinned and said, "Two *days!*"

Holy shit! I thought. "I've been here for *two days?*"

"Yup! And, we're gonna keep you here for at least another twelve hours to see if that nasty old 'Mr. M.' comes back to knock you on your butt again," she added, turning to walk away.

"Wait, ah, Lieutenant? Is there any way I can get in touch with Sergeant Royce at the 4/9th?" I asked impatiently.

She turned back briefly. "He's been over here to see you about a dozen times while you were out. I'll give him a call and let him know your fever finally broke."

"Thanks a lot."

I couldn't believe I had just lost two days of my life, especially when those two days were at a time and place that meant so much in my life. Lying there in an Army hospital bed made me immediately thankful for a lot of things. The first—and most obvious—was that I was in the care of American doctors and nurses. What if this had happened while I was alone in Bangkok or during my two-night trip from Thailand to Vietnam? I was also thankful that I was with Sergeant Royce when the first symptoms appeared. His caring and quick response were most likely very instrumental in helping me pull through.

But, then there was the problem of me being at the 25th Division as an unauthorized *guest*. Other than the tongue-in-cheek emphasis by the nurse, referring to me as *Mister* Reilly, so far there didn't seem to be a problem with my presence. I only hoped that Royce or Top Miller weren't in trouble because of me.

Even though I was exhausted and ached all over, I was determined to get out of the hospital as soon as possible. I didn't really know how serious my presence was as an unofficial noncombatant, or if it was even an issue, but I could imagine the commanding general and a squad of MPs coming to get me. Worse yet, my imagination had Sergeant Royce and Top Miller sharing the same olive drab paddy wagon with me.

But, if I was to escape the hospital undetected, I couldn't do it alone. All I was wearing was a pair of Army green boxer shorts. A quick look around my bed revealed no other clothes, just a pair of clog shower sandals on the floor under the hospital bed. If I left wearing only those two items, I would be stopped by the first officer or sergeant I encountered, asking why I was out of uniform. And that would only be the start of the interrogation.

Besides, I didn't know how big the hospital complex was or where my Quonset hut was located. Hell, I didn't even know where the hospital was relative to the rest of Cu Chi base camp.

I would just have to wait for Royce. I hoped the lieutenant nurse would follow through on her offer to contact Royce. Somehow, I felt she would. My gut feeling was right, because as I was thinking all this, Sergeant Royce came walking through the door of the ward. I saw immediately that he was smiling, which went a long way in quelling my mounting paranoia about the situation.

"How the hell ya feelin', Tom?" were his first words.

"A little tired, but I think I'll live."

"You scared the shit out of me the other day," he said, gently shaking my shoulder.

"Sorry about that, I really am."

"Well, the captain and lieutenant say you're gonna be all right. Problem is, you might get a relapse today or tomorrow. They say it depends on what kind of malaria you contracted."

"I feel okay, now, and I'd feel a whole lot better if I could get out of here," I said.

"No, you'd better stay and let them keep an eye on you, at least 'til tonight," Royce said, obviously concerned.

"But did you or Top get into trouble, you know, for bringing me in, a civilian?"

"Fuck no, don't worry about it. I talked to the trauma doctor, Captain Davis—she was the one on duty when I brought you in. She was a little surprised at first, but now she's cool. I explained why you were here in Nam. Actually, she was kind of touched by the story. She'll take care of your records, so nobody will know you were ever here. Far as she's concerned, she figures if they take care of local Vietnamese civilians, they sure as hell can help an American civilian."

"Great, thanks again for everything," I answered, amazed once again at all the help I was receiving, especially since I had just dropped into these people's lives unexpectedly.

"How the hell did you get malaria anyway? Didn't you get any shots or at least take the 'big orange pill' before coming over here?" Royce asked me.

"Yeah, I took all my shots before coming, *including* one for malaria. But they warned me I needed more time for them to take effect. By the time I got the shot, I couldn't change my departure date from the States. What's this 'orange pill?' "

"We get a bunch of shots too, before coming here, and one of them is probably for malaria, but then once we're here, we take these big fuckin' orange pills—they're like something you'd give a horse. Seems to do the trick, though. We also go through a ton of bug spray when we're in the field," Royce explained.

"You get malaria from mosquitoes, right?" I asked.

"Yeah, and there's about eighty billion of 'em per square meter in the boonies."

"I know. I felt like I was being eaten alive when I was in Cambodia about a week ago."

"Well, Tom, you take care. I'll find out when they're gonna release you, and I'll come back to get you then."

"Thanks, and be sure to find me some clothes."

"That's affirmative," Royce said, as he turned to leave the ward.

Shortly after Sergeant Royce left, my attention was drawn to a very young-looking GI patient who was slowly walking down the row of beds in my direction. He was dressed in a white T-shirt and white boxer shorts, which looked out of place, since the only underwear I had ever seen while in Vietnam were the standard issue Army green variety.

He was walking with the aid of a metal cane that he held in his right hand. His right leg, above the knee, was heavily bandaged to the bottom of his skivvies. It appeared that this young soldier was either cautiously exercising his wounded leg, or was just bored by being bedridden too long. He would stop every couple of beds, smile, and make small talk with his fellow patients.

When he approached my bed at the end of the ward, he stopped and gave me a curious look. "Are you a helo pilot?" he asked, staring at me.

The question surprised me. What would give him the indication I was a chopper pilot? "No," I answered.

"So, are you CID?"

"No. Why do you think I'm a pilot or a criminal investigator?" I asked him.

"Well, sir, I heard the nurse call you *Mister*, so I figured you were a warrant officer. Most helo pilots and El Cids are warrant officers," he replied.

Now I understood his questions and confusion. "Actually, I'm a civilian, and you don't have to address me as 'Sir' or 'Mister.' My name is Tom Reilly," I explained, sitting up and extending my hand.

He moved closer to me from the end of the bed and shook my hand with his left, while teetering on the cane with his right. "So, you're a reporter?"

This kid just wasn't going to quit until he knew my whole life history! I was beginning to feel like a mystery guest on the old *What's My Line?*

television quiz show. "No, no, I'm just a civilian who came over here to find out how my brother died. What's your name?"

"I'm PFC Algood, James Algood," he answered proudly.

"What happened to your leg, Jim?" Now it was my turn to question him. Maybe I wouldn't have to tell this friendly, but overly curious new acquaintance my life story after all.

"I got it fucked up out on patrol last week. Took some shrapnel and a piece got stuck in the bone. They got most of it out, but they might have to go back in, so I'm still here. Might even have to go to Japan or maybe even back to the World, but I don't think it's bad enough for that," he explained, seeming somewhat saddened his wound wasn't serious enough to get him a ticket out of the war.

"Does it hurt much?"

"Sometimes, but they give me pills or a shot to help the pain. It hurt like a sonofabitch the first couple of days. But now they want me to exercise a little more each day. Seems to be getting better. With my luck, I'll be back in that damned Ho Bo Woods in a couple weeks."

"How long do you have left?" I asked, against my better judgment.

"One hundred-seventy-four days and a wake-up," he said optimistically.

At least he was starting the second half of his tour, I thought to myself, so I hadn't asked such a demoralizing question after all.

"How long do you have left?" he asked me.

Great, now for the demoralizing part. I decided it was best to avoid a direct answer. Apparently this young PFC, who was probably a year younger than me, wasn't comprehending that I was on my own schedule. "Well, uh, I'm kinda on my own time, so I'll be here a while yet," I tried to say with some degree of diplomacy.

"So, when do you plan on going back to the World?"

"Depends on a few things, but I'll most likely go back sometime next week," I said with as much empathy as I could, considering his five and a half months left in country.

"Holy shit!" he cried out. "You're only a week short!" Obviously he put everything in the context of his own situation. "You're gonna be back in the World next week?" It was like I was some sort of celebrity to him. He just couldn't believe he was in the presence of someone who would be leaving Vietnam so soon.

"But you said yourself your wound might get you out of here, to either Japan or the States," I said, trying futilely to add some encouragement.

"No, I just know I'll be humpin' the boonies next month, while you and a lot of other guys are back home." Algood was really getting dejected.

"Actually, next month I'll be in basic training," I told him to help ease the disappointment and self-pity he was feeling at that instant.

"*What?*"

I explained about my Delayed Entry Enlistment into the Army that was awaiting me when I returned.

"Let me get this straight. You're a civilian, but you come over here to Nam. Then, when you get back from Nam, you're going into the Army. You're one crazy dude! What are you gonna do then, come back over here again for a combat tour? You're a crazy fuck!"

"No, I probably won't come back over here. Maybe I'll go to Germany or someplace. Besides, you'll probably have the war won by then," I said, trying to humor him.

"Well, put 'er there," he said, sticking his left hand out again to shake mine. "I've seen some really strange shit since getting drafted, but nothing tops this shit with you!" Algood was half-laughing as he turned to hobble back towards his bed. About twenty seconds later, I heard his voice as he was passing by another patient several beds down the ward: "There's a crazy motherfucker down there on the end, but at least he's one week short!"

After the brief exchange with Algood, I realized how much I really felt for the guys serving in Vietnam. Supposedly, the war was de-escalating. The U.S. government's policy of "Vietnamization" was in full swing, allegedly turning the war over to the ARVN, or South Vietnamese forces. However, it seemed very clear that Americans were still fighting and dying each week with regularity. All I had to do was look around the hospital ward. These guys weren't here all bandaged up because of car accidents or sports injuries. They were here because an enemy was shooting and maiming them with bullets, mines, and mortars. I'd like to see the response a Washington politician would get if he came to Cu Chi and told these guys the war was really winding down, and that Vietnamization was really working.

That's why it was so difficult for me to tell someone like PFC Algood that I could go home anytime I wanted. They could overlook the fact that I was here, or even for what reason, but the tough part dealt with the going home, which was something they could *all* relate to. Going home was all these guys could think about.

I spent most of the rest of that day dozing off and on in my hospital bed. This was, I suppose, a defense mechanism—I really didn't want to talk to any of the other patients. I was somewhat embarrassed at being at the 12th Evac Hospital as a civilian. I'm sure a few of the other patients were there because of illness, rather than the fact that pieces of metal were embedded in their bodies, so the malaria wasn't the source of my embarrassment. No, what really affected me after talking to PFC Algood was that I was in Vietnam on my own accord, and I could leave when I wanted. Most of these guys, especially the younger ones, were draftees like Algood. They had no choices at that point in their lives. And I knew Algood was right. Most of these guys sharing my ward would most likely be patched up and put back out in the field. It was as if getting a nonlife-threatening wound wasn't a high enough price to pay; maybe the next time they could get a bigger wound, or worse. I simultaneously felt sad for and proud of the guys over there.

Throughout my day of napping, I was fully aware of the nursing staff and even some doctors coming in and out of the ward administering to the other patients. Once I heard a few muffled screams of pain, which quickly turned to sobbing, as a team of nurses rotated a patient in his bed about halfway down the ward from me. I closed my eyes and hoped that my malaria symptoms wouldn't come back, so I could get the hell out of this room of suffering.

I was awakened late in the day by the same lieutenant that had attended to me earlier that morning. "How do you feel, Tom?" she asked, again shoving a thermometer in my mouth.

It took a few seconds for my faculties to return. But when I became coherent again, I was delighted to discover I felt fine. No chills, no fever, just a little tired yet. "Unh, unh," I nodded to her.

"Good! Looks like you're back to normal, at least for a civilian," she winked, as she removed the thermometer and began writing on the bedside chart.

"Can I leave now, Lieutenant?" I asked anxiously.

"Yup, you can. I'll go call that friend of yours. He's got your clothes, anyway. If I can get in touch with him, he'll be here shortly." Then turning to leave, she looked back, smiled, and said, "You be sure to take care of yourself out there; I don't want to see you back in here again."

"Hopefully, you won't see me again, but thanks again for your help." I got the feeling she said the same parting sentiment a lot.

About half an hour later, Sergeant Royce walked into the ward carrying a bundle wrapped in plain brown paper. In his other hand he carried a pair of jungle boots. "How ya doin', trooper?"

"I'm fine and ready to leave here—if you have some clothes for me."

At that, he tossed the package in my lap, as I sat up in the bed. "Open it," he instructed.

Inside the package was a neatly folded fatigue uniform, both shirt and pants, along with a new change of underwear and socks. Holding up the shirt, I saw something extra. A new 25th Infantry Division emblem had been sewn on the upper left shoulder, and another patch, bearing the name REILLY had been sewn over the right breast pocket. Both new patches were in the combat style of black and green.

I looked up at a grinning Sergeant Royce. "I can't wear this!"

"Hell if ya can't! Isn't your name Reilly?"

"Yes, but I really can't wear the Tropic Lightning patch, I'll get in trouble, won't I?"

"Fuck 'em! The way Top and I see it, you not only survived malaria while here, but you also lived through a mortar attack. That's enough to be considered an 'unauthorized honorary' member of the 25th, at least to Top and me. Besides, if your brother was here, he'd agree, too. So, that settles it. Get dressed and I'll take you out of here!"

Chapter 15

Back to the World

Even though I only spent slightly more than two days at the 12th Evac Hospital, most of which I couldn't remember, it was good to walk out of there with Sergeant Royce. He had a jeep parked just outside. On my way out, I was able to say a quick good-bye to some of the hospital staff, who had helped me through the malaria episode.

I never again saw the female captain I vaguely remembered being in the ER when Royce brought me in. When I asked about her, Royce suggested that due to my "unauthorized noncombatant" status, we should just leave the hospital as quickly and quietly as we could. This meant not making a fuss over finding her. Besides, Royce said he had already thanked her, and added that he was looking forward to seeing her again in a more "social way," as he put it. I could see why he and my brother Ron got along so well. I told him I was happy to be able to help him with his private social calendar, even if I did have to suffer through an attack of malaria to do it.

"So, if you feel up to it, I'll give you a quick tour of the camp before it gets too dark," Royce suggested.

"Sure. I'm just glad to be out of the hospital and back with you."

"Oh, by the way," Royce said, reaching into his shirt pocket and pulling out a small envelope, "here are some pills you're supposed to take to keep the malaria away. They gave them to me so there wouldn't be any record of you. Follow the instructions on the outside."

I took the envelope and looked inside. Sure enough, there were a dozen large orange pills.

For the next hour Sergeant Royce drove me around the Cu Chi base camp. We drove passed the 25th Division Headquarters, complete with a small parade ground in front, emblazoned with a huge red-and-yellow Tropic Lightning insignia in the middle. Upon seeing this, I thought it was a good thing the enemy didn't really have an air force to speak of operating in South Vietnam, because that insignia would look like a huge bull's-eye from the air.

Next, we drove through the mechanized infantry area, where, Royce explained, were dozens of parked APCs (armored personnel carriers) and other assorted AFVs (armored fighting vehicles). From there we went to the 25th Aviation Battalion. Royce pointed out this was the unit that did most of the helicopter missions in support of the infantry units. There were about twenty Huey choppers and their Cobra AH-1G gunship cousins parked a good distance apart from each other in a large field.

I explained to Royce that I was really interested in these, because they, unlike in any other war in history, were a distinguishing feature of the Vietnam War. Apparently photojournalists felt the same way, because the American public back home was getting a full dose of the use of helicopters in this war. Of course, there was no way of minimizing the important role of the chopper in this type of warfare, but, sometimes I felt the topic was overpropagandized by the government. It was like the government wanted the public to think we must be winning the war, because we were using these machines with their advanced technology against a ground enemy wearing only black pajamas and carrying rifles.

Nonetheless, seeing those Hueys and COBRA gunships up close was a thrill for me, and I made mention of that to Sergeant Royce.

"Would you like to take a ride in one while you're here?" he asked.

"Sure would, as long as no one got in trouble for it!"

"I'll see what I can do."

We continued our tour, with Royce showing me some of the perimeter fortifications around the base camp. Except for those heavily defended positions and the million or more sandbags, I saw that Cu Chi was like a big, sprawling military base back in the States that simply had been dropped in the middle of a foreign country. But even though Cu Chi had a PX, barbershops, and even a bank, you could *feel* that it was not a Stateside base. The sense of imminent danger was always present, unlike the Stateside bases I had visited with Ron. As I noticed earlier, it even had a different feel than Long Binh Post, which wasn't all that far away, distancewise. Somehow, you just *knew* you were closer to the war while at Cu Chi, even if the mortars and rockets weren't coming in over the perimeter wire every night.

Royce completed our tour just around sunset, and we returned to his company area. I still felt weak, as we grabbed some chow at the mess hall and went up to his hootch for a beer. I hoped this evening, unlike three nights ago, wouldn't be interrupted by a mortar attack.

"Naw, that doesn't happen very often anymore. The other night Victor Charlie was just harassing us some. I'm sure you'll get a good night's rest tonight," Royce reassured me when I voiced my concern to him.

At lights-out that night, I had to admit that I felt pretty proud of what I had accomplished thus far in Vietnam: I had made it to both of Ron's units, and got details about his death; survived a trip across the Ho Chi Minh Trail, a mortar attack, and an episode of malaria; and, there I was with one of Ron's old friends, wearing a uniform shirt with an honorary combat patch and my name sewn on it.

Considering I had no idea what I would find, or how I would fare before setting out on this journey, I was quite satisfied with the outcome. But now that it was time to go home, I hoped getting back to the World wouldn't be as harrowing an ordeal as getting to Vietnam had been.

Sergeant Royce was right, there were no more interruptions from the VC that night. I awoke just as he was coming back into the hootch after shaving. I awakened cautiously, hoping there would be no more malaria symptoms—and there weren't. I had taken one of the orange pills before going to sleep and had promised myself to keep taking them as prescribed.

I had breakfast with Top Miller and Royce. Top was glad to see that I was feeling better. He was probably sweating as much as I was—not from malaria, of course, but from the possibility of having to explain my presence to the brass if my condition had gotten worse, or if they found out I was there.

As he ate, he went over the previous day's duty report with Royce. The bulk of their company was still in the field. After three days, there had been no confirmed contact with the enemy. The only real activity encountered was finding a partially hidden cache of supplies, which they blew up along with some nearby enemy tunnel entrances.

Except for some nervous firing the first day, which injured one soldier, the unit had only sustained minor injuries from "humpin' the bushes." One guy got a poisonous snakebite and had to be Medivac'd back to the base hospital.

Top seemed both disappointed and pleased at the lack of activity in the field. On one hand, his unit wasn't getting an enemy body count; but on the other hand—and more important to Top—he didn't have any of his own unit's body bags to deal with, either.

He told Royce the plan was to keep the companies out for another twenty-four hours, then bring them back if no enemy contact was made. I got the feeling that Royce was relieved this mission had turned out to be nothing of substance. I could tell he was torn between being out with his platoon and "baby-sitting" me at base camp.

Knowing that I had already taken up enough of Royce's and Top's time, plus the fact that their company would be returning shortly, I decided it was time to leave. These guys had been so good to me—I didn't want to overstay my welcome. "How would I go about getting back to Saigon from here?" I asked, sort of throwing out that I was ready to depart.

"I'm sure we could work something out for you. You need to get to the civilian airport?" Royce asked.

"Well, actually, I left most of my things, including my civilian clothes in a big suitcase at the Long Hotel near Tu Do Street. I really have to go there first, then to the airport."

"Do you already have a return ticket and reservation to the States?" asked Top Miller.

"I bought a round-trip ticket on Pan Am in the States with an open return. I'm pretty sure what time their daily flight leaves for Manila. I just thought I would show up and take my chances," I told them.

"So, you want to leave for Saigon tomorrow?" Royce asked.

"If that would be okay with you guys, yeah, I would. I've done everything I came here to do, so I guess it's time to go home. Don't forget, I have to report for basic training in a few weeks, anyway."

"Let me work on gettin' you some transportation down there tomorrow. I'll let you or Royce know this afternoon. I've got an idea that just might work out okay," Top said, getting up to leave the mess hall.

Later in the morning, Sergeant Royce let me go with him to the base PX. He needed a few toiletries and a carton of cigarettes. As I tagged along beside him wearing my full jungle fatigues, nobody really noticed my "uniform" was missing rank insignia or the "U.S. Army" patch over the front left breast pocket. But again, since I obviously wasn't Vietnamese, nobody really cared.

While we were in the store, Royce asked how confident I was that the suitcase I left at the Long Hotel would still be there when I returned. The point he was making was that maybe I should purchase a change of civilian clothing to wear on the plane—just in case. He even offered to buy me—with his own money—some clothes from the PX's limited supply of civvies. Not wanting him to do this, I reassured him I was "relatively" certain my suitcase would be at the hotel for me to retrieve.

"Okay, Tom, but that may be a first," he said pessimistically.

We bumped into Top Miller back in the company area that afternoon. He said he could get me to Saigon the next morning—by *chopper!* Of course, it could only take me to the MACV part of the airport. I would have to take a taxi from there, downtown to my hotel, and then another taxi back to the civilian part of the airport.

Top explained the Aviation Battalion was sending two Hueys down to Saigon to pick up some new colonel and his aide at Tan Son Nhut's MACV airbase. Since they were flying down empty on the relatively short flight, I could hitch a ride. Top said he'd already pulled the strings necessary for me to ride along. The two choppers were scheduled to leave at 0830 hours the next morning.

A ride in a Huey! This is great, I thought to myself. I'd never been in a helicopter before, so being in one in Vietnam would be an exciting experience—even if it was just a short "milk run" down to Saigon.

Just after breakfast the next morning, I said good-bye to Top Miller and thanked him for his help. Then I grabbed my rucksack, and Sergeant Royce drove me by jeep over to the Aviation Battalion. We bypassed the Flight Ops building and drove around to the edge of the field where two Huey helicopters had their engines and rotors warming up.

In the open side door of the chopper nearest to us was a soldier in fatigues, flak jacket, and green flight helmet. He was sort of lounging with one leg hanging out near the chopper's mounted door machine gun. Another guy, also wearing a flight helmet, but clad in coveralls, was standing near him talking. I could see a third flight helmet bobbing around in the cockpit through the curved windshield of the Huey.

Royce and I walked up to the door gunner and soldier in coveralls. He asked, over the rotor noise, if these were the two helos scheduled down to Tan Son Nhut at 0830 hours.

"That's affirmative, Sergeant," yelled the guy in coveralls. I could now see the bar insignia of a warrant officer on his collar. "Is this the passenger?" he asked Royce.

"Yeah. They told you his status?"

"Yup! Funny lookin' clothes for a civilian," the pilot said, grinning at me.

At hearing the word *civilian*, the door gunner sat up a little straighter near his gun. I took this not as any extra show of respect, but more out of curiosity.

"Well, board and get yourself strapped in. We'll be leaving in a few minutes," the pilot yelled to me as he climbed into his craft.

I turned to say good-bye to Sergeant Royce before boarding the chopper. "I'm not authorized on this, am I?"

"You're not really 'authorized' to be on base, either, but what the fuck, you're here, aren't you. Besides, it won't matter anyhow, as long as this chopper doesn't crash, nobody will know you're on it. Come to think of it, if it *does* crash, nobody would know you're on it either—except me!" he laughed.

"Thanks for everything, Sarge. I'm glad I came to see you. You helped me fill in the blanks about Ron."

"Now get your civilian ass on that chopper and have a good flight back to the World! And don't forget, there's two things you need to do for me and your brother."

"What's that?" I asked.

"First, when you report for duty, make goddamned sure you don't come back over here. You get your ass sent to Germany or Hawaii, any place but here! Got it?"

"Yeah. What's the second thing?"

"You make sure you go back and finish your college degree. That was important for your brother, and I'm telling you the same. You make something out of your life. That'll be a tribute to him."

"Okay, okay, I got it! I'll do both of those. I promise."

Just then the Huey started revving faster and the door gunner yelled for me to get on board if I wanted the ride. I shook Sergeant Royce's hand tightly as he backed away, hunching over and holding his cap against the force of the rotor's downdraft.

I clambered into the main part of the chopper and sat in the middle of a bench seat that ran across the inside of the fuselage. The door gunner showed me how to get strapped in. But before harnessing himself into his position to man the machine gun, he grabbed an extra flak vest, folded it, and placed it under his butt. Even though the noise level was increasing, he yelled to me that the extra flak vest was for "a little extra ass insurance." Then he said something to the pilots in his helmet microphone, and we began to lift off the ground.

The chopper hovered for a few seconds above the ground, then slowly began a forward movement with the nose tilting downward. I gave a final wave to Royce on the ground, which he acknowledged.

Soon we were climbing and picking up forward speed. I looked out the other open door opposite the gunner and could see the second chopper taking off as well, but slightly behind us.

Being strapped into the middle of the straight bench made me feel as though I was on some carnival ride, especially when the nose was tipped in a downward angle. As we gained more altitude, the craft leveled off, creating less strain on my seat belt. The noise of the engine and rotors, as well as the vibration of the entire machine, went right through to my core.

Shortly after we were airborne, the door gunner leaned over and pointed out one of the open doors to a huge mountain in the distance that seemed to rise out of nowhere. I had seen some of the same peak from around the base camp in Cu Chi, but now had a much clearer view.

"That's Black Virgin Mountain. Least that's what we call it," yelled the door gunner over the noise. "Been a lot of action on that mountain. Charlie doesn't like giving it up to us!"

Even though I knew we were flying over allegedly friendly territory, that is, if such a thing existed in South Vietnam, I felt like a sitting duck. The chopper was certainly flying at a good forward speed, but it didn't seem that fast from inside. Plus, the open doors and seemingly thin protection afforded by the floor and walls led to a real feeling of vulnerability. And I was in the middle of the fuselage and not dangling half out the chopper like the door gunner. Hell of a way to earn about three hundred dollars a month—tax-free or not!

Leaning to one side and looking out, it looked to me like we were flying along a main road leading southeast from Cu Chi down to Saigon. I wondered if it was the same road I had traveled from Long Binh a few days before. But, because of the noise, I didn't want to yell any questions to the Spec-4 manning the machine gun.

After flying for only about thirty minutes, I could see what I guessed were the outskirts of Saigon. As if on cue, both choppers banked sharply to the right, then back again to the left after a minute or so. I could tell we were descending gradually, as we continued forward.

"We're comin' in for a landing at Tan Son Nhut," the door gunner yelled at me.

I didn't know if that meant I was supposed to do something special, so I just made sure my seat belt was on tight and I had a firm grip on the strap of my rucksack.

As we were descending, I could see what appeared to be a massive cargo-type airport. There were several hangars and warehouse buildings off to one side. On the other side of our approach were a dozen or more various-size cargo planes, including several C-130s painted in camouflaged patterns.

The place was bustling with mechanized carts and forklifts. A large civilian-type 707 was parked on the tarmac a hundred yards from our position. I didn't recognize the carrier, but it had an American flag on its tail section.

The pilots landed both choppers on a blacktop section outside a hangar just as another civilian-looking 707 was taxiing to a stop nearby.

"We're here," yelled the door gunner. "But don't leave yet. Wait 'til the engines are down and the rotor stops," he cautioned me. His instructions seemed very formal and in stark contrast to the newscasts showing soldiers jumping out of Hueys into elephant grass, while the pilot maintained a hover about eight feet off the ground. I reasoned this was a much safer and more civilized landing than those done in combat. I just hoped these guys knew where we were and could point me to the main gate so I could catch a taxi to Tu Do Street.

It took about ninety seconds for the large horizontal rotor to complete its final rotations and come to a complete stop. As soon as it did, the gunner got up and made sure I was properly unbuckled, then he helped me off the chopper. The pilot also climbed out of the Huey behind me. It occurred to me I never did see the face under the third helmet, riding in the copilot position. He seemed to be busy with checklists or something, both before and after the flight.

"Do you know how I can get to the main gate and get a taxi?" I turned to ask the pilot.

"You see that big warehouse-looking building over there?" he said, removing his sunglasses and pointing. "Just go around the other side of that building, and you'll see the main gate. Should be taxis just outside."

"Thanks a bunch," I said to the pilot, as I shook his hand and nodded good-bye to the door gunner.

"You take care now, and good luck!" the pilot replied.

I set off across the tarmac in the direction he had indicated. Just as he had said, once rounding the building I saw the main gate about a hundred yards farther. I fell in behind a few other fatigue-clad GIs and walked right out of the gate. The MPs on duty were obviously more concerned with those entering the airbase than with those leaving.

I felt an immediate sense of being alone as soon as I walked out of the sprawling American military section of Tan Son Nhut and into the Vietnamese street. For the last week I had been cared for and supported by some very special Americans while on their turf. Now, once again, I was having to fend for myself in a completely foreign culture. My only solace was that I would be on my own just long enough to get my suitcase from the Long Hotel, change into my civvies, and get back to the Vietnamese-controlled civilian section of Tan Son Nhut airport that afternoon. No problem. I'd be on a Pan Am flight later that day heading for home—hopefully.

There were, of course, several taxis of various sizes and shapes parked outside the main gate. Several drivers were out of their vehicles actively soliciting the American GIs for rides. One such fellow approached me instantly. "Number One taxi, Number One ride. You want girl?"

"No, no girl. You know Long Hotel near Tu Do Street?" I asked, assuming all the drivers knew where Tu Do Street was and could drive there blindfolded.

"Yes, yes. Tu Do Street. Long Hotel. Tu Do Street Number One!" the driver declared, as I got into what looked like a flawed mechanical experiment that had tried to merge a VW bug and a Renault. At least it looked like it could get downtown better than some of the other contraptions being offered for hire.

I had barely closed the door, when my overly patronizing driver jumped behind the wheel, turned, and asked, "Change money?"

"No, just drive to Long Hotel." I could see things hadn't miraculously changed in Saigon since I had left about a week ago.

The driver seemed disappointed, but at least my answer got him to focus on his driving through the busy streets of Saigon rather than trying to make a quick fortune in the world of high finance. Before long, we pulled up and parked in front of the Long Hotel. Taking out my wallet to pay the driver, I realized I hadn't spent any cash during the entire time I was with Ron's friends at Long Binh and Cu Chi. The only purchase of any kind in my presence had been for toiletries and cigarettes, which Royce had bought at the Cu Chi PX, and that he paid for in MPCs—the Army money—rather than in dollars or piastres.

I still had some local currency in my wallet, which I used to pay for the taxi. I didn't dare let the driver see the U.S. greenbacks I had, or he wouldn't have let me out of the car until I changed some money with him. It was the right move on my part. The transaction went smoothly, and I exited the taxi.

Walking into the compact lobby of the hotel gave me a feeling of déjà vu. It was very familiar, yet seemed like months since I had last been there, even though it had only been a week.

The elderly, rotten-toothed grandfather was alone behind the counter. At first he thought I was just another American GI entering his establishment. I wasn't wearing the same rather unique clothing I had worn during my first stay there. My "jarhead" cap had been replaced with an Army fatigue cap, and my light-colored civilian jeans had been exchanged for regular fatigue pants.

Not that he would have recognized me anyway. The only response he gave me was to hold up a well-worn piece of cardboard, indicating both the nightly and *hourly* room rates in piastres and MPCs. He did this, while not making any eye contact, but merely reaching behind him for a key on a wall rack.

Remembering that the old man spoke no English, and since I had to ask about a matter other than his limited routine could handle, I knew I need-ed his grandson, Johnny, to help me. "So, Johnny here?" I asked the elder-ly desk clerk in slow, deliberate words.

He abruptly looked up at my face for the first time, apparently curious about me knowing the younger boy's American nickname. He stared at my face momentarily under the bill of my Army cap, then he looked at the name patch above my uniform breast pocket.

I sensed the man suddenly realized who I was, or at least that I had some previous history with his dingy little hotel. But his look of recognition was coupled with nervousness, almost to the degree of fear.

The old grandfather hurried into the back room just off to the side of the counter, rapidly speaking in his native tongue. At least two other Viet-namese voices responded to him in the back room, one of which I thought was Johnny's. The excited conversation escalated to angry shout-ing. Soon Johnny emerged with his grandfather from behind the beaded drapes that separated the back room from the lobby. "Mister Reilly, good to see you again," Johnny said, a big smile on his face. His grandfather stood off to the side looking sheepish. "You want room? How many nights?" Johnny eagerly asked, pretending not to know why I was really there.

"No, no room. I'm here just to pick up my suitcase. I'm flying back to the States today."

A distressed look replaced Johnny's pretend smile. "Petite problem,

Mister Reilly," Johnny said in a surrendering and overly concerned manner. "No suitcase here."

"What? I left my suitcase here for you to protect when I went to Long Binh. So where is it?" I hoped he was just confused.

"No suitcase here."

"Where the hell is it? It was a brown American Tourister suitcase. It had my initials on it!" I was getting angry.

"Ah . . . it was *stolen!* Very bad, Number Ten," Johnny said in a feeble attempt to lie.

"You little bastard! You sold it, didn't you!" I yelled at him, grabbing him by the front of his shirt.

"No, no, stolen. Someone stole it! Number Ten, very bad!"

At seeing my anger, the grandfather, looking very frightened, eased behind the counter and reached down for something.

Even at only five foot ten, I towered over both of them. As I continued cursing Johnny and shaking him, demanding my suitcase, I saw something out of the corner of my eye. The old man pointed an antique-looking revolver directly at me from behind the counter.

I could tell this whole situation was futile. I didn't think it was worth getting shot over some clothes in a suitcase, so I released my grip on Johnny's shirt. I directed a few more profanities at both of them and stomped out of the hotel.

Before I was three steps out onto the sidewalk, I heard Johnny yelling defiantly after me, "You Number Ten! Number Ten!"

And we're fighting and dying for these people! I thought to myself in anger.

I noticed the same taxi that had just brought me to the hotel was parked at the next corner. I walked up to it and verified it was, indeed, the same car and driver. Upon seeing me returning to his taxi, the driver smiled through his open window, "You change money now?"

"No! I need you to take me to the Caravelle Hotel, okay?" I just needed to calm down and figure out what to do. The Caravelle was a more civilized and international establishment. Maybe from there I could telephone Pan Am and check on today's flight to Manila and eventually back to Chicago. Maybe there was a gift shop where I could buy some civilian clothes.

"No problem, I like you," said the driver, who actually seemed like a pleasant fellow. Of course, when compared with the last locals—who had pointed a gun at me and called me "Number Ten"—he would have to appear relatively pleasant.

When we pulled up in front of the Caravelle, I asked the driver to wait and gave him a good tip to do so. I didn't know at that point what my next move would be, but assumed whatever it was would require some reliable transportation. I was back to handling those kinds of logistics for myself now, after having been pampered by my brother's friends for the last week.

I walked into the Caravelle's lobby, which was busy with a mix of people; none, however, were wearing Army fatigue uniforms. I waited until a desk clerk was available and went to his station, which was at the end of the long reception counter.

"May I help you, sir?" he asked in English, but with a strong Vietnamese and French accent.

"Yes, I was wondering if you could help me telephone Pan Am airlines. I already have a ticket and would like to fly to the States on their next flight. I think they have one leaving for Manila this afternoon sometime."

"Are you a guest at our hotel?"

"No."

"Are you American military?"

"No, I just need your help, okay?" I said, semi-pleading.

The smartly dressed desk clerk looked at me curiously for a moment, then opened a drawer behind the counter, looked at a list of phone numbers, and jotted one down on a small piece of notepaper. "Here is the number to Pan Am's local office," he said in a professional tone, as he handed me the piece of paper.

"I was wondering if you could dial it for me, possibly?" I asked, since I wasn't sure exactly how to work the pay phones in Saigon.

The desk clerk shot me an indignant look for a second, but not being able to figure out who or what I was, decided to back down and help me. He stepped over to a nearby European-style phone on the counter and dialed the number. When the other party answered, he spoke briefly in Vietnamese, then handed me the receiver. I nodded my thanks as he stepped away to help another customer, who probably appeared to be more important than me.

"Hello, is this Pan Am?"

A soft female voice, in impeccable English with only a slight Vietnamese accent, assured me that it was.

"I'm an American civilian and have the second half of a round-trip ticket from Saigon to Chicago. I would like to use it on today's flight," I explained, relieved that I was actually talking to someone who was a link to home for me.

The Pan Am agent did some checking for a few moments, then returned to the phone. "Yes, sir, we have seats still available on today's flight. You will travel via Manila, Guam, Hawaii, San Francisco, with a final destination of Chicago."

"Yup, that's the one. Will you reserve me a seat on it? My name is Tom Reilly. And by the way, what time does it leave this afternoon?" I asked excitedly.

"Actually sir, it doesn't leave this afternoon. The flight's scheduled departure is eleven forty-five."

"You mean eleven forty-five, *this morning?*"

"Yes sir."

I hurriedly looked at my watch to see it was already ten-fifteen, only ninety minutes to flight time. I didn't see how I could possibly make the trip back to Tan Son Nhut and get through immigration in time. But, I also didn't want to spend another night in Saigon if I could avoid it. "Can I get on that same flight tomorrow?" I asked, feeling frantic.

"No sir, that's not a daily flight. The next is in two days, and that flight is full," she said in a calm professional voice that was beginning to drive me crazy.

"Book me today, I'll try to make it!" I said slamming the receiver down and running out of the hotel lobby.

Fortunately my taxi was still waiting curbside, although the driver was casually standing outside the car chatting with someone. I ran and jumped into the backseat, yelling, "Tan Son Nhut Airport, *beaucoup* fast!"

The driver saw my frantic behavior and responded accordingly. He stopped talking to his friend in midsentence and jumped in behind the steering wheel. In a second we were out in the busy traffic of late morning, a cloud of blue exhaust trailing behind the rear bumper.

"Beaucoup fast! Beaucoup Ps!" I encouraged him, as he weaved in and out of traffic.

Then I realized that he had picked me up earlier that morning outside the U.S. military's Tan Son Nhut *airbase,* not at the *civilian* airport. Fearing he would take me back to the same place, I felt I needed to clarify my destination to him. "Tan Son Nhut *airport,"* I said as he drove.

"Yes, yes, Tan Son Nhut."

"Not U.S. military Tan Son Nhut. Civilian Tan Son Nhut!" I told him, wondering if he knew what the word *civilian* meant. I could tell by his face that he was confused. "You no take me to MACV airbase. No take me to U.S. military. You take me to Vietnamese Tan Son Nhut. To Pan Am," I said to him in a deliberate, slow cadence.

All of a sudden the light came on in his head, "Ah, you go Pan Am?"

"Yes, Pan Am to United States."

"Okay. I take you Pan Am Tan Son Nhut. Pan Am Number One," he smiled at me in the rearview mirror, barely missing two girls on a moped who we passed at high speed on an open boulevard.

Good, I made him understand where I needed to go!

However, the thing that would not be readily understood when I got to Pan Am were my clothes. Obviously, there was no time to stop and buy a civilian change of clothes. If I missed today's flight, I would have to spend several more days in Saigon, which would allow me plenty of time to shop for clothes, but I really wanted to get on that 707 *today*.

Not only was I wearing military fatigues and jungle combat boots, I now had a 25th Infantry Division patch on my sleeve and my last name sewn on the front of my shirt. My shirt was also becoming adorned with large, pancake-size sweat rings under each arm. With only the "U.S. Army" patch and insignia of rank missing, I looked like a deserting draftee. But would a deserter be stupid enough to wear his fatigue uniform and attempt to fly a commercial jet out of Vietnam? I really didn't know the answer to that.

Then there was the fact that I had no luggage other than the small Army surplus rucksack I was carrying. The contents inside were no less incriminating: shaving kit, camera, and a bunch of Ron's personal notebooks and photos. The kind of stuff a deserter would take with him while AWOL.

But then I remembered what was in the outside pocket of the rucksack. That's where I kept my travel documents: round-trip ticket from the States and my *passport*. Of course, the passport did not show an entry date into South Vietnam, as I was first denied entry, then came in through the back door, so to speak. But there was a dated visa stamp that I had obtained from the South Vietnamese government in Bangkok. All three documents *had* to prove that I was a civilian and not an Army deserter, right? I'd just have to take my chances, which was nothing new for me on this trip.

The driver was doing an outstanding job of weaving his taxi in and out of the late morning traffic. A few times he saw congested areas ahead, so he cut through side streets and back alleys, as if he raced through this route every day. Finally, he pulled up to the front entrance of Tan Son Nhut. I looked out the window to verify this was *not* MACV's Tan Son Nhut, and was satisfied it was the *civilian* airport instead. Several small units of

ARVN troops guarded the entrance. Several wore the white QC helmets, indicating they were the Vietnamese version of military police.

My taxi was stopped briefly as we entered the main gate, but then was waved through by the Vietnamese guards. I checked my watch and was relieved to see I still had forty-five minutes until departure time. Now, if I wasn't hassled much by immigration, I felt confident I could still make the flight.

"Pan Am, you go there," my driver said, pointing to the entrance door I should use.

I wasn't sure how much money I had left in piastres, but quickly handed the driver all the local currency I had in my wallet. "Enough?" I asked him impatiently as he thumbed through the bills.

"Good, good! You Number One, Number One!" he said smiling. Apparently I had given him more than enough cash to cover the trip and a good tip for his fast driving.

As I grabbed my rucksack and exited the taxi, I thought it curious that I had gone from "Number Ten" at the Long Hotel to "Number One" by the taxi driver, all in about an hour. What had happened to the numbers between Ten and One en route to my rise in glory? It didn't matter.

I entered the terminal and saw that it was only modestly busy as I found my way to the immigration counter for outbound passengers. I thought it would be ironic if the same guy who wouldn't let me into the country nearly two weeks earlier was on duty for the departing travelers. Ironic sure, but I hoped I wouldn't run into him again. He nearly got me killed or taken prisoner by having me divert to Thailand first. At least, if I did see him now, I could proudly show him the precious damn visa I bought from one of his fellow government bureaucrats in Bangkok.

I noticed a couple of other GIs in the immigration area, so I didn't feel so out of place. They were dressed like me, of course, but didn't look like they were passengers. It seemed they were there with some Vietnamese friends.

There were actually several airlines from other Asian countries serving Saigon. I recognized the Royal Thai and Singapore Airlines, but I just wanted to get to Pan Am.

First, I had to get into a short line leading to a gated immigration checkpoint. A couple of Vietnamese civilian police and a few of their military counterparts stood just outside the immigration officer's cage. The officer was methodically checking travel documents and tickets before allowing the passengers to pass further. I was disappointed not to see any other American passengers in the line of six or eight people in front of me.

As I got closer to the checkpoint, I saw the Vietnamese QCs watching me. I just acted nonchalant, as if I made this trip every week. As long as they stayed back, I didn't care. After all, I wasn't doing anything illegal or dishonest. I just didn't want to take the time to explain everything to them, fearing I would miss my flight if they didn't accept my story.

When it was my turn at the checkpoint, I calmly placed my passport and ticket on the counter in front of the immigration officer. He looked at me and thumbed through to the photo page. Then he started thumbing through to the visa section. He found the stamp issued by his own government in Bangkok. He then compared my airline ticket to the passport. I was holding my breath listening to the seconds tick off, but was certain that things were going well.

"You military?" the immigration officer asked me in fairly good English.

"No, civilian. I'm returning home."

"How long been in Vietnam?"

"About ten days."

"Why no stamp showing your arrival?"

Here I thought I should go out on a limb and tell what I judged to be a believable lie. "I don't know, the other immigration officer just looked at my passport, but didn't stamp it," I told him, not wanting to explain the whole story, which he wouldn't have believed anyway. I was still conscious of the minutes ticking away, while he was being so deliberate and precise.

The immigration officer then did something I was hoping he wouldn't do. He beckoned one of the Vietnamese QCs who had been watching this process. He said something to him in Vietnamese, to which the QC turned and ran back farther into the terminal beyond the checkpoint. "You wait," he informed me, pushing my documents aside, but still on the counter near him. He then motioned the person behind me, a local, to step up to him.

Great! I was batting 0 for 2 with Vietnamese immigration officers! I just knew I wouldn't make that day's flight.

I waited for about two more long minutes, and the Vietnamese QC returned with two American MPs, one a staff sergeant. Thank God! Back with the Americans!

Both U.S. MPs looked at me with no expression whatsoever, then listened to the immigration officer, who was speaking quietly to them so I couldn't hear. After listening for a minute or so, the sergeant approached me, still with no expression. "What's your unit, soldier?" he asked, but it was more of an order.

"I'm a civilian, Sergeant. The officer there has my passport with a visa stamp from the South Vietnamese government. I'm trying to fly back to the States on a Pan Am flight that leaves in about half an hour."

With that, the American MP sergeant picked up and examined my passport, also comparing the airline ticket to my identity information. "Okay, if you *are* a civilian, why are you wearing that uniform from the 25th Infantry Division? And what were you doing in Vietnam?"

"I came over here about ten days ago to find out how my older brother died. He used to be stationed with the 25th at Cu Chi. I went to visit his unit there, and they gave me these clothes. I was supposed to change back into civvies, but they were stolen, so this is all I have to wear here."

Surprisingly, the sergeant seemed to be buying my story. "You know it's against regulations for a civilian to wear a military uniform?" he asked, but in a less strict manner.

"Yes, I know that. But sergeant, this isn't *really* a uniform. It doesn't say 'U.S. Army' like yours or have any rank showing," I said, at the risk of him thinking I was a smart-ass.

The MP sergeant walked back over to where his partner was checking a clipboard with paperwork. "His name on the list?" he asked the other MP.

"No, Sarge, don't see it," his partner answered.

The sergeant turned back to me. "Okay, you seem alright. At least your name doesn't show up yet on the active AWOL/Deserter List. I'll clear you to pass." With that, the MP sergeant turned to the immigration officer and nodded. The Vietnamese bureaucrat handed me my passport and ticket and pointed for me to pass the security barrier into the departure area.

Whew! I had made it with nearly twenty minutes to spare! I hurried to the Pan Am counter and presented my ticket and passport to the female agent.

"Any baggage to check, Mr. Reilly?"

"No, just one carry-on."

"Aisle or window seat?"

"Window, please," I answered, feeling much more relaxed, now that the check-in was going smoothly. I chose a window seat because I thought I would be less conspicuous in my fatigues to the other passengers.

I boarded immediately after check-in. Just before going out the door to the tarmac, I noticed the same MP sergeant standing off to the side of the departure area, watching me intently. He was actually making me feel guilty for not doing anything wrong.

The big blue-and-white Pam Am 707 was parked not far outside the terminal, and because of the short distance, there was only one squad of ARVN soldiers hanging around between the building and the plane. Either there weren't many passengers boarding this flight, or I was just boarding late, but, in any case, I walked alone out to the 707 and climbed up the stairs to the open door of the cabin.

As I climbed the stairs, I was very tempted to look back to see if the MP was still watching me, but I forced myself not to. I didn't want to jinx the situation. Besides, he had actually treated me pretty good under such unusual circumstances. But damn, I hated being made to feel guilty when I wasn't!

Soon I was buckled into my window seat—sweat rings, dusty combat boots, and all—as the jet started taxiing to the runway. I still half-expected the plane to come to a halt so the American MP and the Vietnamese immigration officer could board and take me off the plane.

My fears were not realized. The 707 was soon airborne, and unless the MP had jumped on one of the wings, I was leaving Vietnam for home.

I sat back and relaxed for the first leg of the flight, which went to the Philippines, watching the Vietnamese coastline disappear from my window as we gained speed and altitude. I was satisfied with what I had accomplished on my journey. My purpose in coming had been to find out how Ron had died, see the place, and talk to those who had been with him the last hours and days of his life. This I had done. But far more than just getting the facts of how my brother died, I got to learn a lot about his life in Vietnam, too. I found out he was well liked by his coworkers and fellow NCOs. I learned about his last girlfriend, although I never got to meet her. I knew he was important enough for someone like her to mourn him as deeply as I did. I knew he was special enough for the guys in his last unit to hold a standing-room-only memorial service for him.

Another thing I discovered in Vietnam was very personal and touching to me. All of his closest friends knew about *me*. These people were aware of who I was and what I was doing, even though they were all strangers to me. This helped me understand the depth of Ron's quiet love and hope for his kid brother—a depth I always somehow thought was there, without ever needing the unexpected validation I got in Vietnam.

I also got a lot more than what I initially came for. I learned a lot about myself on this unusual journey. I knew if I made it home successfully—as it now appeared I would—that I could accomplish whatever I set out to do in life. The enormity of this whole ordeal taught me that I could get through difficult situations in life by relying on my own ingenuity and wits.

Getting in and out of Thailand, making my way to my brother's units, living through the fear of a mortar attack, the drain of malaria, plus using the street savvy and self-sufficiency Ron had taught me, all blended together to produce a confidence in me that I knew strengthened my character.

Yes, it had been a great trip, although it was one I wished I had never had the reason to make, I thought, as I began to doze off, lulled by the purr of the 707 engines.

�֍ ✖ ✖

Before I knew it, the plane was descending for its landing in Manila. There would be a brief stop there, on to Guam, and then to Honolulu, where I would have to deplane and clear U.S. Customs and Immigration. The stop in Hawaii, before continuing on to San Francisco and Chicago, was one I suspected might be the next source of difficulty because of my military uniform. But, at least I would be back on American soil when I was in Honolulu. Hell, I'd felt better in Vietnam just being on the "temporary" American soil of Long Binh and Cu Chi than I had being in Saigon or Bangkok.

The small islands and bays along the Philippine coast were lush and beautiful against the late afternoon sun. A lot of passengers deplaned in Manila, but I decided to stay on the plane for the hour-long layover. I didn't feel like running into any hassles in the airport because of my attire. I was also beginning to feel more out of place wearing the fatigue uniform now that I was no longer in Vietnam. Even real GIs traveled in their Class A dress uniforms instead of in fatigues and combat boots. So far, it seemed that all the people on the flight from Saigon to Manila were Asians or Filipinos, so nobody really noticed this one sleepy American passenger in military clothes. It seemed to me that the Pam Am flight attendants looked at me a bit curiously, but then again, we were flying out of Saigon.

So, yes, I just decided to stay on the plane. I realized I had slept through whatever meal might have been served while we were in flight. I was more thirsty than hungry, so while the plane was on the ground, I walked to the back of the plane for a drink of water and to take an orange malaria pill, which made me think of Sergeant Royce. I sure hoped that he would survive the war with his life and all of his body parts intact. But, at least it seemed like he was there doing what he wanted to do. "No ties, no problems" was a philosophy he had shared with my brother.

Soon we were back in the air—next stop Guam. Just as had been my experience on the flight over, each stop on the way back produced a change of neighboring passengers. Heck, I was on the plane longer than the crew, which I knew from my previous flight from the States, changed every two stops. I was thankful that most of my fellow passengers were foreigners. At least to me they were foreigners, even though *I* was the one traveling through their part of the world. And, because of that, it was less likely that I was expected to engage in conversation with each new passenger who sat next to me.

During the stopover in Guam, I got off the plane with the other passengers, to stretch my legs and see if there was any place at the airport I could buy some civilian clothes and shoes. I discovered the airport gift shop was quite limited—I could have bought a nice tropical-print silk shirt or touristy T-shirt, but felt they would look ridiculous combined with fatigue pants and combat boots. I had always been proud of what I wore in public and didn't really want to look like a clown. I felt more comfortable just wearing the uniform. Since it was very early in the morning local time during the stopover, I knew nothing else would be open. I also realized it was wise not to leave the airport, with only an hour and a half layover. I could try again at the Honolulu airport.

The flight from Guam to Hawaii seemed excruciatingly long to me. Of course, by that time in my journey homeward, my butt felt like it had become fused to my economy-class seat.

Even though my passport was valid, I still thought there could be a problem getting through U.S. Immigration in Hawaii. I knew a lot of servicemen carried civilian passports in addition to their military ID cards. Ron had carried a separate passport so he could travel as a civilian while he was on leave. This was not necessary; he just preferred it that way. Because of this, I feared I could be detained and questioned as a suspected deserter. And, because I had signed up for delayed enlistment, I was certain my name would show up somewhere on Army records if a thorough enough check was made.

But what the hell was I so worried about? I *wasn't* an AWOL GI or a deserter. The worst thing I faced was a couple hours of questioning while my rather bizarre story could be checked out. At least no one would be shooting mortar rounds at me, like they had at Cu Chi. It was just that after all I had been through lately, I just wanted to get home without being hassled.

After what seemed like a million miles of blue Pacific Ocean had passed under my window, the pilot announced our descent into the Honolulu airport. It seemed that nearly all of my fellow passengers were on their first visit to America, and their excitement about landing in Hawaii filled the cabin. I was tired and filled with anxiety, but I also felt some relief about being back in my home country, even if Hawaii wasn't exactly the Midwest.

After landing, we all streamed off the plane, dividing into two unequal lines: one for returning U.S. citizens and one for the foreign visitors. There was a third area for military personnel, but there were no servicemen or women on my flight. Fortunately, I was in the shorter line leading to the immigration checkpoint. I noticed a few uniformed Honolulu police officers leisurely standing beyond the checkpoint. Noticeably absent in this immigration area were military personnel, military police or otherwise.

Once again, I felt very conspicuous in my jungle fatigues and combat boots, still with a thin coating of Cu Chi dust in the eyelets and leather crevices. There were only a couple of other passengers in front of me. One was a very American-looking businessman I had not seen on the flight from Guam. I assumed he had flown first class. The others were U.S. citizens of Asian descent.

Then suddenly it was my turn. I approached the counter with my passport and the completed customs forms firmly in hand, which I had been given while on the plane. The immigration officer was a portly man who looked to be about fifty. His face was well wrinkled, but I doubted if they were laugh lines. He took the documents from my hand before he really looked at me. When he did look up, he said, "You're in the wrong line. You were supposed to follow the signs for military personnel, over there. And why are you traveling in fatigues?"

"I'm not military, sir. I'm a civilian," I answered, in the most polite answering-a-bureaucrat tone I could muster.

The officer raised up out of his swivel stool, probably for the first time that shift, and leaned slightly over the counter looking at me from cap to boots. *"You're a civilian?"* he asked sarcastically.

"Yes, there's my passport."

"Where are you coming from?"

"Vietnam."

"Why are you in an Army uniform if you're not in the Army?" he asked with increasing irritation.

Here we go again!

"It's a long story . . . but this isn't a real uniform. My clothes were stolen—"

"Wait!" he said, abruptly cutting me off and holding up his hand. He

reached for a phone in the corner of his work booth. Turning away so I couldn't hear him, he spoke a few sentences, then hung up. He then paged through my passport, comparing the photo inside to my face. By the time he finished doing this, two Honolulu police officers and an MP arrived at the checkpoint.

Now I was 0 for 3 with immigration people!

"Now, you're gonna go with these guys so they can figure who and what you are. You can tell them whatever story you were gonna tell me," the immigration officer said condescendingly, handing my passport to the MP.

The police led me off to a cubicle still in the immigration area. Once inside, they passed my documentation around so they could all see it. My passport eventually ended up with the MP, who I guessed to be about twenty-five years old. He was the first to speak. "I'm a little confused and hope you can help me out," he said in a friendly manner.

"I'm sure I can explain everything."

"Go ahead, I think that would be a good idea at this point," the MP said, as the two HPD officers stood there expressionless.

For the next fifteen minutes I laid out my entire story for my law enforcement audience, but from the blank looks on their faces, I had no idea if they believed me or not.

"That's quite a story, you should write a book about it someday," the MP said, when I finished with the line, "so now I'm here with you guys."

Then they asked if I would follow them to a police substation in another part of the airport. Although I was in no position to object, I did key in on the fact that they *asked* me to go with them rather than ordering me. It may have only been semantics, but that and the fact they didn't use handcuffs was encouraging.

When we got to the substation, I was again *asked* to wait in a small room that was furnished with just a desk and three chairs. It looked like something out of *Dragnet*. I was nervous because the MP had taken my passport with him. I remembered Ron's warning never to surrender your passport to *anyone* while traveling. However, under the circumstances, I didn't have much choice.

I was also concerned about the time. Due to the usual immigration and customs procedures, there was a three-hour layover scheduled in Honolulu. By the time I was escorted away and asked to wait in the interrogation room, three-quarters of an hour had already passed. If all this could be cleared up soon, I still had plenty of time to make my flight. But I had no idea how long it would take. I was hoping they could just check my name against the AWOL/Deserter List, like they had at Tan Son Nhut, and I could be on my way. I still had to fly to San Francisco, then change planes and take a connecting flight to Chicago, and finally, a Greyhound bus up to Wisconsin. There were still "miles to go before I slept."

Another half hour ticked off, while I waited, still alone, in the room. I felt cheated because nobody even asked if I wanted a cigarette or a cup of coffee, not that I needed either; it just would have been nice to be asked, I mused to myself.

Suddenly the door opened, and the same MP came back, accompanied this time by a first lieutenant and one of the HPD officers from before.

"Hello, Mr. Reilly, I'm Lieutenant Jenkins. I've been informed of your situation. Do you know a Sergeant McHenry?" he asked very businesslike.

"McHenry?" That question really threw me. "I don't think I know anybody by that name."

"Well, he knows you. He's your Army recruiter back in Wisconsin. We just got him out of bed!" the lieutenant said.

I had been so focused on the Army personnel involved in Ron's funeral and those I met in Vietnam, that I totally forgot the name of my recruiter back in Fond du Lac. "Yes, yes, I know him, I just wasn't thinking about him or what his name was," I answered.

"Sergeant McHenry told us 'bout your enlistment in the Delayed Entry Program. That makes you not entirely a civilian, but since you haven't reported for duty yet, you're also not entirely military status, either. You're kinda in *limbo*," Jenkins explained.

Purgatory is more like it, I thought, sitting in the hot seat. These guys were good. I never even thought about my "in-between status," just considered myself a civilian yet. "What happens now, am I in trouble?" I asked.

The lieutenant and MP just looked at each other for a moment. "Well, not really," the lieutenant replied.

With the sound of those words, I heaved a huge sigh of relief. I knew then I could continue my journey home and get on with my life, as long as I could make it back on the plane.

"There is one problem, though," added the lieutenant, causing my just-elevated spirits to take a nosedive. "We have a problem with you wearing those fatigues. Since you haven't reported for duty yet, you're still 'officially' a civilian, and that outfit constitutes a military uniform, almost," he said.

"Do you have any money on you?" the MP asked.

"Sure, I've got some cash," I answered, wondering if he was soliciting a bribe for himself and the other two—a thought I found hard to believe.

"How much do you have?"

I checked my wallet, as well as another secret stash I kept in my rucksack. "I have a hundred and twenty-four dollars in cash, plus more in traveler's checks."

"Good, that's plenty," the MP said, looking at the lieutenant.

"Then you better get him over there and back so he can reboard his flight in time," he ordered the MP.

"What do you mean? Get me over to *where?*" I asked, a bit confused.

"There's a small men's clothing store in the other terminal, mostly tourist stuff. You need to get your butt over there and buy some civvies before you get back on that plane. He'll take you over so you don't get lost, okay?" the lieutenant said, motioning for the MP and me to leave immediately.

This is great, finally a solution to my clothing dilemma, I thought to myself. I felt conspicuous enough at the Honolulu airport wearing this uniform. I knew how self-conscious I would feel arriving in San Francisco, and then in Chicago, looking like I just came out of a combat zone—even though, the truth was, I had!

"Thank you, sir, I appreciate it," I said, shaking Lieutenant Jenkins's hand.

Time was ticking by—I had only a little more than an hour until I had to reboard. I followed the MP, who was walking at a fast clip through the terminal full of tourists in bright shirts, white pants, and colorful leis.

As Lieutenant Jenkins had indicated, the shop catered to men who wanted to buy the latest in tropical island wear. While the MP went to explain things to the store manager, I quickly began going through the racks of shirts. Most of them were splattered with large flowers, fish, or parrots— all with bright backgrounds of turquoise, pink, green, and blue. Not really my taste, especially since I was en route to Wisconsin rather than Waikiki. I quickly chose the tamest one I could find—a pale yellow short-sleeved affair, with some white stitching down the front. Next I chose a pair of white slacks, which was easy—considering the fact that there must have been eight hundred pairs of slacks in the store, all in varying shades of white. A pair of white shoes, white socks, and a cream-colored belt completed my tropical ensemble. I smiled to myself, thinking that, with this outfit, if I washed out of basic training next month, I could always come back to the islands and be one of Don Ho's backup singers.

After I paid the manager, who placed my uniform, cap, and boots in a shopping bag decorated with palm trees and a bright sunset, the MP and I rushed back to where my Pan Am flight was reboarding passengers. After a quick handshake with the MP, I was soon back in my all-too-familiar seat. But this time I felt better about my situation. The only thing that troubled me was how ridiculous I would feel in the tourist clothes when I arrived at O'Hare and when I climbed aboard the Greyhound to Wisconsin. I left the option open to change back into the fatigues if I needed to. At least the military garb would make me look like I was serving my country, not at a luau!

The continuation of my flight to San Francisco, then on to Chicago's O'Hare on a connecting flight, was long, but thankfully uneventful. Upon arriving in Chicago, I saw several servicemen and women traveling in their Class A dress uniforms, and decided it was best for me to keep the Hawaiian clothes on rather than changing back into my dirty fatigues. Both outfits would call attention to me, but I figured the tropical wardrobe was less noticeable, at least from an "official" point of view.

Finally I boarded the Greyhound bus for the last two hundred miles of my journey from halfway around the world. The sun was setting again as the smooth-riding bus headed northwest from Chicago to central Wisconsin.

Looking to the west, at the setting sun, I was amazed to realize I didn't even know what day it was. All I knew was that I had come a long, long way in both distance and experience since leaving these gentle fields of the Midwest a little more than two weeks ago.

In my mind I kept seeing the faces of all the people I had encountered during my ordeal in Southeast Asia—people I had met only briefly, but who were so important in what I knew then would be the most unique and unforgettable two weeks of my life. I wondered what each of them was doing as I remembered their faces.

Finally, the bus reached Ripon. It was late evening. The outside air was crisp and accented by the woody aroma of early autumn. I inhaled deeply, breathing in, once again, the breath of peace—the *absolute opposite* of what was breathed in the war-torn part of the world I had just left behind.

Once again I was saddened that my brother Ron and thousands of other Americans had taken their last breath of life in a faraway place called Vietnam.

Epilogue

I reported for active duty in the Army on my twentieth birthday in October 1970, a short time after returning from my rather "unique" journey to Southeast Asia. I was a model recruit during basic training. I blended into the back ranks of my training platoon, never lipping-off or questioning my seasoned drill instructors. I let all of the other trainees do that, which they paid for dearly with push-ups, low crawls, and hours of being put in the dreaded "dying cockroach" position (you don't want to know!). Ron had taught me well about what to do, and more importantly, what *not* to do in the Army.

In 1970, the Army's eight-week basic combat training (BCT) was heavily focused on fighting in Vietnam, where most of the young recruits still ended up, even though the American involvement in the war was supposedly winding down (tell that to the families and friends of all the men and women who died there *after* my brother).

The experienced drill instructors, who had all served at least one tour in Nam, were trying to teach the young trainees what to expect there. All through basic, I never told *anyone,* cadre or my fellow recruits, that I had already been to Vietnam. I didn't want to call any attention to myself. But on the last night in the training barracks, the night before graduation, the drill sergeants came in and just kind of sat around with my platoon in a general "bull session." This was the first time in eight weeks these experienced warriors relaxed and showed they were also human. Their job with this group of trainees was done, so they didn't have to maintain their fearsome personas. They answered questions from the platoon and talked some about their personal experiences in Vietnam, as well as about what to do and what not to do over there.

Then, one of them asked the platoon if anyone had any relatives or friends who had served in Vietnam. A few of the guys raised their hands, saying they knew people who had been there, one spoke of a friend who had been wounded.

My heart raced, as I slowly raised my hand and told them my older brother had died there just a few months earlier. The demeanor of the two drill sergeants changed immediately. Their expressions softened, and they looked like they had just lost one of *their* brothers. They both said they were sorry to hear about my loss, showing an instant compassion towards me. Their reaction really surprised me, but I appreciated it.

With my heart jumping into an even higher gear, I knew I had to tell them more. "And, I just returned from Vietnam a couple of weeks before reporting to basic training."

Suddenly the looks of compassion on the sergeants' faces turned to looks of pure astonishment. One sergeant asked me to elaborate, so for the next few minutes, I stunned them, and my fellow recruits, with a summary of my recent civilian exploits in Southeast Asia. My story elicited a mixed response, anywhere from respect to awe to bewilderment.

At the end of the evening, the senior drill sergeant, an E-7, came up to me when I was alone and placed his hand on my shoulder. "You know, Reilly, because of your brother's death, you don't have to go to Vietnam, unless, of course, you're stupid enough to volunteer."

"Well, Drill Sergeant, my brother taught me never to volunteer for *anything* if I ever went into the Army. I'm going to listen to him and probably put down Germany as a first choice when I fill out my 'dream sheet.'"

"Good, I'm sure you'll get it. Have a good life, Reilly," he said, walking away.

❋   ❋   ❋

And I did just that. After another eight weeks of military police training at Fort Gordon, Georgia, I received orders for my first choice of duty location. I served as an MP with the 385th Military Police Battalion in Stuttgart, Germany. While I was there, I earned the "MP of the Month" award three times, was promoted to sergeant in a little more than two years, and was selected to become a member of a plainclothes investigative detachment.

The promotion to sergeant was especially important to me. Even though "buck sergeant," or E-5, was two full grades below Ron's rank when he died, I was proud to be another *Sergeant Reilly.*

During my time in Germany I had this burning desire to finish college and keep my promise to Ron. Upon returning to the States, I reenrolled at the University of Wisconsin's Oshkosh campus. But after one semester, I got a job offer in Northern Illinois. For the next several years I went back to school part-time as a night student at Rockford College. Impatient with my progress, I eventually enrolled full-time for the last year and received a bachelor of science degree in 1977.

The week after I graduated, I made the two-hundred-mile drive north and placed my college diploma on Ron's bronze military headstone. Even though it had taken me seven years after his death, I had fulfilled the promise I had made to him about getting an education and graduating from college—something he had instilled in me from an early age. But to me, the college degree was only part of it. Ron wanted me to be successful in life and saw the degree merely as a means to achieving that success.

Over the next several years, I worked hard at becoming successful and I soon became a regional security manager for a private company, covering several Western states. That position became a springboard a few years later for me to begin an eighteen-year career in the disaster recovery field, working post-disaster assignments for major insurance companies throughout the United States and around the world, including Mexico, South America, and in Kuwait, following the Persian Gulf War. I eventually became the managing director of one such international company.

So, in short, I've had a very interesting and successful career. None of this, I'm sure, would have been possible if not for the direction and guidance I got from my older brother Ron during my younger years.

My teenage journey to Vietnam, my success in life, and this book all serve to honor a brother whose life ended far too soon, halfway around the world.

As "Next of Kin," I offer this book as my tribute to *his* name on The Wall.

Index

About the Author

Tom Reilly has spent the last eighteen years in disaster recovery management. He continues to travel extensively and is actively doing research for his next book, entitled *Uncommon Casualties,* another true story about the Vietnam War. He resides in the Atlanta area with his wife, Arliss.